NASCAR
Generations

NASCAR Generations

The Legacy of Family in NASCAR Racing

Robert Edelstein

 HarperEntertainment
An Imprint of HarperCollinsPublishers

HarperEntertainment books may be purchased for educational, business, or sales promotional use. For information please write: Special Markets Department, HarperCollins Publishers Inc., 10 East 53rd Street, New York, NY 10022.

FIRST EDITION

Designed by Joseph Rutt

Library of Congress Cataloging-in-Publication Data

Edelstein, Robert, 1960–
    NASCAR generations : the legacy of family in NASCAR racing / Robert Edelstein.—1st ed.
        p.   cm.
    ISBN 0-06-105079-2
    1. Automobile racing drivers—United States—Biography.   2. NASCAR (Association)—History.   3. Automobile racing drivers—United States—Family relationships.   4. Stock car racing—United States—History.   I. Title

GV1032.A1 E34 2000
796.72'092'273—dc21
[B]
                                                                    00-038887

00 01 02 03 04 ❖/RRD 10 9 8 7 6 5 4 3 2 1

To Loren, my one and only rave.

Contents

The dream always begins the same way.

The man you look up to is living the horsepowered life, winning races, enjoying the obsessive pursuit of speed. You're just a kid, so you get close whatever way you know how, tooling around in the garage, helping that man—your dad, your older brother—get ready for race day. There's a fraternity of you around the country, just boys under the hood.

Dale Earnhardt, Richard Petty, Davey Allison, and Buddy Baker began their careers that way. Dale Earnhardt Jr. and Bobby Labonte did as well.

Driving quickly becomes destiny; the need for sons to follow fast fathers or swift siblings to the racetrack eventually grows to become an all-consuming passion. In some cases, nothing is more important than beating the old man; it's another way of calling attention to yourself, of trying to turn back the clock to make up for lost time. In other cases, beating your father is nothing to celebrate; it doesn't mean you're better than Dad, it only means you're younger. It means he's mortal.

Brothers are a whole other deal altogether. It can be fun topping your brother in a race. Just try losing to him. That's only fun if you're in Atlanta, it's 1996, and your last name happens to be Labonte.

And yet the dream lives and thrives every week in the NASCAR Winston Cup Series circuit, the highest level of NASCAR racing. No one enjoys it more than the fans who follow these family tales and eagerly embrace every new favorite son. The NASCAR generations who take the track on Sundays now are following a long legacy that dates back to the very beginnings of the sport, when legends such as Lee Petty and Buck Baker laid the groundwork for the racers that followed. NASCAR racing has multiples of Elliott and Allison, Wallace and Waltrip and Wood, Baker and Burton and Bodine, Jarrett and Petty. Fifty years ago, there were Flocks behind the wheel; then as now, there are Frances in the boardrooms.

This book follows the winding, triumphant journeys these families have made both on the track and off. There is no other sport on earth that enjoys such spirited competition and camaraderie between the ages.

"When Archie Manning was on the football field, the closest his son Peyton could get was on the sidelines," begins NASCAR President Bill France Jr., who used to stub tickets at the family track in Daytona Beach. "But in most cases, the father that plays football is already out of playing when the son gets old enough. Davey Allison used to go [to the track] with Bobby Allison in the summertime when he was fourteen years old, but he'd be in the truck towing the race car, and when he was there he did odd jobs, cleaned the windshield or got him a hot dog or whatever kids do. They kind of grow up right there on the playing field, practically. And the driver can drive until he's thirty-five, forty years old. Most football players, that kind of winds up their career. [In NASCAR], we've got a long window."

Three Earnhardts have wound their way through NASCAR's fabled dirt tracks and superspeedways. Four Pettys have as well, and though that road has taken the saddest of detours, the legacy remains. The first time Buddy Baker was unceremoniously knocked out of the way during a race, Buck Baker did the knocking. But the first time Buddy won a race, a beaming, moist-eyed Buck threw his arms around his son's broad neck.

Ned Jarrett won fifty races and two championships in NASCAR. To him, they mean little compared to the pride he enjoyed watching Dale Jarrett's consistent run to the 1999 NASCAR Winston Cup Series title.

And for Bobby Allison, there will always be visions of Clifford and memories of Davey. For Kyle and Richard Petty, there is Adam's smile and his deep love of the game.

For everyone who is passionate about stock car racing and the families that have made their name in it, there are the links from one champion to the next, and a timeline worth remembering. And every kid who takes to the track to follow a family dream draws another link to that tradition.

"Our sport is like anything; it had to have somewhere to start from and it had to grow, and as it grew I went through three generations of drivers that I ran with," remembers Buddy Baker. "I hope we don't lose sight of the past because I can remember when I first started driving, racing was my dad, Lee Petty, and Fireball Roberts and these guys would be winners today just like they were years ago. It's such a great sport and it's kinda like the never-ending question: Where did we all come from? Well, you have to know that, too."

1
The France Family, Part One

As long as there were cars around, William France would be able to make a living.

An auto mechanic by trade, France had been able to support his young family—his wife, Anne, and their young son, Bill Jr.—through jobs around their Washington, D.C. home. And as a part-time race car driver, he added to the family pot with whatever winnings he earned.

But by 1934, at the height of the Depression, the Frances had had more than enough of the harsh northern winters. Enamored of the water, the family took off for Florida and a life hopefully filled with trips to the beach, a warmer climate in which to work on cars, and a chance for Bill France to pursue his dreams of speed.

As a teenager, he'd watched the open-wheel races taking place near his home and had, on a number of occasions, "borrowed" his father's car to exercise his passion for racing. Because the open-wheel circuit was too expensive for his blood, he turned to the indigenous sport of stock car racing, where even a modest budget allowed one to field an entry.

Driving down the coast, the Frances stopped in Daytona Beach and took a dip in the ocean. Daytona had already established itself as something of a national headquarters for speed. Heading into the Daytona water meant walking over the long, hard, flat stretch of beach that had been the site of some of the world's great land-speed records. In the surrounding towns and nearby states, a man looking to break into the world of stock car racing would find ample opportunity to race. In Daytona Beach itself, Bill could easily return to business as a mechanic, which pleased his sensible wife. The place instantly appealed to Bill's sense of adventure while it also satisfied Anne France's practical nature—and it was warm. The Frances decided to stay.

It would be the first of many good decisions Bill and Anne would make in Daytona Beach.

The next fifteen years of the France's lives now read like a timeline of stock car racing history. On March 7, 1935, British land-speed specialist Sir Malcolm Campbell brought his Rolls Royce-powered Bluebird streamliner to the Florida beach in an attempt to become the first gentleman to drive a measured mile at over 300 mph. Thanks in part to the winds in Daytona, he hit only 276.82—a new record, but short of the goal nonetheless. In the dense crowd that day was William France, who had by then become a prominent figure in the Daytona Beach driving scene. Meanwhile, Campbell left that scene behind and took his Bluebird Five to the drier clime of Utah, where he broke the elusive 300 mph barrier—an event which effectively halted the land-speed industry in Daytona. Campbell's departure caused a gap the Daytona city fathers desperately needed to fill.

They did so by running a stock car race on a makeshift 3.2-mile beach-and-road course, with the two long straightaways connected by soft sand at the north and south turns. The challenge for the drivers was to go into those turns just right: Enter too slowly and you risked getting stuck; too quickly and you could turn over. After several laps, the sand in the turns became a coagulated mess. The problem for the promoters, meanwhile, was that, with the lack of a fence around the course, many people watched the race free of charge. In all, the race lost a bundle. France, however, entered the race and finished fifth, taking home a tidy $375. Considering the monthly rent on the France family home was $15, the racing business seemed like it would be profitable.

After a race on the beach the next year finished in the red, it appeared as if Daytona's place in the world of speed would experience a demise as swift as one of Sir Malcolm's Bluebirds.

The turning point for the race, the town, and the sport came when the Daytona Chamber of Commerce asked France if he'd be willing to get involved in promoting the contest himself. By now the owner of his own garage, and a fixture on the stock circuit, France got his car's sponsor, Charlie Reese, to ante up the funds so that he and Anne could promote the event. Thanks to France's ability to lure the finest racers of the day—and Anne's inspiration to, among other things, up the amount of ticket sales by putting signs warning against rattlesnakes in the brush where fans had once watched the race for free—the race made a profit, with France earning an extra $100 for his finish. In the years ahead, France built the beach-and-road course's reputation as a necessary stop on the calendar for stock's elite, who came for up to four contests a year. After World War II, France, with the money he'd earned during wartime work in the Florida dock yards, began to promote races and went about trying to organize the various drivers, track owners, and factions into one solidly-run organization. In his plan, shifty promoters wouldn't run off with drivers' winnings, and competitors could enjoy a safer, sanctioned opportunity to do the only thing that mattered: driving faster than anybody else.

Bill France was going to bring all the disparate sides together and try to make it work financially; to do so, he'd need the one partner with the business savvy to match his considerable vision: his wife Anne. Conservative enough to keep her husband's wildest ideas in check, Anne was also realistic enough to help make Bill's wisest ideas succeed in the most profitable way possible. And considering her levelheaded approach to business, convincing Anne of the credence of a project became step one toward making it happen.

By the end of the 1940s, Bill France was in a position to set his plan in motion and begin his quest to create some necessary order out of stock car racing chaos. A few years after that, his other most enduring dream, that of replacing the beach-and-road course with his sport's definitive speedway, was underway. The latter project would be the ultimate professional test of NASCAR's first family, and a tribute to Bill and Anne's mix of promotion and prowess. Speedway construction would also provide an opportunity for their oldest son to help clear the land, giving Bill France Jr. a chance to learn a new side of the family business from the ground up.

• • •

On the outside, William and Anne France may have seemed like an odd couple. At six feet four, Big Bill, as he would come to be widely known, was a gregarious bear of a man with a commanding presence that seemed to explain his nickname more than his size did. On the other hand, Anne B., as she was known to friends, didn't garner that same kind of attention—and she wanted it that way. Several inches shorter than her husband and five years his senior, she preferred the background to Big Bill's foreground, and in her comfortable place out of the spotlight, she made her own mark.

On the inside, the pair were a match, a potent mix of wit and wisdom. Big Bill had a warehouse of ideas; his sizeable talent lay in his ability to see realistic visions in the unlikeliest places. His wife became the ultimate sounding board and, once an idea had been agreed upon, his chief financial officer.

"It was the ideal partnership. It was probably one of the most perfect complementary situations you could ever find," says their granddaughter, Lesa France Kennedy, now executive vice president of the France family-owned International Speedway Corporation (ISC). "I think that if you put the qualities of each individual on a sheet of paper, they would be totally different, totally complementary. And it would make up probably ninety-nine percent of all the qualities you'd need in a perfect person to transact business—or do anything else, really. It was amazing. My grandfather was a visionary and my grandmother made sure that it all stayed right on track. And I think they trusted each other, they trusted each other's instincts and so they were willing, if you will, to compromise in some situations. There was a lot of give and take from the business relationship standpoint.

"But it wasn't just a given," Kennedy continues. "It wasn't, 'Well, he wants to go do this and I'm sure that's fine.' It was, 'Well, I'm gonna explain all my points first; if he's gonna listen to all of them, then we'll see what he thinks.'" Adds Kennedy's father, Bill France Jr., "My father had a pretty good knack for analyzing the short-term benefits against the long-term negatives—or a short-term negative that would turn into a long-term benefit. He had a pretty good knack of picking and choosing and sorting that out. My mom—

somebody told her [this] one time [and it] became her creed almost, and that is, 'Don't let your business run out of cash.'"

Anne maintained her hands-on approach to race promotions, a business that would naturally have its share of hurdles to overcome before it became constantly viable. But at its roots in Bill France's imagination, the idea of creating a weekly proving ground for drivers had universal appeal. In the years before the second World War, stock car racing had been between drivers in what had most assuredly been "modified" cars. The sport had sprung from the battles of moonshiners who met on dirt tracks on the weekends and tried to decide, in all their horsepowered glory, who was fastest, with each driving cars that had been tinkered with to help them get through long moonshining runs.

After the war, the dirt-track battles began anew, but France understood that the sport's real appeal lay in its common-man touch. By creating a "Strictly Stock" division for cars that could go straight from the showroom to victory lane, France proposed that anyone could join in the fun. Given the upheaval of the Depression, followed by the renewed hope of postwar America, there was something instantly winning about a sport where anyone with a regular family car, or access to one, could race against all comers. All Bill France needed was for everyone else—from car manufacturers to the average consumer—to realize this and the rewards would begin.

"It was not viewed as a legitimate sport when they started," states Jim France, president and chief operating officer of ISC—and Bill and Anne's second son, born in 1944, thirteen years after Bill Jr. "Not compared to other entertainment sporting-type events out there; baseball, which was there when they started, was the leading thing, but in motor sports, even, the open-wheel Indianapolis series was the recognized motor sports activity and stock car racing in the South was at that time kind of viewed or referred to as an outlaw event, and I think their taking that and organizing it and building the credibility of the sport was very important for a lot of people."

The money the Frances made from their race promotions allowed Bill France to dream big. On December 14, 1947, at the Streamline Hotel in Daytona Beach, France gathered many top competing track owners, promoters, and drivers and proposed they form an organization that would help make stock car racing more profitable for all concerned. In time, driver Red Vogt christened the new league the National Association for Stock Car Auto Racing (NASCAR). It didn't take very long to elect a president.

With each test—whether it was a lack of factory involvement in the sport or the near unionization of the drivers by the teamsters—Bill France managed to defuse controversy and increase public and professional awareness of racing; meanwhile, Anne kept the books and handled ticket sales. Through the 1950s, NASCAR was in its infancy and experiencing growth spurts; new tracks sprang up and another generation of drivers came in to refresh the competition.

Bill France's next big idea, the other major notion he'd be most remembered for, faced some stiff resistance from Anne at first. But France convinced her that, ultimately, all the effort and debt they'd need to get into in order to build the most famous speedway in stock car racing would pay off in a big way. France's dream was to create something bigger than Indianapolis Motor Speedway. The project would test their patience and determination. After France first voiced his idea in the early 1950s, it would be several years before he and Anne had the loan in hand to begin transforming an enormous swamp near the Daytona Beach airport into the Daytona International Speedway.

"They were going to build a racetrack and they were determined to do it and that's what was going to happen," states Lesa France Kennedy. "And all along they didn't know exactly each step of the way how it was all going to work out. I don't think they knew all the details in between because the plan ended up being something very different from their original plan, but that's how they got there."

Construction began in the spring of 1958, and their oldest son, twenty-five-year-old Bill Jr., was a member of the team.

"We worked at the track from basically day one, clearing the land," he recalls. "I was probably too young anyway as far as getting the lease all done and all of the paperwork; they were trying to sell bonds and all of the different capital they were trying to raise; I didn't have the background in those days to attempt that. So I was more on the construction side, hands on, along with everybody else that was working, building the track. It was seven days a week for about fourteen months. We went from seven 'til dark; every Saturday and Sunday for a whole year.

"You could start really visualizing it as it started coming out of the ground and you could see the banked turns and the sides of it. When we first started, it was knocking trees down and it was just a mud hole. It was a little difficult then to envision just what it was gonna be like."

Ultimately, a lap at the D-shaped oval at Daytona would come to stretch for a whopping 2.5 miles; it was nearly twice as large as the 1.38-mile track at the other largest NASCAR superspeedway at that time, in Darlington, South Carolina. And adding to the excitement, and the possibility of high speeds, were the 31-degree banked curves. The track instantly became a groundbreaking mecca of stock car speed. Up until then, the fastest qualifying run for any paved-track race in NASCAR history was 117.4 mph. For the inaugural Daytona 500 in February 1959, polesitter Bob Welborn clocked in at 140.1 mph. The track had seats for 41,291 people—and counting, as Bill promised his wife he'd keep adding to the stands and therefore the bottom line, every year. After the first race, which produced a photo finish—one that required calling in photos from outside sources because France hadn't set up a camera at the start-finish line—Lee Petty had notched the inaugural win, and Bill and Anne France had yet another bona fide victory on their hands.

As a boy, Bill France Jr. shared his father's passion for speed. He would occasionally tag along to watch his dad race, and he'd soak in as much information as possible on style and substance behind the wheel in preparation for his own eventual runs.

"I was probably like most kids that thought they wanted to be a race driver," he remembers. "I wasn't a good football player and I tried to play a little basketball and that didn't really go anywhere. I used to see [my father] race when I was little. So like the Dale Jarretts, with their father Ned Jarrett, and the Pettys, and the Earnhardts now, it's a natural progression. You think you want to be a driver. So that was the main driving force."

But contrary to the path taken by the Earnhardts and the Pettys,

Bill Jr. ultimately gave up the ambition; like his father, he discovered his destiny led to a different arena.

"I spent a little time in college and I went into the Navy during the Korean War. Then when I came out, I was working in our business side of the sport as well as hoping to drive a race car," he says. "I found out very early on that you either had to do one or the other; you couldn't be out parking cars, for instance, and getting the people in, and then run inside and put a helmet on and run the first heat and then go back out and park cars again."

He performed a great many functions for the business, working at the racetracks doing everything from selling tickets to flagging races to selling snow cones. Through time and effort, he was becoming more familiar with the inner workings of NASCAR.

What had to be one of his more pleasant responsibilities was recruiting bathing beauties to serve as racetrack representatives in victory lane. The task became all the more memorable when, at one track, he signed a particular lifeguard named Betty Jane Zachary who caught his attention; months later, the lifeguard became Betty Jane France.

Jim France went through a similar transformation, beginning with his early indoctrination into the wonders of life at the track while still a toddler, when NASCAR too was young.

"I basically grew up around racing and racetracks," Jim says. "From my earliest recollections, I enjoyed the flavor of being at the racetracks. When I was young, we would move up to the Carolinas every summer and I can remember sliding up and down the red clay dirt banks with [NASCAR's one-time chief scorer] Joe Epton's kids at the old Raleigh Speedway behind their grandstand there; every Saturday night at Bowman Gray Stadium in Winston-Salem— it was a natural part of my rearing."

Also natural was his desire to race. His interest lay more in motorcycles, and he rode in amateur contests for a number of years before fully immersing himself in the family business.

"I never tried any professional racing; I never really had the time," he says. "My brother did a little bit of racing early on, but the business grew to the point where he couldn't devote the proper time you need to try and drive race cars and be competitive and do all the other things needed to put on the event. And when I came along we were farther down that road than we were when he started."

NASCAR had firmly established itself, gaining a stronghold in the south. Superspeedways were being constructed, slowly changing the face of the sport as dirt tracks went by the wayside—at least as venues for the top tier of racing. And by the mid-'60s, Bill France Jr. and Jim France had become much more integral arms of the business of NASCAR. While Jim shared his mother's disinterest in the limelight, Bill Jr. became a visible representative. If he had once picked up pointers while watching his father race, working closely with him day-to-day gave Bill Jr. some much-needed background and on-the-job training.

"I know of some other father-son relationships that weren't very good and the son couldn't hardly do anything that the father [approved] of. I never had that problem," he says. "[For us], it couldn't have been better from that standpoint. We had a good relationship."

Big Bill France, long retired as a stock car racer, had one more opportunity to get behind the wheel in the late 1960s. He was making an unexpected run, driving alone on the track, and going for an important victory that would require less speed than finesse.

The track was the second great superspeedway Bill and Anne France christened, the 2.66-mile oval at Talladega, Alabama. The Frances' preparations for a huge debut weekend in September 1969 were severely dampened. Many drivers claimed Talladega was too fast and that it ate up tires too quickly.

In an attempt to stall the union initiative before it even started, France made a brilliant move. He borrowed a car from legendary owners Holman and Moody, and entered the race as a driver. Then France took to the track for a practice run and reeled off a lap at about 170 mph. When he got out of the car, he told the drivers that surely, if a man pushing sixty could drive that fast on Talladega's new track, the sport's elite drivers could do so without any overt threat of personal harm.

To counter France's tactical masterpiece, the drivers decided to sit out the day anyway, and drain the race of its prestige. But France pressed on and said the race would go on regardless; the drivers themselves would miss out on a great event. And the NASCAR president fired the final salvo when he promised the crowd that all ticket holders would also be entitled to free entry for a future contest at either Talladega or Daytona. The first Talladega 500 might not have proved memorable in terms of participants—it gave Richard Brickhouse his only Grand National victory in a thirty-nine-race career—but it earned Bill France the appreciation of race fans.

By the time Bill France engineered his solution at Talladega, a monumental change had begun within NASCAR. Even though it would be several years before the racing world saw the retirement of the sport's founder, his oldest son had already begun to assume much of his father's responsibilities. As executive vice president, Bill France Jr.'s contributions grew annually. In doing so, Bill Jr. also began to earn the trust of the top drivers on the circuit, many of whom were contemporaries who appreciated his sense of fairness and pursuance of vision—qualities that had made his father so effective. That's not to say everybody felt he'd be able to instantly come in and lead the sport to greater levels of success. He was, after all, following in big footsteps.

"Anytime there's a change in somebody that's in a key slot, you're always going to have the speculation going on out there about, 'Is he the right guy? Can he get the job done?' or what have you," Bill Jr. recalls. "You're going to have that even if you go totally to the outside and bring somebody in. Different people then go on and make comparisons of their strengths and weaknesses or one thing or another. If you come in as a sibling or the next generation, I think you get probably more scrutiny just because you've got the same last name and everybody's saying, 'Well, you know, you think the kid's got it?' So I had all that to go through. And looking back at it, it wasn't that bad."

The scrutiny began in earnest when William France officially retired as president of NASCAR in 1972, naming his thirty-eight-year-old son successor. Whatever the reaction from fans and drivers, Bill Jr. had the benefit of his father's confidence, which appeared to be immediately well-earned. The new president presided over and brought about some enormous changes in the sport's growth. In 1972, R. J. Reynolds agreed to sponsor NASCAR's senior series, then renamed NASCAR Winston Cup Series. Other sponsorship opportunities also began to present themselves, hitting an early peak in Richard Petty's association with STP. And several years later, Bill Jr. finally led the sport into the age of live national broadcast television when he and CBS agreed to the first-ever flag-to-flag airing of the Daytona 500 in 1979. The late-going tussle between Cale Yarborough and the Allison brothers made for spectacular Sunday afternoon viewing and set the stage for the contracts that now link NASCAR with a number of prominent network partners.

Perhaps as important, Bill Jr. and Jim France created a relatively seamless transition from one generation to the next. Big Bill and Anne's legacy was safe in the hands of their oldest son, who inherited what his younger brother calls "Dad's promotion and organizational skills and Mom's financial and conservative approach to things. He's a good blend of both of their best traits." And perhaps the best of those traits are finding their way into Bill's children, Brian and Lesa, both vital parts of NASCAR business today.

"[My father] certainly didn't have the kind of personality Bill Sr. did; on the other hand, he brought some discipline to things," says Brian France, now senior vice president for NASCAR. "I think he wanted us to, then and now, operate like a professional sport and a business—not that Bill Sr. didn't, but I think my father is a little bit more disciplined about things. So that was a good evolution."

2
The Allison Family

The Legend of the Alabama Gang

Donnie Allison couldn't believe it. Half a lap from the finish of the 1979 Daytona 500, the ever-elusive victory in his grasp, and it had all gone wrong.

Twice before he'd come close; he'd entertained thoughts of having his name forever inscribed on the Harley J. Earl trophy and being given the privilege of hoisting its broad, unwieldy replica over his head before the cheering throng. Each time something had led him to misfortune. Nothing, however, would ever rival this.

It had come down to Allison, a highly regarded competitor and racing journeyman with twelve years of NASCAR Winston Cup Series experience, against the popular, determined Cale Yarborough. Allison headed toward turn three and saw Yarborough, going low to make the pass, in his rearview mirror. Allison tried to block him from doing so and in all the jockeying, the pair bumped and bumped again, bouncing off each other relentlessly in the pursuit of position. They popped doors until the unthinkable occurred: The cars, their drivers attempting in vain to regain control, suddenly skidded off the track, down onto the infield. Fifteen seconds behind them, a stunned Richard Petty, who'd been looking at third-place money, suddenly found that his attempt to keep Darrell Waltrip behind him held significantly more meaning. Petty, the acknowledged king of stock car racing, managed to hold off his brash young opponent and sped past the scene on the infield to take his sixth Daytona 500 checker.

Afterward, the camera focused on the cars of Yarborough and Allison, sitting inertly where they'd stopped. With NASCAR President Bill France Jr. having negotiated with CBS to air this first-ever flag-to-flag live broadcast of the great American race, millions at home were enjoying the play-by-play. But stock car fans weren't the only viewers that day by a long shot: The severe snowstorm that had knocked out travel plans for a good part of the eastern seaboard ballooned the ratings with an audience hungry for a diversion. They got one.

By now, Yarborough and Allison had been joined at the scene by Donnie's older brother, Bobby. In previous years, the brothers had raced and helped each other at countless venues throughout the country, from local dirt tracks to Daytona's prestigious D-shaped oval. Earlier in the Daytona race, the Allisons and Yarborough had been involved in a spinout, which had set both Yarborough and Bobby Allison back; the incident had given Donnie a greater hold on the lead. There in the infield, an incensed Yarborough blamed the older Allison brother for causing the first accident, which had, essentially, set up the occasion for this one.

Bobby, whose career-long motto spoke of never taking a grudge from one race weekend to the next, tried a creative approach to solving this disagreement.

"I think I questioned his ancestry, not totally sure, but I think I did," he says. After more heated discussion, Yarborough felt inclined to hit Bobby with his helmet.

"And I said, I've got to get out of this car and address this right now or run from him the rest of my life," Bobby says. "So I climbed out of the car, and with that, Cale Yarborough went to beating on my knuckles with his nose. And that's my story, and I'm stickin' to it."

Cameras, which had focused on Petty's victory lap, abruptly returned to the infield to train on a decidedly different scene between Yarborough and Bobby Allison. Many of the wide-eyed, uninitiated at home had begun viewing with little idea of this moment in NASCAR's rich history, coming after years during which the governing body had tried to find a balance between the sport's hard adolescence and what they hoped would be a more lucrative future. There had been attempts to tame the game's wilder side while simultaneously allowing it to maintain its edge and the rugged individualism of its stars.

At the heart of that historic struggle stood Bobby Allison, a driver forever determined to do things his own way. As a result, Bobby hadn't always been able to count on getting consistent top-quality rides enjoyed by the likes of Richard Petty, but then, some of his favorite victories had involved less-than-stellar equipment driven past its capability by a talented driver. With his brother, he shared a reputation as a formidable competitor, though in terms of success and pure commitment, few drivers in NASCAR history would ever hold a candle to Bobby Allison. In previous years, he and Petty had given the sport some extraordinary thrills during classic struggles that redefined NASCAR's limits of intensity. Years before that, the Allison brothers brought their own hard-charging excitement to fans who saw them rise through the ranks to the sport's top tier.

And on this day in Daytona, Bobby Allison got into a scuffle—for himself, sure; his brother, certainly; and, most importantly, for the principle of the situation. It's hard to find a moment that had a greater impact on the popularity of the sport than this one. Before the thousands on hand and the multitudes at home, Bobby fought the good fight, a symbol of the old days, which was enjoyed by fans of the future who were just catching up on some fresh, new lore being added to NASCAR's slice of Americana.

Had those same fans come into the sport even ten years earlier, they would have appreciated the moment's significance. In the 1970s, it seemed as if opposing, larger-than-life stock car characters waged great battles every weekend; looking back now, as the dust of age continues to rework their images, it only serves to raise their profiles higher. Out-and-out heroes valiantly met folks of equal talent but somewhat less buffed reputations, and when these characters rolled into the smaller towns across the land where they were destined to meet up, those towns were enlivened by the wonder of the spectacle. There was a lot of boasting and challenging—the only thing the competitors seemed to have in common was that each believed he was right. There was Richard Petty, the beloved, no-nonsense sheriff of the game, countering David Pearson, the sullen loner who always seemed invisible, until it came time to settle up. Buddy Baker and Cale Yarborough were like two outlaws from out of town; Baker quick-witted and just as speedy on the track, Yarborough a master of horseplay and angry when crossed. Running the sport, keeping it clean his way and earning the respect of all who entered and left was Bill France, a judge holding court with a firm but fair temperament and a grin forever coming to his lips.

And from town to town, there was only one gang.

They were an unassuming bunch, three guys who, in the early 1960s, had earned a name for themselves as competitors to be feared. They didn't ask to be called a gang; they weren't even originally from Alabama. But once the Alabama Gang started, they weren't about to argue over the matter when there was plenty of racing to be done.

"Red Farmer, Bobby, and myself all came from Miami, Florida, and we moved to Alabama like vagabonds almost," says Donnie Allison. Bobby, who had a modified car and was doing a lot of driving in Miami, took his brother to Alabama, where they discovered the driving was incredible and the pay for finishing second or third often was better than what they were used to receiving for winning. One Thursday night in 1959, they left with little funds but enough to buy a fifty-cent basket of peaches in Central Florida that would have to serve as sustenance for the whole trip—or until they made some money at a track. They arrived in Alabama the next day with confidence in their hearts and five meals' worth of peaches in their stomachs and headed for Birmingham's Dixie Speedway and its quarter-mile high-bank paved track. Bobby and Donnie unloaded their car and Bobby drove a heat race, a semi-final, and a feature, finishing fifth in all three. He went to the pay window and was counted out a total of $135. In Bobby's words, the brothers thought they had died and gone to heaven. Even if it wouldn't put them into a different income bracket, they were assured of eating steak instead of peaches. They also got the idea that perhaps a change of location would serve them well.

The brothers convinced Farmer—a driver Bobby had worshiped and worked for—to take some vacation time from his regular non-racing job and tag along. "The week that he got there began a series of races over a holiday where we ran eight times in seven days, and Red Farmer won like seven of the eight races," Bobby recalls. "He was really strong in those days, and it was a perfect situation for him, perfect timing. So we all migrated to Alabama. And as things got going in Alabama, Red destroyed his one car, so I built a new car for him. His car then appeared very much like mine, so our cars, all three cars, were the same style cars—by then Donnie was running pretty good. Donnie was running the car that my [older] brother Eddie was working on out of Miami. So if there was a major event somewhere, we'd all get together and go."

The Allisons and Farmer were frequently the class of the field at these modified circuit events, pushing past the other competitors and taking each other on for dirt-track victories. It was about this time that a promoter gave them their nickname. "Pretty soon we would come into one of these tracks for a special event, and one of the competitors would say, 'Uh-oh, here's that Alabama Gang,'" Bobby remembers. "And so we were graciously handed the title."

"Well, then that caught on in the media—what little media there was at the time," adds Donnie. "Every racetrack we went to promoted 'the Alabama Gang's coming.' And at the time, personally, none of us really felt like being a gang. But I talked to Bobby later on and we thought, hell, we *were* a gang, because we took the money. So it was an appropriate name. You know, we'd finish first, second, and third, or right in the front at every race."

"And, you know, that's the mission," adds Bobby. "And my own attitude was that Red and Donnie also needed to be behind me."

Bobby's love of the competitive spirit developed when he was about nine and his grandfather took him to see his first stock car race. The bug bit him exceptionally hard; by the time he was in high school, he was getting to the track any way he could as a spectator while looking for a chance to race. He got one, and in his third week in the amateur division, he won all of $12. "But that didn't matter—I had won a race, and it convinced me," he says, "that this was something I had a future in."

The future looked short when he needed to secure his reluctant mother's permission to keep racing. Eventually, she said yes. "She thought it was for one night; I thought it was for a hundred years," he says.

Wanting her son to go to college and become a doctor instead of a driver, she raised the particularly galling threat that Bobby couldn't race under her roof. Bobby, who found the bed warm and the food delicious, solved that dilemma by racing under a different name. Before very long, his father finally spoke out and told Bobby that if he was going to race, he should use his own name and do his best.

From then on, Bobby went about making the deal work, racing wherever and whenever possible. His older brother Eddie was already in the business as a mechanic, and in short order, Donnie, who is less than two years younger than Bobby, joined in as well. But there was something different about watching Bobby. He drove with passion and abandon; behind the wheel, he did not suffer fools gladly, passing other people with impatience en route to victory. Not that he wanted races to end—he would have been happy behind the wheel all day long.

"If I heard of a race that I could make by driving through the night and get there in time to line the car up and make the start of the race," he states, "then staying up all night and the miles were just no problem."

Even though both brothers were tough to beat driving modified cars in the early 1960s, Bobby always believed his younger brother didn't have the same determination to succeed behind the wheel. And on one particular night, he went that claim one better. Bobby had won two elimination rounds of a particular series of races and, due to a conflict, a determined Donnie was set to run the finals for his brother; during the race, he crashed out. When Donnie got out of the hospital, Bobby told him he would never have what it took to drive a race car. Sibling knockdown dragouts have occurred for much less, but Donnie felt the sting of the dare and ran with it. He has always claimed that that moment truly led to the start of his career in earnest.

In 1967, Donnie's first year running NASCAR Winston Cup Series full-time, he ran twenty races, earned four top-fives and seven top-tens, and finished sixteenth in the standings. He was voted Rookie of the Year.

• • •

The Allison brothers maintained a code of honor during their years in professional racing, one best summed up as "Do the right thing." Of course, the right thing often meant different things to different people. For the Allisons, it meant standing up for your principles even if that sometimes took you further away from the best winning ride available on the circuit. Both brothers got into more than their share of tussles with owners over whose way to win was the right way. But all told, some of the most successful owners of the day—from Junior Johnson to Holman-Moody to the Wood Brothers—employed at least one brother at various times and then parted ways. Yet, both brothers kept getting offered great rides from the best because of their ability to find success—especially Bobby. Where Donnie always yearned to win, Bobby was obsessed by it. Donnie never once ran a full NASCAR schedule, driving more than twenty races only once in fourteen full-time seasons and starting a total of 242 contests to his brother's 718; Donnie's desires found him seeking victories in many different avenues, including IndyCar racing. Bobby wanted to taste the glory of a prestigious Grand National title. He came into NASCAR racing in 1966, after the departures of Ned Jarrett and Junior Johnson and the death of Fireball Roberts had left an enormous chasm in a sport that thrived on its heroes. Already, David Pearson had entered the ring to do battle with Richard Petty, the son of a NASCAR Winston Cup Series legend and inheritor of a business acumen that made him the most successful driver of his time. Allison, who had risen the hard way through the junior circuits, often scraping to put his ride together in less than stellar conditions, was the kind of working-class hero fans could easily grow to love. He was not a driver to be crossed. In fact, when Donnie Allison comments on his own reputation as something of a fighter, he claims that of the seven on-track fights he was involved in, Bobby started five of them.

On the surface, that might seem unlikely, considering Bobby's leaner build and his younger brother's larger, broader form. In their prime, Donnie had the more exaggerated features—a large, lopsided grin over a soft chin—compared to his brother's more chiseled profile and intense gaze—and one could picture Donnie's squint-eyed smile turning more easily into a sneer. True, Bobby Allison did more than his share of damage, but instead of using his fists, he was part of many of the most impressive metal-to-metal clashes in NASCAR history.

He set the tone for his intensity with the skirmishes that would forever remain the most heated of his career: battles with Richard Petty throughout 1972. Theirs was a classic struggle: two of the best drivers in the best equipment money could buy (for once, Allison had a terrific ride, driving for Junior Johnson in a Coca Cola-sponsored Chevy) in an escalating series of clashes. Petty was five years removed from his twenty-seven-win 1967 season—the greatest single year by any driver in history—and he was the defending Grand National champion, having won twenty-one races in 1971. Allison had notched eleven wins in 1971 after finishing the season in second place in 1970, losing to Bobby Isaac by a mere fifty-one points. His search for a season title was fast becoming the statistic that mattered most to him. In 1972, he would prove just how eagerly he wanted that title to prove the value of the Allison pedigree.

The battles between the drivers began late in the season and raged from week to week, with accusations of foul play constantly tossed back and forth from both camps. When the season results were counted, both Petty and Allison had each led a remarkable thirty out of thirty-one races. Allison finished with ten victories to Petty's eight; Petty finished out of the top ten only three times; Allison four times.

To say that numbers tell little of the story, as impressive as they are, is to understate the tale. Though the pair had had their on-track differences in 1966 and 1971, they were running smoothly in 1972 until the September 10th race at the Richmond Fairgrounds, in Richmond, Virginia. Leading the rest of the field by eight laps, Petty and Allison found themselves too close for comfort with about one hundred laps remaining. Petty bumped Allison on turn two of one lap and Bobby bumped back even harder on turn four. The latter hit sent Petty careening toward the railing with nowhere to go but up. His No. 43 Plymouth vaulted toward the wall; he ricocheted off the wall, bounced back onto the track, and retained the lead. Allison posed no threat for the rest of the race, which Petty won with ease. The stage, however, was set.

Two weeks later at Martinsville, Petty beat a clearly dominant Allison by climbing on the curb to the inside and knocking his rival's fuel cap loose—this after miles of the most spirited racing between the two rivals, which had the crowd on its feet.

At this point, both drivers denied the existence of a feud between them. That would change one week later in North Wilkesboro during a race that found them four laps over the rest of the participants, trading the lead back and forth in an amazing short-track frenzy. With three laps to go, Petty bent Allison's fenders with a powerful blow. One lap later, Allison returned the favor and sent the King into the wall on a pass. Petty climbed a guard rail to try to retake the lead, but failed to get enough momentum. He finally made a last pass when Allison, his cockpit filling with smoke, swerved to miss sections of Petty's bumpers which were sitting on the track—in a what-goes-around-comes-around maneuver, Petty went low, past his own equipment and Allison, and took the victory.

By the time the season ended a few weeks later, Allison and Petty had made up somewhat, and the former had set a NASCAR record that will probably never be broken: Over two seasons, he had led at least once for thirty-nine consecutive races. That was nice, of course, as were the victories, but a Grand National title still eluded him as Petty took home his then-record fourth win in the annual derby.

Allison also lost his ride with Junior Johnson at the end of the season, and in 1973 he went back to driving for himself, which he'd done before joining up with Johnson. He finished seventh in points.

From 1968 to 1972, some of the brightest years of his career, Donnie Allison won six races and had thirty-four top-five finishes in only seventy-one starts. Years earlier, while running modifieds, he developed a desire to try out Indy cars. In 1970, he finally convinced his friend A. J. Foyt to lend him one for that year's running of the Indy 500. Donnie put in a full week and pulled off some numbers for the ages: Driving a Ford for Banjo Matthews, he won the World 600 at Charlotte by two laps; then he started twenty-third at Indy and finished fourth, earning the race's Rookie of the Year honors.

Donnie had his own journeyman's career, did his share of tussling, won some races, lost some heartbreakers, and like his brother, fought with owners about the right way to produce a winner. For posterity's sake, however, he always ran in the shadow of Bobby, a fate he accepted without jealousy. In their minds, the Alabama Gang had long since been "disbanded," even as the mid-1970s emergence of local Alabama favorite Neil Bonnett would inspire talk of the gang's next generation.

For all his highs and lows, Donnie is most remembered for two facts. First and foremost, there is the forever-haunting 1979 Daytona 500. For his part, Donnie has only been able to watch the race once, and even then he turned it off in disgust. He can talk about how it turned out to be the vital link between NASCAR then and now, about how in just a few minutes, "[NASCAR] went from being a roughneck sport, all of a sudden there were a few white-collar people around there, and it's progressed since then to the enormous thing it is right now"—but he can only really think of it in its purest, visceral terms.

"That particular day was very, very, very, very hard on me," he says. "To be perfectly honest, when the fight broke out I did not fight. Bobby and Cale fought."

That second fact is much easier for Donnie to swallow: Of his ten career victories, four of them—including his first-ever win—involved one-two finishes with his brother.

"All my racing life, most of it was competing against Bobby," he says. "And it was really weird because in '71 in Talladega, he sat on the pole and I won the race. The next race, I sat on the pole, he won the race. The races that people don't see, there's many, many times when we ran second and third, and third and fourth, when we actually helped each other run second and third, and third and fourth. But I don't know, half of the time it felt good to beat whoever, much less my brother. And of course the media and the outside people probably made a little bit more out of it than we even did."

Even with the competitive edges, the brothers, always close and nowadays closer still, continue to reminisce about their tight finishes, going all the way back to the modified days when it was a worthy struggle just to field their cars.

"The only thing my mother always said is she wanted a dead

heat between Bobby and I," Donnie remembers. "And I told her, 'Mom, that'd never happen.' She said, 'Why not?' I said, 'Because I wouldn't let him win, and I know he wouldn't let me.'"

In fact, after their mothers' initial opposition to the brothers' entry into racing, NASCAR eventually became very much a family sport for the Allisons.

"I think my mom finally found out, I know she found out, that racing people weren't as she perceived them. I mean, there are rogues in everything, but the people I think really shocked her, the [great] way they were," recalls Donnie. "Well, [my parents] got very involved, and over the twenty-five years or whatever it was that they were really interested, they'd become the biggest race fans there were. They'd go everywhere. There's not very many people in this world in any business [who] can say that their parents took a part in doing what the kids did like my mother and father did with us. And my mother's still doing it—at ninety-two years old."

For years, Bobby Allison made the most of his rides, added to his victory total, and finished in the top ten. A NASCAR Winston Cup Series title still eluded him and would continue to until he became involved in one of the biggest rivalries since the days he'd toiled against Richard Petty—this one with Darrell Waltrip.

Like him or not—and many fans didn't at the time—Waltrip was one of the first drivers of his generation to break the logjam of NASCAR Winston Cup Series champions that had defined the 1970s. With the coming of Waltrip, that most fertile era of champions, the days of Petty, Yarborough, Allison, Pearson, and Buddy Baker was giving way to a growing youth movement, dominated at first by Waltrip, Dale Earnhardt, and Terry Labonte.

The old guard was not finished yet, however. For his part, Allison still had that elusive Cup title to earn. But in the early 1980s, he'd somehow have to get through Waltrip to do so.

To make matters even more interesting, Waltrip was running for Allison's one-time boss, Junior Johnson, and in 1981, when Bobby raced for Harry Rainer, the racers staged their first memorable competition for the annual prize. Early in the season, Waltrip was hundreds of points out of the running, and Allison put an exclamation point on his own efforts by climbing from seventh place to first in the last lap to claim the June win in Michigan. Eventually, Waltrip marched back with amazing success; toward the end of the season, he won four consecutive races from the pole, putting himself finally in position to win the title, which he ultimately did by all of fifty-three points over Allison.

The following year, Allison switched cars yet again and drove for the DiGard team, starting the season off right with his second Daytona 500 victory, beating Cale Yarborough. In a move that seemed like old times, the pair had gotten together in the fourth lap; as a result of their on-track tussle, Allison lost a bumper. Later, Yarborough's crew would make the interesting claim that the car had been designed to lose a bumper in order to make Allison run faster. Would that Allison had such an advantage all season: Though he and Waltrip clearly outran the rest of the field, winning a combined twenty of the season's thirty races between them, Waltrip again made a late charge and held a slim 22-point lead going into the last race of the season. With the championship again so clearly in his reach, Allison could only manage sixteenth place in the final race to Waltrip's third-place finish. Again, it was Waltrip's title.

It must have seemed impossible for two drivers to dominate the rest of the field for yet a third year, but when 1983 came to a close, Bill Elliott, in third place, was several hundred points off the pace set by Allison and Waltrip. Finally, it seemed as if the fates were in Allison's favor; late in the season, it was his turn to put on the charge to seal a title. His Southern 500 win that year was the first of three in a row and with six races left, the title was his to lose. Waltrip closed the gap with four top-fives, including a win at North Wilkesboro, but a third-place finish at Atlanta kept Bobby in the lead going into the final at Riverside. The car ran poorly that day, but when that race was run, Bobby Allison had capped off the best three-year stretch of his career with the one win he'd always wanted.

After the race, the rain came down in buckets; it fell hard on Bobby's parade, hard enough so that he couldn't celebrate the way he wanted to. Fittingly, he adapted, and in a little Italian place in Riverside, he, his wife Judy, and the team partied good and hard.

Bobby's stretch of good fortune kept alive talk of the good old days, when the Alabama Gang's Allison brothers first came onto the scene, a pair of young modified drivers who always made something out of nothing. It was good publicity to keep the name going, first with Neil Bonnett and then with a host of other drivers who shared the geography, if not the drive.

But a few years down the road, the Gang's next generation would be the talk of the circuit, thanks to the emergence of its true inheritor, in name and spirit. And as much as Bobby Allison forever embraced the love of winning and driving as few others have before or since, there would be nothing in his career to ever match the joyous thrill of racing against Davey.

Two Lives Worth Remembering

Bobby Allison made a career out of facing challenges from the best drivers of two generations—Richard Petty and Darrell Waltrip—but during the 1988 Daytona 500, Allison saw both those drivers fall out of contention, leaving Bobby, at age fifty, to vie for the trip to victory lane with a great challenger from yet a third generation. This driver, however, was the only one Bobby ever faced with whom he felt an odd mix of competition and kinship—his twenty-six-year-old son, Davey. There is no knowing the wild complexity of thoughts that must have passed through him during those final high-speed moments, as he tried to keep himself ahead of his boy, the defending NASCAR Rookie of the Year and one of the undisputed princes of his sport.

One thing Bobby certainly didn't feel was reassurance that he would definitely win. True, he had the greater amount of experience, but Davey could have conducted a seminar on his father's insistent, consistent driving style. While much of it had rubbed off, Davey also countered his adoption of Bobby's intensity with the lesson of patience, earned well through hard-won—and sometimes hard-worn—seat time. Yes, Davey worshiped his father, but that wouldn't make him back off, not when winning would prove something to the old man.

On the other end, Davey had more than just his father's skills to overcome. Bobby had a real streak going, having won a Twin 125 qualifier and the NASCAR Busch Series race during Speedweeks; if that wasn't enough, he'd also won the annual Speedweeks fishing tournament.

Through lap after lap, they drafted together, like a son forced to follow his father on the highway because he doesn't know where they're going. Davey plotted his move, waiting for the laps to fall away so that if he did make the pass, there'd be little time for the reeling Bobby to recover.

He waited a long time, until there was less than half a lap to go: Winning would take a spirited, daring move. Bobby knew this all along; setting up a fake, he inched over and offered his son the low part of the track. Davey took it and ran wide open; for an instant, coming out of turn four, it looked as if they might come even, but Davey didn't have enough momentum, as Bobby had known all along. Seconds later, Davey watched his father earn the checkered flag and win the day. Not surprisingly, when all was said and done, Davey crossed the start-finish line beaming. It had been almost thirty years since a father, Lee Petty, had beaten his son Richard for a NASCAR senior circuit victory. That this newest occurrence happened at Daytona, of all places, spoke volumes about the historic talents of the Allisons.

Davey called the race his most memorable moment on track. Four years later, after winning the Daytona 500 himself, he said his victory paled in comparison to his second-place finish from years before. With the victory lane celebration on that February 1988 day, and the warmth, camaraderie, and acceptance between the two men, it's easy to see that, had nothing ever changed for Davey Allison, he would have felt the same way about the result today.

The same goes for his father—had nothing ever changed for Bobby, the memories of those final laps would still bring him insurmountable pride and joy. But as every long-time fan of NASCAR knows, things changed more drastically than reason should have allowed for both men, along with Bobby's other son, Clifford. In four years, Bobby's two young sons would be tragically gone. They have left in their wake enormous gaps that still remain: in their family, in the sport, and in their lost potential.

For Bobby, after all the facts of his later years are tallied, one bitterly unfair one remains: Thanks to his accident at Pocono four months after the Daytona 500 win—and his subsequent memory loss—there are significant days now irretrievably lost. One such day is his race for the ages with Davey. He knows what happened because he has seen it on television. But the images coming through do not register.

"To win that race at age fifty and to have the best young man in racing be second behind me, and have that young man also be my son, has got to be the greatest achievement anybody could hope for. But that race still seems to not want to come back around," he said in 1993. "I remember the twenty-four-hour race in '88, the Australia race in '88, and also an outlaw, non-sanctioned race I did at Texas World Speedway—I sat on the pole for that and won the race, and somehow the memory of that comes back. But the Winston Cup race continues to be covered up with dust."

That the 1988 Daytona 500 turned out to be the golden experience of Davey Allison's racing career is not surprising considering that for years, he wanted nothing more than to be able to run on the same track as his father. Born in 1961, the day before Bobby Allison made his first Daytona 500 start, Davey immersed himself early in the dream of inheriting the mantle of the Alabama Gang, leading his friends on bike rides through the back roads at home in Hueytown, Alabama, dreaming of checkered flags and glory. Not long after that, he began working in his father's shop, and felt ready to run some local races as a teenager.

"When Davey said he wanted to go into racing, [his mother] and I told him that he had to have a high school diploma," Bobby recalls. "So he went to summer school between junior and senior year. And he finished his schooling in January so he could start working on his car and be ready for the racing season. I thought that was an indication of sincere commitment. This boy talked constantly about being a racer. I would try to help him some, but he was an employee of my race shop, and he had duties there he had to take care of. After working hours, he had use of the equipment and the facility, and I could make a comment about the selection of the equipment. He really followed through on those things."

Bobby wanted his oldest son to earn the privilege of racing, as he had. While Davey began to develop his natural talent behind the wheel, he was also green and had his share of fender benders using his less-than-stellar materials. That began to change in 1979 when he started driving Limited Sportsman events in Birmingham.

"In the first part of his racing career, I didn't think he'd make it," recalls Davey's uncle, Donnie. "I told his daddy several times. We had a pretty good conversation one night, Bobby and I. And I said, 'Why don't you give that boy a car, a piece of equipment that suits him,' and he said, 'No, he's doing all right.'"

Donnie, who had grown very close to Davey, rectified the situation by giving him the frame to a Nova he had. Davey built up the car and finally had the right ride. "That was my good race car," says Donnie with a smile. "And he came on Tuesday, put it together, raced it on Friday, and won his first race. Then he went Saturday night and won again. His father came home on Monday and said, 'Maybe you're right.'"

Davey was starting to live the dream he'd always claimed he would. Along with his old biking friends from youth, who became his pit crew—dubbed the Peach Fuzz Gang by the family—Davey readied to blaze a trail on the Automobile Racing Club of America circuit. In 1983, the season his father won his only NASCAR Winston Cup Series title driving the No. 22 DiGard Buick, Davey ran a limited number of ARCA races and won four times, driving his own No. 22 car. His wins that year included the race at Talladega, his hometown superspeedway, where his father had won three times and his uncle twice. Davey was getting some engines from his father's friend Robert Yates, and the Allison name became a popular one on the ARCA circuit. In 1984, at twenty-three, Davey won ARCA Rookie of the Year; the next season, he subbed in three NASCAR Winston Cup Series races. Unbelievably—considering his inexperience at that level—he earned a top-ten.

Two years later, in 1987, thirty-odd years into a brilliant career, Bobby Allison experienced what was for him a strange emotion at the race track: awe. Two months into the new NASCAR Winston Cup Series season, there was no denying his son's talent and ability. With little fanfare—especially compared to the pressure-filled reception that greeted Davey's friend Kyle Petty on his NASCAR Winston Cup Series debut eight years earlier—Davey established himself as the best rookie his sport had seen since Dale Earnhardt began his full-time ride in 1979. Less than two weeks shy of his twenty-sixth birthday, he became the first rookie ever to qualify on the front row of the Daytona 500; a week later, he won the pole at

Rockingham. Seven weeks after that, he interrupted Earnhardt's streak of four victories by winning his first NASCAR Winston Cup Series race in a familiar setting: Talladega. For the Firecracker 400 at Daytona on Independence Day, Davey won the pole and his father won the race. In all, he won two races, five poles, nine top fives, and Rookie of the Year honors driving twenty-two races in 1987. Perhaps more important, he earned the long-sought approval of the one man whose life he'd tried to emulate.

There was something all too familiar about Davey's driving style, the determined march to the front, matched with a stalker's patience—that latter quality gleaned from watching Uncle Donnie. He was the complete package, a handsome kid with a great smile, a warm appeal for fans, and a beloved name that allied him to a favorite son of the sport's prime years. With Davey, the Alabama Gang was assured a continuation of its lore for another generation.

Of course, the reigning generation wasn't through yet. At Daytona in 1988, Bobby Allison got to win the big one in the best of circumstances. He still figured to have some good racing years left; there'd be more times like these, days spent challenging his boy and watching him become a champion.

Lap after lap, Davey Allison circled the track at Pocono, still under caution, looking for some sign. A mere four months after Bobby had won the day at Daytona, he cut a tire on the first lap and had gone solidly into the wall. The day ended his driving career.

When Bobby was knocked out of commission, the family was devastated. He had always been the center of the Allisons, the family's prime decision-maker. Now, a scant few months after sharing his father's moment of triumph, Davey felt he needed to assume the reins.

It would be a period of uneasy growth for Bobby's oldest son. The profitability that had brought about new growth issues across the top tier of professional sports had come upon NASCAR, and Davey, a popular and successful driver, found himself more successful than his father had ever dreamed of being. While he enjoyed his stardom, there were more responsibilities at home. Bobby had always been his son's inspiration; now, given his father's condition and new reliance upon his son, the tables had turned. The pressure became hard to bear, and it ate into Davey's focus at the racetrack. In the summer of 1988, he met the woman, Liz, who would become his second wife in 1989; within a year, he'd be a father.

Although he won some races and had success, people began to wonder when the payoff might begin to outweigh Davey's enormous potential.

Looking back with the benefit of time, Davey Allison's 1992 season, with its brilliant highs and mesmerizing lows, can still leave one speechless. That he even made it through the season intact was an achievement; that he thrived, especially in the face of renewed family tragedy, explains more than anything his endless appeal.

Coming off a career-high third-place NASCAR Winston Cup Series finish in 1991, Allison finally seemed to have everything in order. A great crew chief in Larry McReynolds, a long-standing relationship with team owner Robert Yates, and the best Ford in the field were all reasons for optimism, confirmed when Davey began the season with a win at the Daytona 500. Then Bill Elliott established some early-season dominance of his own, winning the next four weeks straight. The tour then stopped in Bristol, where Davey received the awful news of his beloved grandfather's death. Pops Allison, Bobby's father and the patriarch of the Alabama Gang, had, with his white beard, been the symbolic head of Davey's Peach Fuzz Gang when his grandson first dreamed of stock car glory. Davey, still leading in points despite Elliott's success, came to the track with added incentive to win.

He didn't come close. In a race where crashes ate up an inordinate number of laps, Davey fell victim himself when an oil fitting broke loose on his car, pouring oil under the wheels and sending him into the wall. The crash put some considerable hurt on his ribs and shoulder.

Regardless, he was back on the tour's next stop at North Wilkesboro and even won the race, offering a belated dedication of the win to his grandfather.

After reinjuring his rib cage the next week in Martinsville, he came into Charlotte for the running of the Winston All-Star race, the first NASCAR superspeedway event held at night since 1955.

Dale Earnhardt had taken the lead from Kyle Petty at the restart with four laps remaining in the final ten-lap dash. The two battled into the last lap with Allison lying in wait behind them, seeking the inevitable move among the leaders. It came when Petty made a run to the inside on the backstretch. Trying to block him, Earnhardt swerved and the pair drove as low as the track would allow off the third turn. When Earnhardt couldn't hold his position and Petty eased up a touch, Allison saw his opening.

Momentum carried him down to Petty's inside off turn four. With Earnhardt now out of the running, old friends Allison and Petty struggled for the lead. Davey tried to hold his line, Kyle tried to block. They were yards from the finish when the door-to-door touching began. They came together once before the finish and then again at the checkered flag, with Davey inches ahead of Petty. But thanks to that last touch, Davey spun out and hit the retaining wall just after the flag.

Davey was still chasing the same championship dream his father—and every driver on the circuit—always shares. So one week later, he was back in the car, starting seventeenth for the Coca-Cola 600 in Charlotte, finishing fourth and keeping his lead in NASCAR Winston Cup Series points.

He gave himself a bit more breathing room with a win from the pole on June 21st at Michigan. Two races later, the tour returned to Pocono, the site of his father's last race. Davey clearly dominated, leading almost two-thirds of the going, before everything dissolved.

A long pit stop set him back during a caution and after a restart on lap 147, he began making his way back through the pack. In trying to pass Darrell Waltrip, the two cars made contact. Waltrip kept going; Allison went airborne.

Davey slid sideways and headed for the grass, where his car dug in and flipped several times.

Davey required some surgery. But a day later, he declared himself fit enough to at least start the race the following week at Talladega. For the first time all season, he had fallen behind in NASCAR Winston Cup Series points, and despite the hurt, he didn't want to stop.

●   ●   ●

By 1992, Bobby Allison's recovery had been on an upswing. "God, I struggled," he says, recalling the early times after Pocono in 1988. And though Davey's influence had a lot to do with his father's progress, the insistence of Davey's younger brother, Clifford, that Bobby get out and stay active proved to be an enormous asset as well. Clifford, after years of having more fun than anything else, had finally embraced the idea of working toward the goal of using his considerable natural talent behind the wheel.

"They were two unique young men, very different in lifestyle," Donnie Allison says of Clifford and Davey. "Clifford had a way to finagle around and get out of work. He was a very, very good lad but he was shrewd. And I think this hurt him later in his racing, because there were some very good opportunities that he didn't take advantage of because of the work ethic."

He had finally begun to turn that around—and he and Davey, four years his senior, had also started to grow closer as well. With Clifford encouraging Bobby, the latter grew more active in securing a ride for his younger son. When Clifford began driving NASCAR Busch Series races, Bobby was about as happy as he could be; his two sons were often at the same location on the different circuits and Bobby couldn't help but show some optimism.

Davey was relaxing in the garage at Michigan the day Clifford set up to do some practice in preparation for qualifying. Bobby watched his son drive off, radioing back with "Dad, we're gonna get 'em."

They were the last words Bobby Allison would hear his son Clifford say. A crash on turn four ended his promising young life.

After finally thinking there'd been a turnaround in family fortunes, the Allisons once again wallowed in grief, with Davey and Bobby going through pangs of guilt, wondering if they could have done something to better guide Clifford's career. Yates encouraged Davey to pass up the Michigan race to mourn his brother. The driver instead knew racing was the only way he could honor him and he started the contest. After finishing fifth, he immediately left for home.

It must have been a relief that, after Michigan, Davey returned to racing with very little incident. His body mending, he tried to get himself back in the running for the NASCAR Winston Cup Series title, even though Bill Elliott had built a commanding lead over both him and Alan Kulwicki. But with some late-season collapses, Elliott started to relinquish that margin and after Davey took the second to last race of the season, he brought a slim thirty-point lead over the ever-consistent Kulwicki into the final race in Atlanta.

With Elliott hovering another ten points back, the championship could turn on a single bit of fortune, and for Allison, after a season of such devastating turns, there remained a good shot at some redemption. He needed to finish fifth or better to win what it had taken his father decades to claim. It would also be the final race of Richard Petty's illustrious career—and the first of Jeff Gordon's—giving Allison a chance to clinch the title at the retirement party of his father's biggest rival.

Everything went according to plan for three-quarters of the event; Allison stayed comfortably in the top five, and even though Elliott was out in front, it didn't matter. Only a mishap could reshape the picture.

The mishap came on lap 254. Already laps down and out of the running for victory, Ernie Irvan, experiencing tire trouble, lost control of his car and brushed the wall. After bouncing off, he ricocheted right in the path of the unsuspecting Allison. Davey, with nowhere to go, went into Irvan.

Though both drivers were unhurt, Allison's championship chances were about as healthy as his damaged car. He got back in the race again, although several laps down; now, he needed Elliott and Kulwicki to end their days prematurely in order to have a chance.

The two opponents not only stayed out of trouble, they ended up finishing one and two, with Elliott winning the race but Kulwicki leading the most laps by one. That single-lap difference became the most important statistic in the closest NASCAR Winston Cup Series championship finish in history. Gaining five points for most laps led in a race allowed the popular Kulwicki to win the NASCAR Winston Cup Series championship by a mere ten points. While Kulwicki enjoyed his backward "Polish victory lap," followed by an extra lap for the King, who had brought his car back after a crash, Allison could only shrug off the day in the background. It seemed, somehow, a fitting end to a season packed with frustration and sadness.

Unfortunately, the pain was not nearly over. Davey healed up in the off-season, but not long into 1993, NASCAR had to face an awful tragedy when Kulwicki perished in a plane crash on April 1. The event shook fans and competitors terribly. At a time when the sport was starting to be dominated by multicar teams, many fans regarded Kulwicki—who owned his car and raced on a tighter budget—as a genuine working-class success story. His death robbed the sport of a great champion.

In the Allison family, the dust had begun to settle a bit. Bobby's recovery, which had taken a powerful setback due to the loss of Clifford, was back on track, thanks in no small part to Davey's encouragement. As the season progressed, Davey ran well and kept himself consistently in the hunt for the 1993 NASCAR Winston Cup Series prize. And on the plane ride back from New Hampshire, after the inaugural running of the race in Loudon, Davey and his dad talked about their rich past and bright future. Bobby cherished the trip and its further confirmation that he and his older son had grown even closer in the months following Clifford's death.

The next day, Davey and Red Farmer—his lifelong friend and his father's Alabama Gang partner—took off in Davey's helicopter for the quick ride from home to Talladega to watch their friend Neil Bonnett's son, David, test a car. Davey looked forward to the next week's race, in Pocono; it had been a year since his incident there and Davey wanted some payback at the track where his family had seen such hard times.

The winds blew hard as Davey and Farmer prepared to land in the Talladega infield, and the ride suddenly grew turbulent. Davey, losing control of the craft, tried to regain it, but the helicopter shook and turned on its left side, falling to the ground. Davey, who had hit his head, lay unconscious. Medics removed him and rushed him to the hospital; the Allison family arrived for an all too familiar vigil. Unbelievably, Davey Allison was gone.

The following week, Dale Earnhardt, loving son of another NASCAR legend, won the race at Pocono. Afterwards, he stopped at the start-finish line and joined his race team in a prayer; then, with tears in his eyes, he took a flag bearing Davey's number, 28, and drove a Polish victory lap to honor the sport's two fallen stars. He would need a minute to compose himself before driving off to victory lane.

For Bobby Allison, the further tragedy—and, to some degree, solace—after Davey's death was their renewed bond. Once again, Bobby had begun to think there might still be a day, far off, when he could run a team with Davey at the wheel.

After the season, highlighted by Dale Earnhardt's sixth NASCAR Winston Cup Series title, Bobby Allison and his wife Judy headed for what would be Bobby's emotional induction into the International Motorsports Hall of Fame. At that point, it seemed the honors he earned had less to do with his speed than his endurance.

"I still cry a lot," he said, sitting with Judy the day before the awards. "When we lost Clifford, it was really really tough, but a lot of people helped and Davey helped me. Davey had been a special son from real early on anyway. He and Clifford were quite different young men. Clifford was the one who looked for the fun things, the things to play with. Before he died, he was really applying himself, but his basic lifestyle was looking for the fun in life, and Clifford got killed working. From very early on, Davey planned what he wanted to do, he was very well focused and he worked. And Davey got killed playing. And that's the irony of life."

Bobby Allison emerges from the rear garage area at Pocono in July 1999, and takes some time out from talking with the team of fellow Hueytown, Alabama, native Jimmy Kitchens, an ARCA racer he is working with and advising. There is a deliberate quality to the way he moves through life now. The hitch in his gait is part of it: He walks carefully, as if doing so is a therapeutic exercise. When he addresses a question that makes him dig back, he raises his hands awkwardly, still trying to understand the scope of what has occurred. But he does his best to look forward.

"I am fortunate there are some things I do enjoy doing," he says. "I really enjoy flying, and owning and operating my airplane gives me an accomplishment that's special. And so I try to focus on the positive.

"It's eleven years since I was busy racing, eleven years since my career ended, and people are still really nice to me," he continues. "I was in California on Wednesday and in North Carolina Tuesday, and had an autograph session. People turned out in big numbers, and the thing that I'm also pleased about is, people ask how's my mom, and how's my brother Donnie, and how's the rest of the family, [older brother] Eddie who they knew a little bit, and Tommy, my younger brother, and of course Tommy's son, Tommy Jr., was with Davey, and so it's very, very complimentary for people to regard the whole family as special."

Among NASCAR fans, few families will ever be embraced with as much affection as the Allisons. And although some of that has to do with a deep outpouring of sympathy for the hand fate has dealt them, it has as much to do with the family's triumphs and the enduring working-class hero reputation of the Alabama Gang.

For his part, Bobby is tied for third among all drivers in history with eighty-four wins; to that he can add being named NASCAR's Most Popular Driver six times (1971–1973, 1981–1983). In 1998, as part of the sport's golden anniversary celebration, both Bobby and Davey were chosen for the list of NASCAR's 50 Greatest Drivers. Davey earned the accolade with nineteen victories and sixty-six top fives. Those would be successful numbers for a full career; the fact that they came in only 191 races run over six-and-a-half full seasons makes the figures extraordinary. Fans still celebrate the legacy of Davey's No. 28 car with souvenirs and placards and legions of competitors speak to his enormous talent. Though you can't call it a sure thing, few would dispute that Davey, so close to winning the championship in 1992, had an excellent chance of securing NASCAR's great prize had he lived to keep driving. Less of a stretch is the idea that he, too, would one day have been voted Most Popular Driver. As his proud father has since stated on a number of occasions, "What greater compliment could a parent have than their son is loved around the world—and that was Davey."

3
Buck and Buddy Baker

Eighteen-year-old Buddy Baker's first NASCAR race looked to be a real nightmare. He was running last at the Columbia, South Carolina, dirt track and he couldn't understand why. It seemed the wrong place for the son of the formidable two-time Grand National champion Buck Baker to be driving, but any observer could see Buddy couldn't keep up the pace. Granted, he shared that track with the greatest drivers of the day, Ned Jarrett, Tiny Lund, Lee Petty, and Buck Baker among them. These racers had battled each other for years both on and off the track, collecting trophies and winnings to go along with bruises during the early days of NASCAR racing. Buddy Baker bitterly watched through his windshield as the cars sped ahead of him, then watched them again even more bitterly in the ugly déjà vu of being lapped by the field. At one point, he took a turn too wide, and the lead car, attempting to make a pass, bumped him out of the way and almost into the infield. Buddy regained control quickly enough to notice that the offending driver, the first one ever to lay a bumper on him, was his own father.

Disappointed at his situation, Buddy came to one conclusion: There had to be something wrong with his car.

A few days earlier, he'd set into motion the plan that landed him in this mess. He had been in the shop, working on his father's car, and after putting it off long enough, he finally decided to approach his dad about doing some driving himself. It seemed natural enough: He'd grown up talking racing with his dad at the breakfast table, discussing strategy since the time he'd been old enough to understand anything about it. His father had been winning races in NASCAR since 1952, and like Lee Petty's son Richard, Buddy had grown up in a house used to winning. Buddy now felt that same need to carry on the family tradition.

However, it would not be easy bringing up the subject. "My dad was pretty stern," he says now. Buck Baker, a compact man with piercing eyes under jet-black hair and furrowed brows, enjoyed his reputation as a racer to be feared. Even now, the one-time city bus driver from Charlotte, North Carolina, describes himself during his on-track days as "A guy who'd like to run over you and then say, 'Excuse me.'" Buddy, on the other hand, was tall and broad in a gentle bear kind of way, with a twinkle-eyed easygoing manner and a good sense of humor. Afraid of his father's reaction, he sidled over to the man twice during that afternoon at the shop, starting to bring up the subject before skulking off with a "Never mind." By Buddy's third approach, he could see his father getting angry.

But he was completely unprepared for the reaction he got.

"I went, 'Dad,' and he said, 'What do you want?' I said, 'You know, I'd like to start racing.' To my amazement, he said, 'Well, there's an old car over there in the corner and all the parts are over there. Get some people up and we'll help you get going and we'll go down to Columbia next weekend.' And I went, 'Cool!'"

It felt that way until he qualified the car toward the back of the field and found himself on race day driving the equivalent of a lemon. While driving, he went over the week's events in his head, trying to figure out if he hadn't set the car up right. That's when he saw his father waving him in from the pit area.

Due to mechanical trouble, Buck Baker's car had stopped in mid-race. Stuck without a ride and not wanting to miss the chance at a good payday, Buck figured he'd take his chances driving his son's car in last place. As Buddy tells it, he surrendered the wheel and Buck left the pits in a haze of smoke.

It took a number of circuits, but Buck Baker unlapped himself and then deftly pursued the leaders. The race, however, ended too quickly for him; he finished third in a contest he clearly might have won had his equipment been a match for his talent and drive.

The whole event left Buddy Baker deeply embarrassed.

"Like all kids, we think we're equal to fifteen years of racing experience," he says. "On the way back home I said [to myself], 'You know, you got a lot to learn, kid.' Because I had really gotten a lesson at an early age and I was glad. I realized that anything worthwhile takes a lot of dedication, a lot of hard work. It was quite awhile before I felt that I was even competitive, but that made the day when I started running with the lead cars that much better."

Ten years before his first race, Buddy had watched his father run with the leaders and often run off with the win during the early days of his classic NASCAR career. Some of Buddy's favorite memories include being swept up by the excitement of the action and the crowds as an eight-year-old on a February afternoon in Florida.

"When [my dad] ran at Daytona, when he went down the paved part of the beach course, I'd run across the sand dunes, watch him go by, then I'd run back across and watch him come down the front straightaway," he says. "At the end of the race, I was almost as tired as he was."

Like Richard Petty, Buddy had watched his own father drive in the first-ever NASCAR race in Charlotte in 1949. Seven years later, he watched again while his dad, driving for legendary multimillionaire owner/taskmaster Carl Kiekhaefer, won the first of his two consecutive Grand National championships. In 1956, the second and last year Kiekhaefer emblazoned the Mercury Outboard Motors logo on those Chryslers, his cars won thirty of fifty-six races on the schedule. Buck Baker won fourteen of those on his way to a championship. In 1957, Kiekhaefer departed from NASCAR racing, but Buck Baker was smack in the center of his prime; he went back to owning his own cars, won ten more contests, and claimed the annual prize once again.

Buck enjoyed elite status in the highest ranks, having won the respect of his fellows since the days he'd run in the modified division ranks in the undisciplined era before NASCAR organized stock. "I'm kind of a pioneer you might say," he declares, a veteran of contests when races were often one hundred miles instead of five hundred, run on much smaller tracks with a slower, brutal pace. The driving was more "intimate," to say the least, and with the stakes lower, racers ran for pride more than anything else. In pre-NASCAR days, a stock car race promoter might run off with the purse—an all-too-frequent occurrence—or a winning driver could end his day earning barter instead of dollars. "It's real shocking to hear they get a million dollars," Buck says of some of today's more lucrative races. "Back then you could get a fifth of wine and a ham." All factors combined for a much rougher atmosphere that was quite different than what the standard racing fan is used to today. Buck Baker thrived in such an environment.

"Hell, a hundred miles back then was a whole lot rougher than five hundred miles is now," he boasts. "You used to drive thirty minutes and fight thirty minutes."

"But it's like anything else," says Buddy Baker. "That's the only way you get rules and regulations, because when it first started out it didn't even have a sanctioning body and then NASCAR comes in and gets everybody together. Bill France came in and offered them an opportunity to keep the playing field pretty even and guarantee the purses and have the fire equipment and the stuff that makes a race and they had to grow, too. I mean you look at some of the first NASCAR races and see how far they've come.

"The current-day race car driver is highly educated, most of them have been to college, have engineering degrees, but because it started out as a my-car-can-outrun-your-car type thing on a little cut-out track in somebody's backyard and it grew to the sport that it is, it's like talking about how basketball got started with a peach-basket hoop."

When Buddy Baker joined the business that made his father a champion, the way of speed had already begun its biggest transformation, from the more strategic yet caustic business of short-track racing to the all-out, big-business reality of superspeedways. Unlike his father, Buddy found the unconstrained menace of the high-bank asphalt tracks suited him perfectly. After years of developing his skills, it was clear that something happened to Buddy Baker when he got behind the wheel of a car at a grand palace such as Daytona or Talladega. The benign guy you could share a drink with during the week became a road warrior once he got on the track, running in the front of the pack whenever possible and always going wide open. As a result, he too frequently ended his day in the infield, in the pits, or somehow out of the action, perhaps partly due to the toll his car suffered from his style.

"I would have loved to have had the opportunity, with my driving style, to have driven in today's society, as far as the attrition," Buddy says. "Unfortunately, I was along in that time when you could almost guarantee that of the top ten cars there would be three or four of them that would go out with mechanical problems. That never bothered me; I'd just run it wide open, half turned over all the time."

After driving for his father for several years, he ended up as something of a journeyman, going behind the wheel for a number of owners, building his resume and skills and often finding that he managed to get more out of a less-than-perfect car than many would have thought possible. He also found that by the mid-1960s, he could beat his father more frequently behind the wheel. In 1965, when his dad was forty-six, Buddy topped him in the Grand National standings for the first time, finishing ninth to his father's seventeenth.

"That was not a goal of mine," he admits. "I can remember the first time I actually beat my father in a race and it didn't have the feeling that you would think, because he was still my hero and he always has been, in a race car, and for me to beat him I said, you know, it's like in any sport. We all have our time; you just run the calendar back and make him twenty-four like you are and he'd kick your fanny. That's the way I looked at it. I never did really run a competition with my dad; I still don't. Whether I beat him or lost to him, it didn't have a feeling of being happy or sad. For so many years I looked out the windshield at him and then I looked at the mirror and the feeling was never any different."

The only difference would come if he ever got the chance to beat not just his dad, but everybody. At one point, he nearly got the opportunity to drive a factory car for owner Ray Fox, but that situation vanished unexpectedly to Buddy's infinite disappointment. He began to wonder if he'd ever find himself paired with a machine to match his demeanor as the stretch of time before his first trip to victory lane grew longer.

But Fox, one of NASCAR history's most accomplished engineers, had long been impressed with Baker, and tapped him to drive one of his cars for the National 500 in Charlotte in October 1967.

"The funny part was, I bragged to people that if I ever got a shot in a good race car, I'd show them where I was supposed to be. So the day I was supposed to drive for Ray Fox the first time, I drove up to the front gate at Charlotte and I kinda looked at it and thought, 'Whoa, boy—now you done all the talkin'; now back it up.' And I got in the car and I went out [in practice] and I ran as hard as I could, but I came in and said, 'You know, I'll be able to pick it up as soon as I get used to the car.' And [Fox] said, 'Well, if you do, we're gonna be awfully tough because you're about half a second quicker than anybody that's ever been around here.'"

Finally behind the wheel of the perfect car, Buddy Baker had one huge obstacle to face in Charlotte: the unstoppable hemi engine of Richard Petty. In 1967, Richard and his mechanic brother Maurice were in the midst of the greatest season in motor sports history. When all the races had been run at season's end, Petty would compile twenty-seven wins and a total of forty top-ten finishes in forty-eight starts. Two weeks prior to the Charlotte race, in North Wilkesboro, Petty had achieved the unthinkable by notching his tenth victory in a row. His impressive run was the talk of the circuit.

Baker, a good friend of Petty's, wasn't even thinking about records. With his obvious penchant for the major speedways, he didn't even run a full schedule and missed a number of the tracks where King Richard had been compiling his grand numbers. And Petty had not seen what Baker's car could do.

He wouldn't get much of a chance in Charlotte. Thanks to an accident, Petty wasn't a factor in the race, and by the end nobody else was, either. When the checkered flag went down, it was Buddy Baker who had earned it, easily outdistancing Bobby Isaac by about a lap. It had taken a long time for Baker's first trip to victory lane. In all, he'd waited over eight years and driven more than 200 races before tasting the thrill of a win. Perhaps the best part of all was the way he was greeted in the winner's circle.

"I had a car that could *fly*," he remembers. "I won four times at Charlotte but that first one, you never forget it. And seeing my dad—at the time he had a broken leg, but he was standing right as I drove into the winner's circle, on a pair of crutches, with a smile, and I guess it was the first time that I felt like I got his approval. To me, that was as important as winning, to see his face when I drove into the winner's circle."

Recalls Buck Baker, "I was on crutches and I threw the damn crutches down and hugged his neck and told him I was real proud of him."

"It was just a very special day, you know?" Buddy continues. "It still is. You can't explain to the average person unless you just say, bottle up everything that you ever wanted to do and put it in some type of formula. That's what it's like for a race car driver when he wins his first major race. The years that you worked getting there and the aggravation and everything is forgotten. It's like, okay, here's your peace pill. This will work for awhile."

The next year, Baker enjoyed one of his finest seasons: one victory and another eighteen top-tens. He soon parted with Fox, but his reputation was solidified: Owners had seen what he could do when given the right equipment.

"What was funny, though, is as I got better cars, I got 'smarter,'" he says, chuckling sarcastically. "Everybody'd go, 'Now you're using your head, you see.' You know, it's kinda like, it'd take a pretty bad jockey to look bad on Secretariat."

Through the mid-'70s, he often found himself posting top-tens, making a racing afternoon interesting and building a name as one of the circuit's most popular drivers, a favorite for fans who enjoyed an easy smile matched with a wide-open style that reminded them of the old days. On superspeedways, Richard Petty, David Pearson, Cale Yarborough, Bobby Allison, and Buddy Baker were the new legends. Their car numbers, scrawled on placards, were held up at the tracks where fans by the thousands cheered or booed the good guys or the bad guys. "Richard Petty was always the good guy," Buddy says. "Cale and I, we were good, some."

Mixed in with these heady days, Baker dealt with a pressing concern that brought him a great deal of angst involving his father. By this time, Buck Baker was at the tail end of his driving career, ready to hang it up, running only on occasion. At times, it seemed like one occasion too many to Buddy, especially during a 125-mile race in Daytona where, of all things, he and his father were involved in an incident together.

"I'll tell you, it was the scariest moment of my life," he admits. "My dad was in a car that was not up to speed and just as I lapped him, my engine let go, he got in the oil and got into the outside wall and all I could see in the mirror, through the smoke out of the back of my car, was his car and stuff flying everywhere."

Perhaps the only good thing about Buddy losing his engine was he could coast to the garage area and run to check on his dad. "I can remember going in and just going, please, please let him be okay. And, I'll tell you, when I saw him sitting up, whatever else happened didn't matter. I was just, 'Whew.' That's when I said to myself, one of us has got to quit."

When it came to goals in stock car racing, Buddy Baker wouldn't have considered a NASCAR Winston Cup Series championship to be near the top of the list. With his strengths being the faster, major tracks, he would often concentrate on winning superspeedway races through the year. He also discovered early on that he could easily make more money testing cars for owners on superspeedways than he ever could competing. Testing was a lucrative business that suited Buddy: If an owner wanted to see how his car handled under the most strenuous conditions, who better to put behind the wheel?

There was only one race Buddy dreamed of taking the checker for: the Daytona 500. Before Dale Earnhardt toiled for twenty years to earn his most prized victory at Daytona, Buddy Baker held the ignominious distinction of making the most attempts with the most near-misses. In fact, Earnhardt probably has nothing on Baker, who claims to have run about 40,000 testing miles at Daytona.

"I think it fit my driving style as well as any place I've ever been," he says of the fabled track. "My love of that speedway—I used to test there so much, it was like a track in my backyard. [The 500] became an obsession with me, year after year."

And year after year he fell short—if the race had been the Daytona 450, he states, he would have won about sixteen times. In 1980, in his eighteenth attempt, he finally had a car that was worth what he could put into it. Soon after the green flag went down, the question of whether Buddy Baker would break his hex seemed moot; more to the point was, how brilliant a run could he have. He not only finally won the race, he also shattered the existing speed record for the track, covering the distance at an average of 177.602 mph, a figure that still stands today.

It seemed only fitting. Ten years earlier, testing Goodyear tires at Talladega, Daytona's sister track, Baker became the first man to travel over 200 mph in a stock car.

The same year that Buddy Baker captured Daytona, his father opened the Buck Baker Racing School, where would-be racing professionals, curious corporate guests, and anybody else looking for high-speed thrills could attend classes; the school now offers lessons in Rockingham, Atlanta, Richmond, and Bristol. No doubt it has seen its share of executives with disposable incomes in search of a boyhood thrill, but the school has made its reputation as a training ground for a number of the sport's beloved names: Among them are Jeff and Ward Burton, Joe Nemechek, Tony Stewart, Bobby Hillin, Lynn St. James, and most notably Jeff Gordon. After retiring with the kind of numbers that made him a shoo-in for 1998's NASCAR 50 Greatest Drivers list—636 starts, 46 victories, 44 poles and two championships in a 26-year career— Buck had found the perfect challenge for a racing vet.

Buddy would himself face the retirement question a scant eight years later. On May 29, 1988, at Charlotte, he made contact with Bobby Allison—who had sped across the track to avoid spinning driver Eddie Bierschwale—and went into the wall. The event led, in time, to Buddy's retirement from the sport.

"I was out almost a full year before I was able to compete again and the only reason I ever ran another race was to tell myself I don't want to do it anymore," he says. "I didn't want a doctor or friends or even family members to make up my mind."

Before long, he got right back into the sport that, as with his father, had given him his livelihood. He entered the sportscasting booth in the 1990s while still keeping a foot in the game by continuing to test cars. He provided expert commentary for TNN and CBS, often teaming with strategist Ned Jarrett.

What remains for Buddy Baker are the memories: a 30-year career with 19 victories and 40 poles, a place alongside his father on NASCAR's 50 Greatest Drivers list, and races against three generations of drivers—including battles with the experts from his own generation, with whom he explored new limits of tenacity to the delight of fans. At the seed of these remembrances are his mornings at the breakfast table while still a boy, talking business with the father-turned-teacher who always set the example and made the most lasting impression. It's those discussions that have always fueled his need to succeed, even now.

"I admire things about my father," Buddy says. "He was one of the most determined people I've ever met. I think the biggest thing is his never-give-up attitude. That takes you a long way in this world. If you get to a point where good enough is good enough, then you don't need to be out there. When you need to always excel or try to excel and you hear a guy say, 'Well, I had a fifth-place car and I drove it to fifth'—that's the same as saying, 'I'm happy with fifth place.' Nah, I like to hear a guy say, 'I took a fifth-place car and ran second with it.' To me that's important. That old half-full, half-empty crap: I mean, c'mon. You still got half a glass—keep *pouring.*"

4
The Bodine Brothers

Geoffrey Bodine does not want to go hunting. He does not want to stay home, go on vacation, rest, take a boat trip—nothing. Geoffrey Bodine only wants to race. He is fifty but he feels like forty and he's ready to go. He'll race even when there is no race to run. Cars, trucks, whatever. To hear him tell it, you would think Bodine—voted one of the fifty greatest drivers in NASCAR history by virtue of longevity as much as success—was reciting a classified ad under the heading "Driver Available."

"I'm in good shape, I'm mentally tougher than I've ever been, and I have the experience of a veteran driver," he states. "Put all those things together and you oughta be really good out there. I feel good enough right now that I can race forever. My kids are grown up, I don't have to worry about taking them to the ballgame. I want to race and I spend almost one hundred percent of my time thinking about racing, and I think I have some positive things that should help me be successful where these other guys have young kids and have boats and they go hunting and they have other distractions. And my kids are right there with me—they want to race. They see their uncles out there, they see their father still out there, they want to be a part of it. But they know how hard it is. They know the highs and the lows of this business, but they still want to be a part of it. It's in their blood just like it's in mine."

Bodine's effort, his nonstop desire, is all about blood. Behind him are his father and grandfather, who built a racetrack in their hometown of Chemung, New York, when Geoffrey was only a year old. Alongside Geoffrey, grudgingly at times but a bit more comfortably these days, are his brothers, Brett and Todd. Brett is ten years younger and more easygoing. He's had his own highs and lows in a thirteen-year NASCAR Winston Cup Series career, but there's no escaping that his lowest point on the track involved a confrontation between him and Geoffrey, played out in front of millions during one of the most high-profile races in the sport's history.

Todd, five years younger than Brett and removed from any of that fray—or as removed as one can be when he's stuck in the middle of an argument—watched both his brothers race and win in junior divisions and struggle with consistent success in the NASCAR Winston Cup Series; meanwhile, he has managed to maintain a strong showing in the NASCAR Busch Series while waiting for a long-overdue break that will bring him back up to the top tier of racing.

Somewhere ahead of Geoffrey Bodine, in the future, is his plan to build a team for his twenty-one-year-old driving son, Barry, and Barry's mechanic brother, Matthew, who is twenty-seven.

So Geoffrey Bodine runs to win as always, but he also runs to carry on the family name in a sport where, every race weekend since 1982, there has been at least one Bodine in the field in a NASCAR Winston Cup Series or NASCAR Busch Series race. It's as if Energizer batteries would be a perfect sponsor for one of the Bodines. But that's another thing they all run for: the perfect sponsor, whichever one it is at the time. Geoffrey and Brett, inheriting their father's entrepreneurial gene, have each owned their teams during their racing histories. Todd has had several different rides in his travels. In this day and age where a legendary racing name can be a tremendous asset, the Bodines are still driving for legendary status. There is a lot of traffic ahead of them.

"I want to win and at the same time I want to keep that legacy going with my sons," says Geoffrey. "You can do both. My sons are the future, like Earnhardt Jr. and Jason Jarrett. But there's a lot I can still do here in the program and I can still win. I haven't let myself go. I want to be like Michael Jordan. I want to make the last shot of the last game. I wanna win the last race of my career and then say I'm gonna retire. That would be the ultimate."

• • •

Once upon a time, the ultimate for Geoffrey Bodine was winning the Daytona 500. The desire was not an atypical one, but Bodine had been dreaming it since the days when his parents put him and his older sister in the station wagon and drove the two days from upstate New York to Daytona Beach to watch the grand race. Bodine still recalls it all with zeal: the wait to stay at the Holiday Inn, the eight-millimeter movies of the races—he still has them—which he shot from the back of the station wagon, and of course the week and a half of school his parents allowed the kids to miss in order to show them this annual piece of Americana.

Given NASCAR's geographic history, it might have seemed an odd dream for someone from upstate New York, but Geoffrey began getting his racing chops beginning at age five in the micro-midget class at the Chemung Speedrome. His father, Eli, who also owned a farm, a dairy store, and a bakery, owned and promoted the Speedrome.

"I'm the luckiest guy in the whole world because my grandfather and father built a track, I grew up at that race track watching racing, I worked with my father at the dirt track so I drove the water truck, picked stones, and worked every day of the week in the summer with him," Geoffrey recalls. "I would not trade those days for anything; of course at the time I was like, I don't want to get up and work today, because when you're a kid you want to do other things, but when I look back, they were the best days of my life. And what an education: I had my father owning and running a race track, I had my uncles who raced. So I worked with my father, I'd go to the garage and help my uncles with the race cars, I learned the racing business from my family. How many kids can say that? I learned promoting a race track, running a race track, operating a race track from my father and mother, and I learned the racing part—building cars, engines, driving—from my uncles. I got a bachelor's degree in auto racing from my family."

The Bodines' track established a toehold for stock car racing in a vastly unexplored territory and though it helped grow the town back in the 1950s, stock car racing was still decades away from the days of the Winston Million. Recalls Brett Bodine, "My grandfather and my father were pioneers in motorsports in the United States and saw it through the tough times when it wasn't accepted or popular. . . when it wasn't the 'in' thing to be involved in racing. I remember times when I was growing up and my dad was operating our race track that he would actually have to buy advertising space in the Sunday paper to get the results in. If it wasn't for people like my father, who continued to push to get auto racing recognized and accepted, the sport wouldn't be where it is today."

Meanwhile, in Chemung, the brothers Bodine, each in their time, cut their teeth at the Speedrome. "My entire life, Saturday afternoons in the summer and Saturday nights, we were racing," recalls Brett fondly. "That was accepted, that was part of my life."

Geoffrey, still fueled by his Daytona dreams and his successes on the home track, graduated to the Modified division, and for a time, he tasted success that no other driver has ever experienced. Throughout the '70s, his aggressive style and nearly total commitment to the craft of building and racing cars paid off in whatever rewards the division offered. Testament to his success is the line he holds in The Guinness Book of World Records: During the 1978 Modified season, Bodine won an incredible fifty-five races out of a scheduled eighty-four.

"When everyone else was going to the clubhouse to have some beers after the race, I was driving home to work on my car for the next night," he says of those days. "People thought I was a snob, but I was determined to make the big time some day."

Brett also harbored dreams of greatness; he started racing hobby cars in Chemung the year before Geoffrey's miracle season. There began the parallel in the Bodines' careers, with Brett following Geoffrey's moves a few years hence, learning his own path by first stepping into his big brother's footprints. Geoffrey moved up to the NASCAR Winston Cup Series in 1982 and won Rookie of the Year honors by virtue of three top-fives, nine top-tens and one pole. Meanwhile, Brett was at the midpoint of his own successful career in Modifieds, hoping to get the break that might propel him into the NASCAR Busch Series, where his brother also drove, racing for Rick Hendrick. Fate—and his brother—were obviously in Brett's corner: He got his shot when a spate of bad weather presented him with the chance to earn his name.

"Geoff had qualified a Busch car for a race at Martinsville,

Virginia, and due to that race being rained out, he was not able to come back and drive the car because of his commitment as a driver on the Winston Cup circuit," Brett begins. "So he kinda went to bat for me and went to Rick Hendrick and said, 'Look, the car's there, you spent the money, the tires are bought, why don't you let Brett drive it? He knows the race track, he's raced the Modified division there several times.'"

Hendrick agreed and Brett paid him back by winning the race.

"They were very hesitant to do it, but because he was my brother they gave him a chance," says Geoffrey. "He ended up starting his career down here."

The brothers from New York were where they'd dreamed of being. These were the headiest times; success bred unquestionable status as rising stars in their sport.

With their success, however, came the knee jerk of jealousy. Although there wasn't talk of it between them, Brett's rise into the spotlight meant he was jumping out of his brother's shadow and it made for uncomfortable times. That Geoffrey was generally reserved and Brett more outgoing was only part of the story; with a ten-year gap between them, Geoffrey and Brett were really experiencing sibling rivalry for the first time. They'd never competed against each other as kids since they'd spent little time together.

"Closer-age siblings would grow up having competitions," says Todd Bodine. "They probably [go] out in the backyard to see who can throw a ball the farthest. We didn't have any of that growing up. It makes a difference in the way you perceive it as an adult. I believe Brett feels the same way I do."

Brett adds, "Geoff and I are not as close as some brothers and families are. Todd and I are probably much closer than Geoff and I just due to our age." In the early times of their success, in a very public forum, the professionally aggressive older brothers would have to deal with going head-to-head in a sea of other drivers.

In 1986, those issues might have seemed less important than the great triumphs Geoffrey and Brett were living through. Brett made his NASCAR Winston Cup Series debut and finished second in points on the NASCAR Busch Series circuit. That same year, Geoffrey lived the dream he'd always wanted.

At the 1986 Daytona 500, the stage was set for an exciting dash to the finish between Dale Earnhardt, a one-time NASCAR Winston Cup Series champion, and Bodine, who'd won three races to that point. In a contest that would be remembered more for what didn't happen than what did, Earnhardt added to his Daytona hex by doing the unexpected: He ran out of gas with three laps remaining. With the Intimidator out of the contest, Bodine drove himself to victory lane. At age thirty-six, he'd earned the grail.

As the late '80s moved into the early '90s, Brett's full-time NASCAR Winston Cup Series deal led to his first win in the 1990 spring race at North Wilkesboro; he finished the season ranked twelfth. Geoffrey captured the 1987 annual International Race of Champions (IROC) title—beating out a collection of the best drivers from the NASCAR Winston Cup Series and three other types of racing, competing against each other in equally set-up stock cars in four tracks around the country. In Geoffrey's best year, 1990, he won three races—the second time he'd done so—finishing the season in third place and earning over $1 million. He had made his mark.

In the next few years, another challenger who would give Bodine pause was none other than his little brother, Todd. The racing bug bit Todd for the first time after Brett's crew snuck the thirteen-year-old into the pits for a race on a local track. And when Brett won the race, it changed everything. "That night gave me a whole different perspective of what it was all about, why these guys work so hard every night—and that was a pretty big deal for a thirteen-year-old to hang out with a bunch of grownups," he says. "After that, I started [working with] Brett just sweeping up the shop and cleaning the car, whatever I could do, hanging around the race shop."

A few years later, the family moved to Massachusetts, due in part to the demise of the Speedrome, and Todd continued his education on the road. He learned fabrication from the legendary Hop Harrington and moved to Connecticut after high school graduation in 1982 to practice that art and work on Brett's cars. He also built his first car and started racing, following Brett down south when the latter began treading the path to the NASCAR Winston Cup Series. For years he learned the automaking art, developing the ethic instilled by his brothers.

"Todd is fifteen years younger than I am and I think he expected Brett and I to help him in racing and he was kinda lazy, didn't want to work, he was the baby of the family, thought everyone was gonna hand everything to him," says Geoffrey. "Brett and I realized that if we did that it was gonna ruin him, because we both had to work really hard to get here, so we got together and said, all right, until he shows he has that determination to be in this sport, let's make him struggle a little bit. When he started working hard and started to build a race car, that's when we began helping him. So I guess we instilled that you've got to work for what you get in this business, and believe me, he turned out to be a great mechanic and obviously a great driver."

Todd put in his time as a crew chief in the NASCAR Busch Series for Billy Standridge, drove some late-model stock, and worked as a fabricator for Bobby Hillin while driving in the Sportsman series. By 1990, he was running some Busch races himself, ready to move up to a full schedule the next year, having earned the respect of everyone on the track because of the time he'd logged off-road. Behind the wheel, he plied his trade with a kind of calculated aggressiveness. Observers believe his style could best be described as a mix of his two older brothers'.

In 1993, Todd ran ten NASCAR Winston Cup Series races and was set for a full-time ride the next year. The ultra-competitive Geoffrey Bodine would now have to deal with the possible conflict of driving door-to-door with some all-too-familiar faces.

"At first I didn't like that because I'm quite a bit older than [my brothers] and I used to take care of them when they were kids," he admits. "I didn't have the competitor's spirit in me toward them, but they did toward me. They wanted to beat their bigger brother. I've learned to get that feeling toward them, but at first I didn't like racing with them. I didn't like to pass them. I was like, 'Oh, man, I've got to pass my little brother.'"

In the early 1990s, there was still a feeling in some NASCAR circles that you could own your own team and successfully operate in the NASCAR Winston Cup Series elite. With the right business-minded approach, a driver could keep the tenuous balance between commerce and competition, pleasing sponsors by being amiable off the track and ambitious on it. True, the multi-team cars, with their bigger budgets and facilities, held a distinct economic advantage, but for the few independent-minded drivers, the idea of retaining full control was a great lure. And it's not as if there wasn't a reason to think one could succeed, as Alan Kulwicki proved by winning the NASCAR Winston Cup Series title driving solo in 1992.

Both Geoffrey and Brett Bodine, with racing and the entrepreneurial spirit in their blood, saw the advantage of such an arrangement. Even though Geoffrey seemed less inclined toward the idea than Brett, he made the move first, inheriting Kulwicki's team in the wake of the champion's tragic death in a plane crash on April 1, 1993. Brett, still driving for Kenny Bernstein, with whom he'd started in the NASCAR Winston Cup Series, was considering the same action.

Both brothers felt they needed some kind of change. They had each fallen on frustrating times. For Geoffrey—a top-ten driver six out of seven years at the end of the 1980s—the early '90s found him moving down the rankings. In 1993, driving for Bud Moore the year before he took over Kulwicki's team, he won only one race, in Sonoma, California, and finished a distant sixteenth in the standings. Brett ended up twentieth that same year, his worst annual showing since he first began racing in the NASCAR Winston Cup Series full-time.

The year 1994 started out only somewhat more promising for the family. Todd was enjoying his first full-time NASCAR Winston Cup Series ride, driving for the Stavola Brothers. Geoffrey enjoyed some early-season success with a victory from the pole at Pocono after a pole at Rockingham in the second race of the year, but several less than stellar finishes kept him mired in the middle of the points pack. Brett was still hungry for any kind of fortune. All three brothers had something to prove.

The proving ground turned out to be the hallowed Indianapolis Motor Speedway, home of the inaugural Brickyard 400. For decades, the idea of a stock car competition occurring at the mecca of open-wheel racing seemed impossibly far-fetched, but thanks to an agreement between Bill France Jr. and Indianapolis president Tony George, the great linking was agreed upon and an August 6, 1994, date set. With NASCAR already on its way to becoming the most popular auto racing concern on the planet, the Brickyard 400 symbolized a long-fought—and won—battle for supremacy. Few races had ever been so hyped; few would be as well-watched. And for the Bodines, no day would be as infamous.

Geoffrey Bodine qualified fourth for the race, Brett seventh, and Todd twenty-fifth; in other words, all three were within shooting distance of a possible victory. Indeed, Geoffrey led early on for a number of laps and Brett led for one himself. All signs pointed to a great day.

Not long after the race's halfway point, a caution led the top competitors into the pits. Geoffrey had been leading at that point, but Brett emerged from his stop in front, with Geoffrey now in second. A few laps later, the green flag sent the field back into full racing mode and Geoffrey was ready to return to the lead. What happened next is something the brothers have never spoken of and probably never will. Geoffrey gave Brett a tap to loosen him up, hoping to make the pass in turn three. Brett responded by tapping his brother back quite a bit harder in turn four, on the oval. Geoffrey lost control and spun into the wall. In his rearview mirror, Brett could see his brother's car out of action. Through his windshield, he saw the daylight only a race leader sees.

When he emerged from his car, Geoffrey told the millions watching at home on ABC that, "We've had some personal problems, and he took it out on the racetrack. I never expected he'd do it." When asked for details about a reconciliation, Geoffrey declared that Brett wasn't talking to him.

The race ended with Jeff Gordon taking the checkered flag; Brett wound up second. It was his only top-five finish of the season.

Now, five years later, the race remains a sore subject, so sore that Geoffrey cannot really talk about it. The brothers would not mend their rift for over two years; even now, they still have not discussed the particulars of the race. Brett, looking back, believes the conflict was inevitable.

"Anytime you put competitive people in competitive situations, I don't care who it is, eventually you're gonna have a run-in with them," he says. "If we think we're not, we're kidding ourselves. To think Geoff and I weren't going to find ourselves in that situation throughout our career, it would have been crazy. I mean, sure, you don't want that to happen, it just does. Situations present themselves, possibly bad judgment overcomes the right thing to do. And that's what happens. And ours," he says, with a chuckle, "just happened to be in front of millions of people on national TV in the biggest race in that time in NASCAR Winston Cup history."

Todd, meanwhile, recalls the event and the aftermath as one of the hardest things he's ever had to go through.

"I was smack dab in the middle and I tried not to be," he states. "It was incredibly hard on me to see two people that I grew up watching and respecting, to see what they were going through, it just ate me alive.

"And something I've never said to anybody and something that was never thought about was, I finished ninth in that race—I had a hell of a race," he continues. "I passed more cars that day than Jeff Gordon did. In fact, I had a faster car than Jeff Gordon but because of all the other stuff that went on, I got overlooked. I mean, it's nothing I'm upset about, it just shows you how much can be in the shadow of what's going on. We had two very bad pit stops and I still ended up ninth."

Todd, understandably, did not try to broker a deal to end the rift. "I had a career I was trying to get going in the right direction and I was having success doing it and I didn't want to lose my focus from that. I just basically didn't have time to try to settle some family feud that they were gonna have. There was nothing I was gonna say that was gonna change their minds so I went about my own business—while at the same time treading that thin line."

Things would get worse for the brothers before they got better. For Geoffrey, the dual positions of driver and owner began to take a toll on his home life, culminating in the dissolution of his marriage to his wife, Kathy, later in the 1994 season. He soldiered on for several seasons with mixed results and one important high point: his 1996 victory at Watkins Glen, only thirty miles from Chemung. A series of financial problems with sponsors culminated with his need to sell a majority of the team to businessmen Jim Mattei and John Porter. When things got still worse, Geoffrey was forced to give up the rest of his ownership and, in a searing twist of fate, he was ousted from his ride of the end of 1998, landing with Joe Bessey Motors at the start of 1999.

At the end of 1995, Brett entered into the realm of owner/driver himself, buying the team of legendary driver-turned-owner Junior Johnson. But sponsorship problems plagued him, as well, and he ended up selling part of the interest to Andy Evans before eventually buying that back.

"It's a tough business," says Todd. "The way the sport is going, there won't be many single-car teams left in the near future. I've seen the ups and downs that Geoff and Brett have both gone through with ownership and I'm definitely not pursuing that by any means."

As far as their feud is concerned, the brothers patched things up at the end of 1996, after two years of tension. If time is what healed the wound, it unfortunately had some help from bitter circumstances.

Two days after Christmas, Eli Bodine succumbed after a lengthy bout with emphysema. Seeing their father face death was a wake-up call to Eli's oldest sons, who seemed to agree that life was too short to keep feuding.

"Unfortunately, in life, tragedy or heartbreak usually brings people closer together," Todd says. "You have to keep [things] in perspective. It was the first Brickyard 400, it was probably the biggest race of the century, but it was a race and that's all it was, and I think they finally figured that out and understood that and got over it."

Geoffrey and Brett maintain the incident was a learning experience. "That's history; we're brothers again, we're loving brothers and spend time together," Geoffrey says. "It just took me awhile to feel comfortable racing against [my brothers].

"[Brett and I] try to help each other now more than we used to. I mean, I always tried to help him, but it seems like he'll talk to me about things and he'll try to help me so that's good; that's a plus."

Adds Brett, "I think Geoff and I are a lot closer and probably quite a bit more understanding of the pressure on our relationship brought on by our sport."

The brothers would prefer not to dwell on the past. Geoffrey, for his part, is happy to look to the future. In 1999, he raced against his son Barry in the NASCAR Craftsman Truck Series and is continuing to try to build a full-time NASCAR Busch Series team for him.

"Racing against him, well, it was different," he says. "It was his first race. This kid has not raced very much in his career and he's so good. We weren't door-to-door. I'm looking forward to the day when we go door-to-door because he's a natural. I'm sure, like in that commercial, Mario Andretti talking about Michael [Andretti], 'The first race we ran, we banged wheels, he went on by, he said, Adios, Dada.' Well, Barry will be saying, "See you later, told you I was faster.' He is fast and when we get out there, I'm sure he's gonna blow my doors off one day."

Strangely enough, one gets the feeling Geoffrey would like nothing better. Meanwhile, he and Brett continue their attempt to trek back to respectability in the NASCAR Winston Cup Series while Todd gains ground on the NASCAR Busch Series circuit. Geoffrey has also recovered from injuries suffered in his scary 2000 season-opening truck crash in Daytona. Geoffrey and Brett, so dissimilar in temperament, have fashioned careers that are remarkably similar. And in the glare of more media attention than they probably wanted, it is safe to say that they finally grew up together, too.

"If we bump on the race track, we have to get that squared away as race car drivers," Brett says finally about life with brothers on the road. "And then in the motor home area at the race track, we've gotta still be able to sit down and have dinner together."

5
The Burton Brothers

With fourteen laps to go in the 1999 Las Vegas 400 on March 7th, Ward and Jeff Burton were racing door-to-door at 185 mph. Ward had been leading the race for ten laps and was doing his best to hold off his younger brother, who now clearly had the standout car in the field. Meanwhile, Jeff Gordon was running up quickly behind them, threatening to make it more than just a Burton family outing. Still, the brothers remained in front. Jeff tried to dart ahead and Ward kept him back. He pulled up even again and they stayed side by side, lap after lap.

Ward was unhappy, to say the least. Here he was, the big investment of Bill Davis's single-car team, trying to win only his second NASCAR Winston Cup Series race, his first since 1995 in Rockingham ("This is the longest time I've been involved in any kind of racing and haven't won," was how he put it) and he knew quite well who was trying to thwart his victory. Ward's brother had already won five times in his NASCAR Winston Cup Series career, and as a member of Jack Roush's five-driver racing team, he enjoyed the benefit of a bigger budget and the experienced counsel of veteran teammate Mark Martin on everything from setups to strategy.

For years the brothers had watched each other perform, often from afar as they toiled in different circuits. But this battle would be different: brother against brother on the way to the checkered flag. It was a spectacle fit for Vegas.

The brothers nearly rubbed metal; they charged hard and almost rubbed again. And in the middle of one of the most heated battles of his racing life, Jeff Burton began laughing. Maybe it was the nervous energy, or just the thrill of being there; perhaps he felt secure in the knowledge that he had the best car on the road and the confidence that he would find a way to make the pass. Or maybe the thirty-one-year-old, sandy-haired Burton was feeling the effects of a season that found him already a lot more competitive than he'd grown used to being in the NASCAR Winston Cup Series.

Meanwhile, Ward Burton was stewing behind his steering wheel. At thirty-seven, with jet-black hair and dark eyes to match his wry sense of humor, he was trying not to get too carried away in the moment, although that wouldn't be easy.

"I wasn't too happy to see him gaining on me, to be honest with you," he says. "I knew [Jeff's] car was the only one I had to beat. If I hadn't been in the car, I'd have taken care of it."

Taken care of it?

"I mean, I wouldn't have let him gain on me anymore; I'd have gone back there and stomped his toe or something," he says. "It was aggravating because I knew he was coming and I was driving with every piece of energy I had."

Whatever the outcome, the brothers kept an unspoken pact between them. This day, on national television, they would do their best to avoid a replay of an epic battle from a dozen years before at their hometown track in South Boston, Virginia. That Late Model Stock race ended for the Burtons when both Jeff and Ward made it clear to the thousands of fans—and both their parents— that they were each unwilling to be their brother's keeper.

But on this grand stage at Vegas, they would have to drive wide open yet stay in control, to see who was the better man on this day—without letting the day get the better of them.

"There are a lot of thoughts going through your mind," says Jeff of those laps in Las Vegas. "One of the biggest things is 'Don't mess up.' Don't do something that's gonna put yourself or your brother in jeopardy because the cost of that's way too high. You're better off finishing second, or for that matter, tenth."

• • •

Despite the fact that they work in the same business, the Burton brothers do not have a great deal in common. Ward, an avid outdoorsman, is founder of the Ward Burton Wildlife Foundation. If Jeff is equally rabid about anything, it's the title chances of Duke basketball. While Ward is watching ESPN Outdoors, Jeff is turning to *Seinfeld* reruns. They don't even sound like brothers, with Ward's thick Virginia accent and Jeff's faint one. Given these facts, and the endless pressures of the business, their relationship is bound to be complicated. So the bond between them—the love and respect with which they always speak of the other—could surprise some people. The best way to describe their on-track relationship now would perhaps be the way they choose to do so: They hate to lose, but if they have to lose, they'd rather lose to each other than to anyone else.

The first and third sons of the incredibly competitive John Burton ("Dad is over sixty and still plays tennis like it's the last game of the year every time he plays," says Ward), the boys were united by their fathers' passion for sports, especially a favorite hobby of his, go-kart racing. John was committed to seeing his sons learn the thrill of effort well rewarded.

"We played basketball, football, baseball, soccer, we raced go-karts—we always had fun with it, but we wanted to win," recalls Jeff. "My father spent a lot of time with us in the backyard—anytime we wanted to do something, he was there to go play with us if he wasn't working, obviously, because he worked all the time."

John Burton ran the family construction business, which he'd bought from his father; nowadays, Ward and Jeff's middle brother, Brian, runs it. But on weekends, the family would pack the go-karts and tools in the back of the Suburban and drive to races all over the state of Virginia. Says Ward, "I'm not sure how Mom and Dad put up with it, 'cause I'm sure the three of us fought the whole way there and the whole way back."

By then, Ward had already started to find success in venues more varied than the family backyard.

"My dad took me to a local dirt go-kart track that older men raced at, guys my dad's age," he says. "I had a two-seater go-kart with a five-horsepower motor that I used to ride around the yard and we went up there and the first race—of course they made me start in the rear—I took the lead on the last lap and the second-place guy spun me out on the last lap before I took the checker. I didn't ever know the checker was coming out. Then the feature race, they made me start last and I lapped the field other than about four guys," he says, recalling the easy victory with a satisfied chuckle. "It was an exciting weekend because I was only eight years old, first race, to go up there and do that. I mean, sure, I had a huge weight advantage. Still I passed them all and never raced before."

He continued racing go-karts on weekends until he was sixteen, and he and Brian also punched the clock at the construction company, a responsibility Jeff was able to avoid at the time by virtue of his age. With six years separating them, Ward and Jeff were worlds apart: the older brother, who was thinking about going to school; and (by Jeff's own admission) the younger, snot-nosed kid who Ward didn't want around all the time. But in quick time, they would be united by their pursuit in the next step of their careers.

"I quit go-karts right after I was sixteen, went to college, and then I lived out in the woods for awhile and went back to work for my dad's construction company," Ward says. "And I went motocross racing for two summers, which was the only thing I could afford to do on my own. Meanwhile, Jeff and my father had gone straight from go-karts to Late Model stocks, which I would have loved to have done but my brother Brian and I weren't able to do that."

The timing of what John Burton was able to do for Jeff helped jump-start the younger brother's career, but inadvertently, some good luck rubbed off on Ward. He went to the track one night to visit his father and brother and, while there, a different owner, hearing of Ward's skill, offered him a Volkswagen to drive the next weekend, which he did for two weeks. That led to another ride—a full-time gig in Street Stock, which he took on for a year and a half, during which time he turned a corner in his stock car career. His youngest brother had wanted to race for as long as he could remember and was, with his father's aid, deep into the learning curve that would lead him to NASCAR. Finally, Ward had found the calling as well.

"Once I got into Street Stock, I was always tunnel vision," Ward says. "I was always at the shop working on the car, trying to help do something with the car. I've never been a really good mechanic by any means, but I was focused and trying to pull my weight. Everything else came second from that time on, and when I moved up to Late Model Stock it was a natural progression."

What seemed a bit unnatural was the fact that now, brother would have the opportunity to race against brother. Jeff had been in stock cars for years; Ward had now worked his way up to his younger brother's level. It was a situation ripe for uncomfortable competition. The brothers found themselves thinking more about beating each other than taking on the rest of the field.

It all came to a head one night in 1987 during a race at their hometown track in South Boston. In front of friends, family, and the community at large, the brothers staged a torrid battle on the track that was like a family picnic compared with the tussle they engaged in off of it.

Even now, twelve years later, the brothers can't agree on how the conflict started. "Well, it depends on who you talk to about what happened," admits Jeff. "Basically what happened was, Ward was running second, I was running third, we were both running the leader down. I thought I got under Ward, Ward thought I wasn't under him."

Ward had been chasing the leader and was on his bumper when a caution came out; after the restart, he went back to business. He'd notched only one Late Model Stock victory and was hungry to get his second. Meanwhile, his younger brother was getting too close behind him. Before either of them could react, they connected and spun, and headed off the track, screeching toward a fence.

It was the worst of all possible conclusions. A Burton win looked likely, which would have delighted the local fans; now both brothers were finished for the day.

"Jeff put about a foot under me and knocked me out—and knocked *him* out," Ward says of the on-track action. "And you know, at the time and probably still today, I felt that it was—I mean, we were both learning, you know? I should have protected the inside a little bit more. Jeff shouldn't have drove in it because he didn't have the position. I probably created the situation a little bit and he added to it."

You could say the same thing for what happened moments later when they got out of their cars. In front of the hometown crowd, a frustrated Ward, in an uncontrollable rage, hoisted his youngest brother up by the throat.

He had no intention of letting him down until he saw the familiar face of his brother's chief advisor stamping toward the scene.

As Ward puts it, still somewhat sheepishly, "I had him up in the air with my hands and I saw Dad coming. Just seeing my father I realized that this damn sure wasn't good," he says, chuckling. "It wasn't good for the family and it wasn't good for the fans that came to watch us race. It wasn't a good situation anywhere. It wasn't just a deal where it was only me and Jeff."

As soon as John Burton arrived, Ward put down what he was doing and walked off, unable to calm down and face his family. Strangely enough, even though the anger wouldn't subside for quite some time, the event seemed to break the tension between them, as if the brothers needed to push each other into the fences before they could set about mending them.

"I woke up the next day and felt like an ass, and I think Ward did, too," says Jeff. "We saw each other and apologized—we both felt like we were still right but had embarrassed the family.

"When that happened, I learned pretty quickly that Ward wanted it just as badly as I did. And he learned the same thing about me, and sometimes things have to come to a boil before they really get fixed. He may speak about it in a totally different light, but for me, it was one of those things that make you understand the bigger picture. It doesn't mean you can't still go race hard and still try to win; your brother's leading, you need to go try to outrun him. But you understand his emotions better. You understand that he is a person who cares about what he's doing and you're not the only one that cares. It was an important moment for us as brothers."

That day in South Boston was certainly in their minds as the Burtons tried their luck in Las Vegas. Ward, who'd started the race in 30th spot, made a steady, businesslike climb toward the front and took the lead on lap 45 of the 267-lap race. He continued to run strong and near the front for several miles but at around the halfway point, his brother sped to the front, taking the lead from Jeremy Mayfield and holding it for almost 60 laps, surrendering it only due to a green-flag pit stop and gaining it again a few laps later. Such was his dominance that by lap 211, he was leading the second-place Ward by eleven seconds.

Geoffrey Bodine's blown engine made all things equal on lap 232 and when the race restarted, it was Ward who jumped out to the lead, by virtue of an excellent pit stop, with Jeff Gordon in second and Jeff Burton third.

But Ward's younger brother still had the car of the day, especially in the second half of the race, and after 12 laps, he had passed Gordon and was gaining on Ward. There were 23 laps remaining and it would be brother against brother once again. With 14 laps remaining, they were side by side. For the next four laps, a riveting six miles, they remained locked door-to-door with each trying to outmaneuver the other at close to 190 mph.

"Jeff kept inching up on me and he had been, from the middle part of the race to the end of the race," Ward remembers. "Tommy Baldwin, my crew chief, was saying to me, 'Drive it like you stole it.' I worked the car so hard, I had blisters the size of golf balls. There was no other way I could have done any more than I did."

On two occasions, it seemed Jeff had taken the lead, only to surrender it to Ward. But on lap 257, Jeff moved to the outside on turn two, and then hit the third turn harder than either he or Ward thought he'd have been able to. He stuck it and when the racing straightened out once again, Jeff was finally able to eke by his older brother. Ahead of him there was now only daylight and under him was the best car on the track. He'd been able to make the pass without incident and there would be nobody left to challenge him on that day.

Jeff won by a little more than one second. Between the two of them, Jeff and Ward had led for 182 of the race's 267 laps.

"My job became to go win the race and the guy I had to beat was my brother, and that's difficult because he wants to win in a bad way, and I'm having to take away from my brother what I know he wants," says Jeff, summing up. "You don't really know how to handle that other than go do what your job is to do. It's not easy by any means to race against your brother."

It was Jeff's sixth NASCAR Winston Cup Series career win and it left Ward still chasing victory number two.

"I drove it with everything I had, with all the talent I had, all that car would let me get out of it at that time," Ward says with a sigh. He knows he didn't have car enough to win, but he's willing to admit that he may have also lacked a bit of the killer instinct. There is every indication that that night in South Boston—the family, his friends, his town, his brother—remained in his mind at Las Vegas.

"Could I have crowded [Jeff] a little bit more or something? Maybe. You get to a real thin borderline there between control and out of control. And if you're the one doing the crowding, you can very easily be the one that ends up in the fence. These cars are heavy, they're aerodynamically balanced, and you start changing things and putting cars in different situations, you can lose control. But there was nothing left on the table for me that day."

And does Jeff believe Ward would have been more aggressive against someone else? "I'm sure he would've. Ward used a lot of the race track with me. He did all he could to keep me behind him. There would have had to have been some touching if he would have used any more of the track."

For four laps at Vegas, during some of the most heated side-by-side racing of the season, the Burton family watched the brothers fight the good fight. This time, when all was said and done, they were able to talk about it the next day.

"It was fine," Ward says of his conversation with Jeff the Monday after Vegas. "By that time I was happy with what we'd done, but I would have liked to have been happier. So we just chatted and laughed a little bit but I told him, 'One time I got loose going into three and almost got into ya,' which I did. I had to back in, try to come around. I was just doing all I could do."

Both brothers would prefer not to dwell on the past and indeed, the way things are going for them, there's no need to. In 1999, they were easily in the midst of their career years, with Jeff in the hunt for a championship most of the season and Ward hovering around the top ten in points. And they even had two more opportunities to relive their old memories when Jeff and Ward finished one-two in the rain-shortened Southern 500 and the fall race at Rockingham. The Darlington contest might have brought the same kind of thrills as Vegas had it gone to regulation, and one could see Ward at least had that in mind when he playfully bumped his brother during the last yellow-flag lap on the way to the checkered flag. ("He may have thought it was funny, but I sure as hell didn't," Jeff said after the race with a laugh.) And in 2000, Ward broke back into the win column with his own victory ar Darlington's spring race. These days, the Burtons seek each other out for advice and try to help when they can. Success has a habit of breaking tension.

6
The Earnhardt Family

The Son of Ralph Earnhardt

Twenty-one-year-old Dale Earnhardt lurched forward in the driver's seat and instinctively gripped the steering wheel harder. The tap on his rear bumper was nothing too strong, but it was enough to make him look in the rearview mirror. When he did, he had to smile. Behind him, his forty-four-year-old father, Ralph Earnhardt, kept coming. Suddenly, his dad's car was on Dale's rear bumper, pushing him along as if he needed help to get where he was going. Dale held the wheel, kept the car straight, and hung on for the ride.

Dale had shown up that day in 1972 for a dirt-track race in Concord, North Carolina, with an old six-cylinder car he had put together himself. His dad, arguably the best dirt-track driver of his day, was there with the car he had built, the one with the V8 under the hood. Ralph couldn't help but laugh.

Even if he'd had the right equipment, Dale had no illusions about beating his father. Ralph Earnhardt was in his prime: He'd won hundreds of races and earned the praise of peers such as two-time Grand National champion Ned Jarrett, who thought he was the toughest competitor he'd ever faced on dirt. Earnhardt's record on the Late Model circuit in the '50s and '60s was staggering; many was the time he entered four races in a week and came away with the winner's share at every one. At one point, he had won enough races to be champion at seven different tracks.

Dale had practiced with his father often on the race track, but this was the first time he'd raced with him. For years Dale had watched his father compile his stunning record and dreamed of trailing him into the business. He'd worked in the garage with him and had even quit school against his father's wishes to be there and learn in preparation for racing professionally. And as many things as Dale learned in the garage, he got a lot more out of building setups and watching races, seeing the way his dad and others took a turn and then trying it out himself on the track.

On this day, however, Dale was ready to learn a thing or two about how much fun it could be to race with your father. Ralph had hung there behind Dale for three or four laps, watching him try hard to power his way past the car in front of him, and now the father decided to lend a hand. Once on his son's bumper, Ralph Earnhardt let his V8 talk for him. He pushed his son's car fast down the straightaway and into a turn—Dale has since said that he never hit a corner that hard. When the pushing was done, Dale had made the pass. Then, with typical efficiency, Ralph Earnhardt was gone, speeding down the track to contend for victory.

"That was the one time I did get to race with him," Dale recalls now with a smile. "I've got one picture of that, him and I on the track together in that race, and that's something you remember for life."

The memory is a bittersweet one. In September 1973, a year after their race together, Ralph Earnhardt died of heart failure. Dale, then twenty-two, had lost the man he worshiped, his main inspiration for getting into racing. Just before his father died, Dale had spent two years winning local championships on dirt. But unlike his father, he yearned for a chance at making a name for himself in the higher-speed, higher-prestige world of the NASCAR Winston Cup Series. In late 1973, he began to drive primarily on asphalt tracks with an eye toward eventually facing NASCAR competition. It would be years before he got a legitimate shot at a senior circuit ride, but when he did, he made the most of it. In his first two years, he set records still unbroken more than twenty years later. He has long been considered by many experts as his sport's greatest champion; his seven NASCAR Winston Cup Series championships lend credence to the claim.

And from the time before his big break—the years where he lived virtually hand to mouth—to now, he has conducted himself on the track and off with an image of his father in mind: his father the winner, the advisor, the relentless intimidator on the track. And today father and son are also side by side on the list of NASCAR's 50 Greatest Drivers of all time.

That Dale Earnhardt followed his father's example, advice, and style explains at least part of his great success. He no doubt would have traded it in for the chance to enjoy more time with the man. In lieu of that, he has spent a chunk of the latter part of his career tearing yet another page from his father's primer, this one related to the lesson Ralph taught that day in Concord. Winning races is a thrill, but as Dale is now learning, it's hard to match how much fun it can be to race with your son.

Years before he ever shared a track with his father, Dale Earnhardt seemed to trail him everywhere. They'd travel to races together where Dale could watch and learn, and they'd recap the contests after they were done. Dale and his two brothers, Randy and Danny, would work with their dad in the garage next to the family home in Kannapolis, North Carolina, where they'd see their father build both the winning engines he sold to Grand National teams, and the cars he would use to win his races. When Dale quit going to school, his disappointed dad asked him to reconsider, but Dale already knew what he wanted to do with his life. In time his father came to accept that, and Dale started to earn money in his late teens working on cars during the day, which he then invested in Hobby-class autos he built to race at night. Ralph was not always the most forthcoming man, but over time father and son grew close.

"I just enjoyed my childhood so much, around my dad, around racing," Dale recalls. "The time at the race track was a lot of fun; the time with him in the shop was enjoyable. I learned a lot—wish I had paid better attention and learned more. The times we had one on one, we'd go bird hunting and things like that together, that's what I really enjoyed.

"He was always the kind of person who, if you couldn't pay for it, you didn't need it; independent, did everything himself. He was a stern father but he was a loving father."

He was also a driver who, as far back as Dale could remember, was respected as a champion by everyone from the Late Model Sportsman racers he normally competed with, to the Grand National circuit drivers he occasionally ran against. They had to respect him; at the race track he could find a way into their heads and psyche them out. If Dale grew up to be the most intimidating driver of his generation, it's because as a kid, he watched the art of it practiced every weekend at the track by a master.

Whenever Ralph Earnhardt got to the track for an event, he'd arrive ready. There was, generally speaking, no tweaking the car, no changing the setup. While other drivers would still be doing their best to improve their ride, Ralph was done. He'd stand around stoically, saying next to nothing, never giving them the satisfaction of seeing him tinker. His act put the fear of God into much of the field before the race even began.

Then he'd get on the track, take the green flag, and start running with the leaders, as often as not in second or third place, lurking just behind, as if to imply that there was a whole lot more horsepower under the hood than he wanted you to know about. With a few laps remaining, he'd move up closer, stalking the leader, a spectre in the rearview. Then he'd take the leader on; with practiced precision, he'd manage to jostle the man's car just enough to distract him. Then Ralph Earnhardt would be off to the races, charging toward the checkered flag.

"Ralph was one of those guys that when you unloaded the car, no matter where you were at, he was the guy you had to contend with," says NASCAR veteran Buddy Baker, who raced against both Ralph and Dale Earnhardt in a thirty-year career. "At a place like Columbia, South Carolina, that had a hard, sandy track, he was unbeatable at times. He didn't have a tremendous amount of money and there were people coming in with twice the funds, twice the equipment, and they'd go home scratching their heads wondering what happened. He was just that kind of a guy. If he got to you on the last lap, you could go ahead and plan on being moved, but he'd do it ever so gracefully. You know, he wouldn't knock you out of the way, he'd just touch you enough to get you sideways. I watched a guy one night spin out because Ralph was somewhere behind him and he knew he was gonna touch him, so he just went ahead and went in the corner so hard he spun it out—but Ralph was a good ten car lengths back. The guy didn't know that. Ralph had dropped back because of lapped traffic, and the guy thought it was Ralph up under him and he went way down in the corner and just looped it out himself because Ralph had such a reputation of being there on that last lap. Yeah, he was a great talent."

Earnhardt spent most of his time racing the Sportsman circuit and only made fifty-one Grand National starts over six seasons, coming away with six top-five finishes, including two second-place finishes, without a win. Had he devoted himself to NASCAR's more prestigious races, he would have been a greater factor, but he had no desire to do that. He earned a good living and drove to hundreds of victories, winning the Sportsman championship in 1956.

Then there was his record at Hickory Motor Speedway, in Hickory, North Carolina, the so-called "Birthplace of NASCAR Stars" because it served as home track and proving ground for the likes of Ned Jarrett and Junior Johnson. Earnhardt won five track championships at Hickory, in 1953, 1954, 1956, 1957, and 1959. In one particular stretch, he won seventeen races in a row at the track; after awhile, the feat became so predictable, some fans stopped showing up. Ralph went up to accept the winner's trophy after the seventeenth win and the angry promoter refused to give it to him.

Hickory was also the sight of Ralph's first Grand National NASCAR race, in 1956. At the time, the sport was being dominated by the NASCAR dream team of Chevrolets commissioned by Carl Kiekhaefer, whose cars had already won an unprecedented twenty-eight of the season's fifty-four races. The folks at Ford were none too pleased by this; they tried to stack some races with drivers who might break the lock. Earnhardt was a natural choice for Hickory, and when the race began, the hometown fans cheered him lustily. He repaid them with a wondrous show. While no Grand National rookie has ever won in his first race, Ralph Earnhardt came closest. At one point he charged to the front and led for fifteen laps. Driver Speedy Thompson, already a seven-time winner that season for Kiekhaefer, drove the car most considered the class of the field, and with the race winding down, he proved it by making the pass on Earnhardt. With five laps to go, Thompson pitted for a bit of gas, went back out, and kept his lead with Earnhardt the only driver continuously on his tail. When the checkered flag waved, it was Thompson who took it; Earnhardt crossed the line four seconds later.

The win was not popular and the booing continued as Thompson made his way to victory lane. The promoters and NASCAR officials, perhaps wondering if people thought Thompson had lost a lap somewhere—which would have given Earnhardt the win—recounted their cards. They huddled together with the drivers and after some calculations they proved to all concerned that the race belonged to Thompson. Then, to quiet the crowd, they made an odd request that Earnhardt accepted. Moments later, he announced the results to the crowd over the public address system and, lest anyone think of rioting, let them know he accepted the loss fair and square.

He drove sporadically in Grand National through the early 1960s but stopped around the time NASCAR was making the transition from dirt to asphalt, and from short tracks to superspeedways. Instead, Ralph Earnhardt simply went about his business at local tracks.

By the late 1960s, Dale Earnhardt was driving cars he'd built with his two brothers. Like their dad, they created some fine rides using less than stellar funds. They had grown up witnessing the satisfaction gained from making something great out of nothing much.

"When I started racing, I was racing hand-me-down stuff," Dale recalls. "The guy I drove for was on disability from a leg injury, and he had a couple of race cars he had before he got hurt, and we just worked on 'em, fixed 'em up and got to racing 'em. And I won my first race driving that old car.

"My father would take something that other guys would probably throw away, fix it and make it run and outrun guys with it. Dad always taught us to do the best with what we had and that's what I've always done."

In early 1973, several months before he died, Ralph Earnhardt was advised by his doctor to slow down, lest he succumb to his heart condition. As a man who made his living through speed, he found the command especially hard to accept. In time he had no choice: His condition worsened and he found he didn't have the energy behind the wheel he once had. But he didn't give up, and Dale watched his deterioration on the track and off with a sense of dread. A year earlier, in 1972, Dale had won the points championship on dirt at the Charlotte Fairgrounds; in 1973, he made it two years in a row.

His ambitions were more far-reaching, however. Dale saw NASCAR as a way out, an opportunity to dream and win big. His father, though he had limited experience on asphalt, advised him on some of the differences between the surfaces but also kept stressing the racing fundamentals he'd always taught. Among the bits of advice he frequently offered was, "Establish your territory." It was a phrase Dale accepted like a mantra; ultimately, it would go a long way toward defining his driving style.

While Dale was making moves that would change his path in racing, Ralph lost his life to a heart attack while working on a car. Dale was now without his mentor, his part-time benefactor and full-time inspiration.

Ralph's death, while dealing a devastating blow, also somehow dispelled any doubts Dale might have ever had about continuing to make a go of it as a racer. Years before, he'd begun to consider other professional paths. He even tried to work a regular job away from racing and found it didn't suit him. Eventually, that job helped convince him all over again where he belonged and he was soon back in the garage full-time. With his father now gone, any consideration of a different career seemed out of the question.

From 1975 through 1978, Dale Earnhardt ran a total of nine NASCAR Winston Cup Series races as a freelance driver, earning one top-five and one top-ten; he also raced frequently on the same Sportsman circuit his father had run, adding more years of experience to his resume. It was a frustrating time for someone with bigger aspirations. By the end of 1978, the twenty-seven-year-old driver had three kids and was just managing to make a living.

Any big race was an opportunity to step up and make a statement. He did that at the 1978 Dixie 500 in Atlanta, where he drove a Chevrolet for owner Rod Osterlund and finished fourth. Running third that day was Osterlund's main driver, Dave Marcus, who finished the season fifth in the standings.

Fifth was okay, but Osterlund expected more and was willing to expand the business to get it; he considered going with a second full-time driver. Having liked what he saw in Atlanta, Osterlund felt Earnhardt merited a look for a ride in 1979. The only question was, should he go with the young, untested driver, or hire one of two proven winners—Cale Yarborough or David Pearson—who were both seeking to switch teams and run more limited schedules. Earnhardt would need to learn a few things, but he had youth and some good experience in his favor, along with a great deal of confidence. Ultimately, Osterlund saw Earnhardt as an investment in the future.

The picture shifted drastically with the departure of Marcus, who went back to running his own team after the 1978 season. Suddenly, the untested Earnhardt had jumped from substitute to incumbent with the keys to a quality ride and a chance to make something great out of it. Jake Elder, long known for working well with new talent, became his crew chief.

If Earnhardt was looking for the right place and time for a coming-out party, he couldn't have chosen any better than the 1979 Daytona 500. Richard Petty won that day, his sixth Daytona 500 victory, but Dale Earnhardt had his say at the event by leading the race for a few turns as a rookie. Viewers at home were treated to a call from the announcers about Dale Earnhardt: "This cottonhead from Kannapolis, North Carolina, taking the lead." Looking back now, the race remains the "Favorite Dale Earnhardt racing memory" for something of an authority on the subject, his son, Dale Jr.

"I thought [the identification] was funny—I mean it's neat that you stay tied to your roots like that," he says. "They were kinda surprised at his performance. You look at that now and you think those guys had no clue who they were watching race."

Fans and the media would start to get an idea less than two months later when the tour swung around to the spring race at Bristol, Tennessee, the seventh of the new season. With its 36-degree banking and resulting G forces built in to a .533-mile oval, the Bristol Motor Speedway has seen more than its share of scrapped metal.

It saw a bunch more during that 1979 race, which featured six cautions for 44 laps out of 500. But with the contest winding down, the cottonhead from Kannapolis was trying to make a name for himself as, specifically, the first NASCAR Winston Cup Series rookie to win a race in five years, and only the fourth to win one ever. He was riding second to Darrell Waltrip, and to win, he'd have to not only get to the front, but then keep Bristol masters such as Richard Petty, Bobby Allison, and Waltrip behind him.

Waltrip would be especially hard to beat. The defending champion at the race, he had started off the '79 season with a victory, and after coming in fourth and third the previous two years in the annual standings, he looked at Bristol as a good vaulting point to begin another serious championship run.

He and Earnhardt raced each other hard for several laps when another caution sent the leaders into the pits. Earnhardt changed four tires and somehow Elder, who was Waltrip's former crew chief, managed to send Earnhardt out of the pits just in front of his ex-driver. An angry Waltrip made his moves to take back the lead but Earnhardt kept him at bay, even as Waltrip kept coming, sitting on Earnhardt's bumper, waiting for an error that would render the outcome of the race a foregone conclusion.

Then the error came: Earnhardt, overanxious and smelling victory, came off turn two and brushed the wall hard—but kept going. The contact jarred him, but when he regained control of the car a second later, Dale managed to remain in front and continue his poised run, as if nothing much had just occurred.

A caution came out soon after and Dale and Elder made the joint decision to remain out in position with the rest of the leaders. Dale, weaving slowly through the caution, could tell by the noise on the other end of the radio that Elder was agitated.

"I told him I hit the wall pretty hard and Jake says, 'Ohh!'" Earnhardt recalls of Elder's pained, incredulous response. "So I said, 'It's all right. The car's fine.' I said, 'How are you?' and [Elder] said, 'God, I can't take much more of this.' 'Well, y'all take it easy and everything will be all right.' I was just calm."

He would need to be. For the rest of the race, he'd be chased by three guys who, between them, had scored 261 NASCAR Winston Cup Series victories to that point, with Earnhardt determined to notch his first in only the sixteenth start of his career. But for the first time, the veterans got to see how deeply Earnhardt clung to his "establish your territory" credo: Earnhardt's "territory" cut a swath of track that would be too wide that day for everybody else.

He took the checkered flag in what turned out to be the most competitive Cup race at Bristol in fourteen years; Allison finished second, Waltrip third, and Petty fourth.

"I won the race and Jake was like, 'Whew, man, I couldn't believe that,' and of course I couldn't either,'" Earnhardt recalls with a smile. "But Jake said, 'Wow, if you stay calm racing like that and make light of the deal like you did on the caution, you're gonna be all right.'"

Dale Earnhardt, Terry Labonte, Ricky Rudd, and Kyle Petty began NASCAR Winston Cup Series careers in 1979, when NASCAR was moving away from the rockier realities of its youth, toward a more sportsmanlike game—which would not always be easy at 200 mph. It would leave behind some measure of its "innocence" on the way to gaining prominence, profit, and power in a world dominated by the great demands of ever-increasing corporate sponsorship.

Into this place and time came Dale Earnhardt, the shy, proud, adoring son of a man who had earned his living as a star away from the spotlight. After Bristol, Dale was one win into a career; he could see a chance to earn all the accolades that he wanted and that his father hadn't had the chance to collect. "I think the one thing you have to remember about the Earnhardts," reminds Buddy Baker, "is they start out with a tremendous amount of pure gut determination."

In 1979, Earnhardt began to earn one nickname, the Intimidator, by first being tapped with a decidedly less complimentary one: Ironhead. If his father had once been known for being able to move the man in front of him when a win was in sight, the son would go him one better and drive as aggressively as he felt the need to. For Dale Earnhardt, the bottom line became that he would do anything to win. That's an attitude that can earn you about as many admirers as detractors. Some race fans were forced to feel both ways.

The most famous incident of Earnhardt aggressiveness that season occurred in Michigan, two and a half months after his Bristol win, where Earnhardt ran to a sixth-place finish. He also managed to anger a great many of his competitors—not to mention a few fans—with more bumping than they were used to. Chief among the complainants was Richard Petty, and afterward the King tried to school Earnhardt on the finer points of competing the right way. Earnhardt only shrugged and uttered the proverbial, "That's racin'."

His attitude would be forced to change the following month in Pocono. With almost two-thirds of the season gone, the rookie Earnhardt was, incredibly, fourth in the NASCAR Winston Cup Series standings. But while leading the race at almost the halfway point, he blew a tire going into the tunnel turn and lost control of the car, spun around and hit a retaining wall on the driver's side. The incident knocked Earnhardt out of commission for the near future, it seemed.

While Earnhardt was recuperating and contemplating the possible end of his run for Rookie of the Year, Osterlund hired David Pearson as a replacement driver.

With the threat of losing a ride to the successful Pearson seeming very real to him, Earnhardt decided that four races were enough to sit out and he suited up for the next contest at Richmond. Most fans wondered how effective he could be at less than one hundred percent. The rookie responded by winning the pole.

He needed relief help for that race and the next, getting it from Bill Elliott—another newcomer and future nemesis. Earnhardt was on track for the rest of the season and closed it out with five top-tens, including a narrow loss to Neil Bonnett in Atlanta. When the year ended, Richard Petty had won his seventh and final NASCAR Winston Cup Series title; Earnhardt, with one win and eleven top-fives, had finished seventh in the running. Despite missing four races, his numbers were good enough for Rookie of the Year honors.

Not that he cared very much about that. Never comfortable with the praise and requirements of fame, Earnhardt spent his off-season hunting, fishing, hanging out with his second wife, Teresa, and impatiently waiting for the start of the next season, where he fully intended to win the NASCAR Winston Cup Series championship.

In 1980, Earnhardt did what had never been done before. With five victories, nineteen top-fives and twenty-four top-tens, he became the only driver ever to follow up a Rookie of the Year season with a NASCAR Winston Cup Series championship. In a fitting bit of torch-passing, it makes sense that the year after the King claimed his final crown, Earnhardt won his first. And he won by establishing his territory and making the most of what he had. His father would have been proud.

The ensuing years of Dale Earnhardt's career are often summed up by numbers. He now totals seven championships, which ties him with Petty, and he is often cited as his sport's finest driver ever. After winning many races at Daytona except for the 500, he finally won the big one on his twentieth try, and every member of every competing crew went out to shake his hand as he navigated toward victory lane. Going into the 2000 season, he had totalled seventy-four victories but a large part of his appeal is that he accepts his success humbly. And he can still generate controversy like no one else, as he did with win seventy-three, in the 1999 summer race at Bristol, where he spun out Terry Labonte on the last lap to gain the victory. Earnhardt called the move unintentional. Although the two quickly mended fences, Labonte's initial reply can best be summed up as, "Yeah, that's what he always says."

In 1996, Earnhardt had an ugly déjà vu experience that took him back to the worst moment of his rookie year. While in the midst of a dogfight for the NASCAR Winston Cup Series lead with Labonte, a crash at Talladega left him nursing considerable hurts. And yet seven days later, he started the Brickyard 400 and a week after that, in an incomprehensible show of guts, skill, and determination, he started the race on the meandering Watkins Glen course and led 54 of the first 64 laps before becoming human and placing sixth. While he didn't earn an eighth championship that season, he added another volume to the never-say-quit Earnhardt canon.

But at age forty-nine, seemingly with his best driving years behind him, he is getting a shot in the arm from what may be his greatest thrill in racing: taking on his son, Dale Jr., the twenty-four-year-old two-time NASCAR Busch Series champion, who's enjoying his first full-time NASCAR Winston Cup Series ride—for team owner Dale Earnhardt Inc.—in 2000.

The occasional racing between the two has already been spirited to say the least, but as important, the chance to spend any kind of time together—which was rare during the years of Dale Jr.'s youth—has become a priority for father and son. Given Earnhardt's own history, he knows there's something to be said for just being on the scene with all four of his kids—Kerry, Kelley, Dale Jr., and Taylor. "I'm as proud at Taylor's dance recital as I am when Dale Jr. wins," he says. If he's doing his best to make up for lost time, he's learning that Ralph Earnhardt's driving rules can also be applied to fatherhood: Establish your territory and make the most out of what you've got.

All of which explains why the day he officially signed Dale Jr. to a five-year driving deal in 1998 may be one of the highpoints in a grand career. As he put it that day, "It feels good to finally have a formal contract signed with Dale Jr., but our blood contract has been good for twenty-three years, and that will always be the most important contract I have with him."

The Son of Dale Earnhardt

You could call it a distant replay.

Dale Earnhardt Jr. was sitting in his car at the Daytona International Speedway before the start of the first International Race of Champions (IROC) contest of the 1999 season. With IROC featuring only twelve all-star drivers across the major divisions of racing, this would be Dale Jr.'s first opportunity to race against all the top NASCAR Winston Cup Series drivers at once, including Jeff Gordon, Dale Jarrett, Mark Martin, and his old man. The competitors were lined up on the track, ready to go, and Dale Jr. was just minding his own business when he felt a little jolt from behind.

There in the rearview mirror, the Intimidator looked back at him with a smile. Then came another little tap.

In the highest levels of NASCAR, no one uses that tap with greater efficiency than Dale Earnhardt. It sometimes comes after he's been beaten to the flag in close competition: Like a hard, unexpected slap on the back from a friendly rival, Earnhardt's tap always seems to mean both "Congratulations" and "Don't ever let that happen again."

On the track with Dale Jr., the tap also seemed to mean "You're surrounded by the best here: Use your head and drive hard but safe."

As soon as the green flag waved, Dale Jr. went out hard, with the kind of relentless determination that has made reputations for both his father and grandfather. In a brilliant series of moves, courtesy of quick reflexes and impulsive decision-making, Dale Jr. powered to the lead after seven laps of the 40-lap race.

The lead wouldn't last, however. A bad judgment call left an opening on lap eight and several cars took to the inside and passed him. He worked his way back up in the next lap and had only his father's long-time friendly rival Rusty Wallace in front of him. But Dale Jr. lost control of the car at the first turn of lap nine and slid sideways right into Wallace. The two spun and when the collecting was finished, he was gone from the field. Dale Jr.'s effort had lasted nine laps.

His father took a different tack. From lap 17 to the last lap, he bided his time comfortably in second place, an ever-present spectre in the rearview mirror of defending IROC champion Mark Martin. On the last lap, he moved up to Martin, tried passing him on turn two, and then, off turn four, with the checkered flag in sight, he gave Martin just enough of a nudge to loosen him up a bit, swung aside, and took off, with Bobby Labonte in tow. All three careened toward the start-finish line and Earnhardt passed over in front, one-tenth of a second ahead of Labonte, who beat Martin by inches.

That's where his son, dressed in street clothes, found his father and offered his good wishes. Dale Jr. shook his head over the learning experience. He only wanted to get the lead, he told his father, who reminded his over-eager son about that one racing cliché he already knew well: The last lap is the only one worth leading.

In fact, Dale Jr. was a much quicker study than anyone had anticipated. One year earlier, after a somewhat unremarkable career in Late Model Stocks, he began a full-time ride for his father's NASCAR Busch Series team, after Earnhardt Sr.'s NASCAR Busch Series driver, Steve Park, moved up to drive for him in the NASCAR Winston Cup Series. Dale had planned on letting his youngest son gain a bit more experience before moving into the NASCAR Busch

Series, but with the vacancy, he gave him the ride, some top equipment, and a great team, and hoped for the best. The best is what he got. After having posted all of three total wins in 113 Late Model Stock races, Dale Jr. won seven NASCAR Busch Series races in 1998, along with 16 top-fives and 22 top-tens in 31 starts, a record that gave him a NASCAR Busch Series championship.

After a second championship NASCAR Busch Series season in 1999, Dale Jr. is now a NASCAR Winston Cup Series regular. He entered the series with more hype and anticipation than has greeted any driver in stock history. Not only is he the son of a seven-time NASCAR Winston Cup Series champion, there's also his six-year sponsorship deal with Budweiser, which he signed in 1998, before he had ever driven a lap in the NASCAR Winston Cup Series. And sales of his souvenir products are among the highest in the sport.

For two years, there has been the inevitable talk of how he will stack up on the track and off with NASCAR's reigning star, Jeff Gordon, the matinee-idol handsome, smooth-talking, three-time NASCAR Winston Cup Series champion who is the only driver to end up on a box of Wheaties and sport a milk mustache. By contrast, Dale Jr. is a skinny blond kid refreshingly rough around the edges in his manner, who has direct lineage back to the glory days of America's stock car heritage. The general consensus among many racing analysts—and the great hope of Madison Avenue execs—is that just as Dale Earnhardt battled Jeff Gordon during the early part of the latter's career, Dale Jr. will take on that challenge now.

Not that Dale Earnhardt is going anywhere. He'll be on the track racing against his son, whose continued development as a driver will no doubt bring the sport's greatest competitor mixed emotions. Dale Jr. has been able to thrive under his father's tutelage, but there are still lessons to learn. Among them will be how best to deal with the demands of a star's schedule—the same kind of schedule that, ironically, kept Dale and his youngest son apart for much of Dale Jr.'s childhood. Nowadays, father and son do their best to see each other at the garage and at home. But chances are they rarely have as much fun as they did in June 1999 when, in spirited competition, they grew quite close on the track, racing door-to-door in the final seconds of the exciting IROC race in Michigan.

If that race is any indication, Earnhardt Sr. doesn't plan on slowing down—especially if his son is in the rearview on the last lap. The kid will have to earn it. As Dale said after a 1998 exhibition race in Japan—where he and his son did some mid-race bumping before Dale finished eighth and Jr. sixth—"As a father, I'm proud of all my kids and support them in what avenue they choose. As a competitor, you never like getting beat."

Long before they raced against each other in stock cars, Dale and Dale Jr. shared the same track on one occasion, using much less sophisticated equipment. Dale Jr., all of thirteen at the time, cruised around a track in his go-kart. His father watched him racing his friends one afternoon, and taken by the urge to join in, hopped into a ride and took off after them. The ride he chose, however, had a major power advantage: It was a Honda four-wheeler. And with the laugh of a big kid finding a sneaky way to win, he charged ahead of "the rest of the field."

"It was kinda neat just to see him trying to compete," Dale Jr. recalls. "You never have a sense of how intense he is as a competitor and you could see just a hint of that. It gave an idea of how determined you needed to be to be as good as him. Even though I was only thirteen, I still could tell and see it in his face and his driving."

By this time, Dale Jr. and his older sister, Kelley, had been living with their father and his wife, Teresa—and a succession of nannies—for a few years, after having spent most of their childhood in their mother's home. Dale Sr., on the road a great deal of the time, grew concerned enough about a wild streak he saw in his son that he decided to send him to a military academy for two years. Dale Jr. emerged with a greater sense of discipline, and as he entered high school, he could see himself fitting comfortably behind the wheel of a race car. By seventeen, he was competing, along with his sister, Kelley, and his brother, Kerry, in the Street Stock Division in Concord, North Carolina.

His father had grown up obsessively toiling in the garage, helping to build Ralph Earnhardt's cars, but Dale Jr. took a somewhat more modern approach to his off-road education. There was time logged at a local automotive school; courses at a driving school where he learned from Bill Cooper, who had also given his father some lessons; and his less formal course of studying strategy in races on ESPN and on video. As with his father, Dale Jr.'s motivation came from a desire to gain the respect of a man who was solidly in his racing prime.

"When I first started," Dale Jr. remembers, "it was all for that, no other reason, because I didn't have a lot of confidence in myself to be able to become anything important, and my dad was huge. He had gone to certain lengths to give me good schooling and make sure I had a good upbringing, so I wanted to become an asset to him.

"He knew I wanted to [race] all along. I don't know how much confidence in me he had, whether he had a lot or not. It just took awhile for him to come around."

Part of that process was Dale Sr.'s insistence that his son do as he had done when he began to race, so Dale Jr. prepared the cars himself, worked with his own young pit team on setups, and took the car to the tracks. If this made Dale Jr. slightly annoyed at times, he would later admit it also worked out to be a tremendous asset in terms of learning the craft of racing.

Dale Jr. spent two years in the Street Stock Division near home, driving Chevys bearing the same number 8 Grandpa Ralph had used. With some success, it was time for Late Model Stocks at tracks throughout the Carolinas against, among other competitors, his older brother and sister. It wasn't easy for any of the siblings to deal with the pressures associated with being an Earnhardt on a race track. Kelley and Dale Jr., who'd always been close, were able to help each other keep things in perspective, providing frequent reminders that they were there to have fun, regardless of the repetitive questions from some promoters and local reporters.

Meanwhile, their father was in the midst of his memorable run of NASCAR Winston Cup Series championships. In 1993 and '94, Dale Sr. was winning yet another consecutive pair of titles, bringing the total to seven, and giving him an unprecedented six championships in nine seasons. The glory days kept Dale away from home a great deal, something his youngest son has more recently gained greater perspective on.

"That situation was inevitable," he says. "If he hadn't put forth all that effort in those years to racing, he might not be a seven-time champion. You can't replace those years where he was out of town a lot, but it was for good reason and that's why I can laugh about it [now]. It didn't necessarily do me any harm. I mean, I was always well taken care of. And he was doing what he wanted to do and I'd rather him do that."

Dale Jr. had some strong Late Model showings, and in 1996 and 1997 his dad gave him the keys to the occasional NASCAR Busch Series ride, just to help him become familiar with the inevitable next stop. Things looked encouraging when he finished seventh in a NASCAR Busch Series race in Michigan in 1997. It would be his only top-ten in eight races that year, but given that he drove in lesser equipment than Earnhardt's regular NASCAR Busch Series driver, Steve Park, all looked hopeful.

Those eight races proved valuable when Dale Jr. was given the NASCAR Busch Series wheel full-time in 1998. He'd need all the help he could get. With Park having won three races and Rookie of the Year honors in 1997, Dale Jr. had yet another set of big shoes to fill. His father didn't expect a great deal, but his lifelong friend and frequent staffer Tony Eury Sr., who had known Dale Jr. as a boy and would serve as crew chief, had an inkling that perhaps Dale Jr. could run well with the best, if given some time.

For nineteen years in a row, Dale Earnhardt's February heartache in Daytona happened at the 500, the one race he always managed to lose in eerily frustrating ways, from running out of gas in the late going, to cutting a tire on turn three of the last lap. In 1998, the heartache happened one day earlier when his son ran his first NASCAR Busch Series race of the year in the NAPA Auto Parts 300.

A day later, his father had to run the best race of his life to overcome his long history of disappointment. People kept telling him it was his year, while some critics said his best racing days were too far behind for him to conjure up a Daytona miracle big enough to break the hex.

As usual, Dale didn't doubt he could win, and he set about proving it, starting from the number-four position and staying near the lead for most of the race. By lap 140 of 200, he took the lead; several

drivers challenged, but Earnhardt, a master at controlling his territory, managed to keep all comers behind him as the day wore on.

At lap 198, the stage set for a final battle with Earnhardt still leading, it was hard to fight off the question of how he would lose this
time—something had to happen. Then the smoke suddenly rose
when Jimmy Spencer made contact with John Andretti and the
Daytona 500 became a one-lap dash to the yellow flag. It must have
seemed very familiar to Earnhardt when pole-sitter Bobby
Labonte's car started looming larger in his rearview mirror. But
just ahead was Rick Mast's lapped auto; Earnhardt passed Mast,
who served as the perfect block to keep the Intimidator ahead of
his pursuer. There would be no stopping him from breaking the hex
now—coming off turn four, the white and yellow flags in sight and
victory all but assured, the 185,000 faithful at Daytona rose for the
celebration. And they weren't alone: After taking the checkered
flag, Dale drove the road to victory lane and team members from
almost every crew lined the path to shake hands with the champion, whose eyes grew moist in the moment.

And accepting the trophy, with wife Teresa by his side,
Earnhardt took announcer Ken Squier's urging and paid tribute to
some people who mattered most: his old racing friend, the late Neil
Bonnett; T. Wayne Robertson, president of sports marketing for R.
J. Reynolds, who'd died a month earlier in a boating accident; "My
dad, everybody that's been in racing and been my friend, who
taught me so much and touched my life . . . my mom . . . Dale Jr.—I
hope you're not too sore. Kerry and Kelley, I love you all."

Arguably the biggest victory of Earnhardt's career had been
secured. Now it came time for a bit of the old man's good fortune to
rub off on his kid.

The journey didn't start out very well, with finishes of 37th and
16th in Dale Jr.'s first two NASCAR Busch Series races. But he settled
in quickly after that, running in the top ten for the next six races,
which included his first NASCAR Busch Series victory in Texas. His
victory came in a familiar style. Just after the white flag came down,
Dale Jr. got under leader Joe Nemechek, and then, with a sprinter's
kick, made it to the checker, barely besting Elliott Sadler. The win
gave Earnhardt a slim lead in the early NASCAR Busch Series points
race; as an added bonus, his dad was there in victory lane to greet

him with a hug. During the final turns, the Intimidator was on the radio with Dale Jr.; if the kid could deal with the nervousness of that, he'd be primed for anything. Afterward Dale said his son's victory felt as good as when he himself had won Daytona. He hadn't seen anything yet.

The victory led to a four-race lapse of sorts, but then Dale Jr. began a pace that would vault him to the top of the standings for good. In the sixteen races that followed, he won six and came in second twice. That put him out of reach for every driver but the highly regarded Matt Kenseth, whom many had considered the odds-on favorite to capture the NASCAR Busch Series title when the season began. But Dale Jr.'s second-place finish to Mark Martin in the fall Atlanta NASCAR Busch Series race put him almost totally out of reach: All he needed to do was start the season finale to secure the crown.

Start the race was precisely what he did. He lost his engine 89 laps into the contest, and though he would have liked to have run the whole course, it did give Dale Earnhardt Jr. much more time to dive into the waiting arms of his crew and celebrate.

At age twenty-four, he'd won a sanctioned NASCAR championship, the third Earnhardt to do so. Like his father and grandfather before him, he was creative and determined on the track and humble in victory.

There would be many challenges for Dale Earnhardt Jr. to face. The one he'd need the most getting used to would be racing with his father. "[My racing] is all for my daddy," he once said. "I don't care much about anything else." That may be the case, but he also planned on proving to his mentor that he was worthy of sharing the same track space.

Anyone could see that at an exhibition race in Japan—run a few weeks after the end of the 1998 NASCAR season—that served as their first official contest together. It was just a friendly little race with many of the world's best stock car drivers in the field; no points were up for grabs. But as the day approached, Dale Sr. took on his customary serious attitude and began treating his son like any other competitor.

On the track, there was some door popping between them, and an opportunity for Dale Jr. to pass his father for the first time on the way to finishing sixth to his dad's eighth. Now Dale would have something new to get used to. For his son, however, the race, and the week leading up to it, proved to him that he'd finally arrived.

"That was pretty cool—just practicing with him and being on the race track with him was a lot of fun and just real exciting. To see him next to you and being in competition for position was a lot of fun," he says of the event. "It's something that you don't know exactly how it's gonna make you feel until you get out there, and then you're just overcome with some sense of acceptance and accomplishment because he's the ultimate. What he's doing and what you've seen him doing for years is your ultimate goal. It's something that you get right away as a kid, to do what he's doing and be like him."

In 20/20 hindsight, that race now seems like a simple warm-up for the 1999 IROC stop in Michigan. It would be the fourth time father and son were in the same lineup, with Dale Sr. having already won the first two IROC races of the year. But the finish in Michigan between father and son transcended the standard racing fare. It's fitting that IROC is a non-points situation, since this race offered an amazing insight into the exuberance of competition.

Less than ten laps into the 50-lap contest, Earnhardt had risen from last place to second with only Mark Martin ahead of him. Twice in the next fifteen laps, his son, working to keep himself in third, tried to pass his father for second, running down on the apron, and was rebuffed each time.

Past the halfway point, Earnhardt managed to vault in front of Martin on the inside. Four laps later, his son gained some territory on the inside in a charge to second place. With nineteen laps to the checkered flag, father and son were one and two. "You know, I've been in races where I thought Earnhardt was running first and second and there was only one," three-time NASCAR Winston Cup Series champion Darrell Waltrip said from the booth. "Today, I actually can see it."

For eighteen laps, all the action and jockeying went on behind the leaders as Martin, Jeff Gordon, Jeff Burton, CART driver Greg Moore, and Rusty Wallace fought for position. Meanwhile, Dale and Dale Jr. remained fixed on each other, windshield to rearview. When the white flag came out, Dale Jr. saw his opportunity.

Coming out of turn two, he threatened a move to the inside but it was too early to think of following through. Half a lap later, he faked to the inside and went wide open on the outside line until father and son were door-to-door with Dale Jr. in the lead by a fraction. It would be a drag race to the finish.

They popped doors coming out of turn four. They popped them again and Dale maintained his inside line, eking ahead. At the start-finish line, father had his son by inches.

In victory lane, Earnhardt Sr. emerged from his car to deafening cheers from the crowd; the cheers only got louder when his son joined him there and Dale threw an arm around his son after the most spirited generational racing the sport had seen since Bobby and Davey Allison turned the 1988 Daytona 500 into their own family affair.

"It's hard to top that, I think, in father/son relationships," Dale says. "There's things you might do, go out golfing together, or swimming or boating or hunting or whatever. To be racing your son on a race track at the speeds that we were, that's a pretty awesome feeling, and to win the race, pretty awesome. I don't think you could top it.

"I'm proud of him, you know, of his capabilities, proud of what he can do, his accomplishments, but I'm just proud of him as a dad," he continues. "Of course, I'm awful proud of him when he wins, but I'm more proud of him being able to take defeat, because he takes his bad days as well as his good days, because if he handles himself well, then I've done a pretty good job of him being able to understand life."

After one championship and the near miss in Michigan, Dale Jr. saw an inkling of how far he'd come in his hunt for the necessary tools to be competitive at the sport's top tier—especially in terms of racing life with his father.

"I haven't lost any respect for him, but I do feel like I can give myself a little more credit than I have in the past to be able to compete at his level," he concedes. "I thought at one time, and this wasn't long ago, that it was gonna take a lot of practice to be able to do it as well as he does but it's not necessarily that way anymore. That's a lot of confidence and that's where most of it is, in confidence. I still hold him at the highest standards that I did before, but now I feel like I'm closer to reaching that goal."

Perhaps more than anything else, what thrilled race fans about father vs. son at Michigan was the fact that neither was willing to give an inch in territory—and their cars have the scratches to prove it.

"Most of it is the competitive spirit," Dale Jr. says of the bumping. "If I was in his shoes, I would expect some smart-ass comments from my son. I feel I've still got a lot to learn. We get maybe overly competitive, largely because of the expectations of the fans and the hype that the media makes of it. It's hard not to get mixed up into thinking it's a race between me and him instead of whoever else is on the racetrack. You start thinking, well, that's the only goal, that's the only accomplishment, and it kinda screws it up, but we still have fun on the track, and I try to be smart and safe, and try to do what's best for him and everybody else and not do anything foolish. But every once in a while, you catch yourself doing things you normally wouldn't do, had he not been on the racetrack."

In 1999, everything went pretty much according to plan for the Earnhardts: Dale won more times than he had since 1996 (although he is still chasing the ever-elusive eighth championship) and Dale Jr. learned more, won another title, and built still greater anticipation for his NASCAR Winston Cup Series full-time debut.

From a business standpoint, Dale Sr. has little to complain about. Father and son are also employer and employee, thanks to Dale Jr.'s contract with Dale Earnhardt Inc., and his long-standing statement that he hopes never to drive for any other corporation.

That corporation's success is due, in great measure, to the presence of another influential NASCAR Earnhardt. Dale's wife, Teresa, whose father also ran short track races, is the company's co-CEO. It is Teresa who has helped guide Dale Sr.'s career throughout their twenty-year marriage. "She's a very well-rounded woman in the fact that she's smart, and she has common sense, she's got education, she looks good," says her admiring husband. "She uses her head so well in thinking things out, a lot of people say she's too thorough sometimes, but, you know, we've done pretty good as a team. It's one thing being married and having a wife, it's another thing to have a wife and a business partner and somebody to have time with, too, all rolled into one. It's hard to find relationships like that in anybody's life, whether you're a racer or you work eight to five in an office. It's tough to have that balance. I've been fortunate."

The company began with nineteen employees and now boasts well over one hundred, and runs race teams in the NASCAR Winston Cup Series, the NASCAR Busch Series and the NASCAR Craftsman Truck Series; in addition, there's real estate, farming, airplane, and auto dealership holdings.

Both financially and personally, Earnhardt has created a successful legacy in the sport, a link between his past and his future. And if he's humble about his own professional accomplishments—at last count, seven championships, seventy-four victories, and more than $35 million—he is proud of the part he's played in taking the sound advice his father gave him and passing that on to his own kids.

"After you leave here, all you got is your name, and that's all they're gonna remember about you, and what kind of person you were," he says of the main lesson Ralph Earnhardt taught him. "Wasn't whether you had a lot of money or you won a lot of races. Daddy was always preaching honesty and standing up for yourself: Stand up for your faith and work hard and try to get ahead in life. And that's what I want my kids to do. I'm proud of them, I'm proud of how they've grown up. They've got a place in life and they've got their jobs and they make pretty good decisions."

His twenty-seven-year-old daughter Kelley works for a sports marketing firm; son Kerry, thirty, is racing part-time; and Taylor, his daughter with Teresa, is now ten.

He is close to them all, but there is a special bond with Dale Jr., who is still adjusting to his professional life and trying to make the right decisions. With the constant demands on his time, he continues to look for the free moments to stay focused and in touch with the friends who will keep him honest. He is also very much his own man, speaking his mind with little restriction. "When you get into racing, you gotta grow up pretty fast and you gotta be pretty professional, and I have a hard time keeping my mouth shut a lot of times," he admits. "And I still do today and maybe it'll always be, but it's hard to learn."

In other words, he's very much like his father was at twenty-five. Whatever does come of this most promising NASCAR Winston Cup Series career—whether Dale and Dale Jr. will bump when points are being earned; whether Dale Sr. will be inspired by his son's presence to attack the challenge of NASCAR Winston Cup Series championship number eight, before growing content enough to watch Dale Jr. gain his own glory; whether Dale will ever have as much pride behind the wheel as he did watching Dale Jr.'s first NASCAR Winston Cup Series win in Atlanta in April 2000; whether they'll have even more time to see each other now that they're on the same tour—all this remains to be seen. What won't change are the feelings Dale Jr. has for his father, something unsaid during the years of his youth when Dad was on the road, something reveled in now as father and son travel the same road together.

7
The Elliott Brothers

In the early 1970s, George Elliott was facing something of a dilemma. It involved the youngest of his three red-haired boys, who'd recently started driving delivery trucks for the family's home supply center. Like his two older brothers before him, Bill Elliott, then in his late teens, found great pleasure in discovering how fast he could navigate that truck over the local S-shaped roads near the family's Dawsonville, Georgia, home. While Bill powered through his adolescent rite of passage, his dad was forced to contemplate the best way to redirect the boy's passion for acceleration. "It looked like we were going to terrorize the highways," recalls Bill's middle brother, Dan Elliott, with a chuckle. "So Daddy said, 'If y'all are going to do this, then we're going to do something to keep you off the highways and get into an environment that's a lot safer for you and the motorists on the road.'"

George Elliott's solution was to help finance a stock car operation for the boys. It seemed a natural move, given that he'd dabbled in the world of racing through most of his adult life— "Since long before I came along," says Bill Elliott. "He always owned a race car. He never drove himself, but he just loved that aspect of it. He had cars that went to Daytona as far back as the early sixties."

For a number of years in the early 1970s, he bankrolled his sons' efforts as best he could. All three Elliott boys tried driving for a time before each discovered his niche. The secret to their success, they decided, was teamwork, a concept they learned to practice with as much skill as they applied to the art of making a stock car go faster.

By 1976, George Elliott's three sons had risen through the ranks and were poised to make a run at the premier division of their sport. That year, George would have a car at Daytona once again. In February, the boys, working with limited finances and unlimited drive and effort, brought the fast family auto their dad owned to Rockingham, North Carolina, for their first NASCAR big league race. And on July 4th, they made their debut at NASCAR's home base track in Daytona Beach, Florida. These first appearances may not have been auspicious affairs for the Elliotts, but they signalled the arrival of one of the most successful families in NASCAR history.

The advantage the Elliotts always brought to the track was to be found in the closeness of the brothers's relationships, and their unquestionable faith in each other. The oldest, Ernie, built the engines and served the team as crew chief. Middle brother Dan, four years Ernie's junior, joined his older brother in the engine room, preparing the gears; on race days, he changed the rear tires during pit stops. But the real star of the team—a reluctant one, given his chronic shyness—was Bill, the baby brother, eight years younger than Ernie. Not long after his days of speeding around the North Georgia roads in his dad's truck, twenty-one-year-old Bill Elliott found himself sharing the same asphalt as Cale Yarborough, David Pearson, Richard Petty, and Bobby Allison at NASCAR's meccas of speed.

Nine years later, in 1985, the Elliott brothers, now in a car owned by their famed benefactor Harry Melling, brought the Coors No. 9 Ford to victory lane at the Daytona 500. That would be the first win in a storybook season for the team. It was also the start of a year filled with a vast amount of pressure. Given the level of scrutiny Bill Elliott and company faced in 1985, it took a tremendous effort for the brothers to stay focused, stay successful, and somehow stay together.

But then, says Dan, "This was not the average, run-of-the-mill sibling family. I guess my emotions and feelings run a lot different from other people, but to have been so fortunate to be a brother in this situation, it's almost as if my life were predestined. We all have a respect for each other for what we do. And the common goal for the whole thing is you never want to do anything for the team other than to accomplish wins.

"We just worked toward what we wanted," he adds. "I think most of our feelings came out in our work. And we were very passionate about our work."

Given George Elliott's resume, it's hard to imagine him not being the perfect inspiration for his boys in their quest for stock car glory. He had been, at various times, a Navy officer, an elementary school teacher, and a principal, as well as the owner of a Ford dealership. But his real passion remained stock car racing. For a time, he owned Jeffco Speedway, a renowned short track in Jefferson, Georgia. In 1966, driver Don Tilley took a George Elliott car to the fall race at Rockingham. But his involvement in racing began much earlier, coinciding with the beginnings of NASCAR.

"Daddy had a vision that NASCAR was going to be *the* sport," says his son Bill. "Maybe it wasn't at the time I got started, but it eventually grew into it. And maybe he had the same vision Bill France Sr. did as far as what he was trying to do with this sport and take it where it ranks right in there with all the other professional sports."

During the 1960s, the boys knew little of their father's perspective; to them, racing meant great weekends at Georgia's short tracks. "Daddy was running cars on the local level down here," Dan says. "There weren't any responsibilities [for us] or anything, just go and have a good time. If you tore up, you came home, if you didn't, you ran. And it was just basic Saturday night short track, but it was a simple time. And people didn't have a lot for equipment. You just went to the junkyard, got the stuff you needed. And if you couldn't find it in the junkyard, you didn't race. That was about the only way you were able to do it then."

In the mid–1960s, Ernie Elliot began running a speed shop for his dad, where they sold parts to local drivers at the tracks. Several years later, Bill joined the business and the brothers, despite the large gap in their ages, discovered a common interest in working together and fielding a stock car. Ernie tried his hand at driving, but his first love was engine work. Bill was in charge of setting up the car and getting the chassis built, and in time he took to driving. Their inclination eventually led them to Dixie Speedway in Woodstock, Georgia, where Bill won his first Sportsman division race in 1974. George Elliott was spending his race weekends helping his boys at the track.

"Daddy saw I was serious about doing it, so he bought a pretty good car," Bill says. "Ernie and I started racing on the short track level, then we got more into what NASCAR is, and that's when Dan came along and it was then the three of us working together.

"All I wanted to do was race," he adds. "I never dreamed I'd have any kind of opportunity to go to NASCAR, nor did I know where NASCAR was going to go. I'd heard the names Pearson, Petty, Yarborough, and all those guys, but I didn't follow it. I just was used to my own little world; NASCAR was a foreign entity as far as I was concerned."

That changed in 1976 when the boys, armed with a 1973 Torino their dad bought from Bobby Allison, began to invest their combined efforts into preparing a car worthy of keeping pace on NASCAR's tracks. Fortunately, the sport's multimillion-dollar team budgets were years in the future; given the limitations of the Elliott team's finances, they were only able to run a limited schedule as it was. Today, they would never even have made it out of the garage area.

For several seasons, the team ran as best they could, barely managing to stay ahead of early retirement. Despite the hardship, team strides were providing confidence. At the 1979 Southern 500, Bill finished second; he might have wound up two laps behind Darlington master David Pearson, but the effort did not go unnoticed. Ernie's long hours in the garage were beginning to pay off in the form of better engines. And just when things seemed most dire, the family would discover a new way to remain afloat. To battle the cost of tires, they actually ran on used ones for a time, purchased at discount from Benny Parsons. And when NASCAR regulations demanded cars with new dimensions, George Elliott pumped whatever funds he could into the business to keep the operation running.

"[Daddy] sacrificed a lot to believe in us," Bill says now. "He never was a very affectionate-type dad, but I think we all knew where we stood with him. And I think it took me to later years to better understand him. But Daddy was always there supporting us and that means more than anything."

The Elliott brothers were a team on the cusp of great things. It was clear that Bill knew how to handle himself well on the track; there was the occasional rookie mistake, but his skills were beginning to attract attention. From 1979 through 1981, on little more than the strength of Bill's ability and Ernie's engines, the team scored two top-fives and fourteen top-tens in only thirty-nine races.

"He's probably one of the smoothest and most confident drivers I've ever known," Dan says of his younger brother. "The ability to conserve equipment, draw on your aggressiveness when you need to—and knowing when not to—gave us the edge through the years we had."

One sponsor who took notice was Harry Melling, owner of a successful Michigan-based auto-parts company. Melling came aboard as a sponsor in 1981 and provided enough support to make the Elliotts' competitive. He bought the team outright in 1982 and with the extra capital added to an already hardworking operation, Bill and company quickly turned the corner. In 1983, he ran thirty races (he'd run twenty-one the season before) and ended up third in the final standings (his previous best finish had been twenty-fifth, in 1982). Of those thirty races, he gained top-ten finishes in twenty-two of them, including his first-ever win, on the road course in Riverside, California, at the season finale.

Now the brothers had no excuses, and they took to the task of proving their worth with renewed vigor. In 1984, they ended the year in third place again, this time posting three victories.

They maintained their small team of about a dozen or so crew members, with most of them working long into the night to get the Ford ready for each week of competition. At the center of the operation remained the three brothers who, despite the struggles, grew closer together.

"We were all just content with what responsibilities we had," says Dan. "With brothers it would have to be jealousy among you for there to be tension. And I didn't want to be crew chief. I didn't want to drive. Ernie didn't want to work on the crew and change tires or do transmission and gear stuff like I did, and then I think it just came about that three brothers found three individual roles. And they just happened to work toward a common goal. I think if anybody could be fortunate enough in their life to do that with brothers or family, that's an ideal opportunity."

Perhaps it was the family's rise from nothing that made them fan favorites. On the one hand, there was a certain charm about Bill, with his halting speech and shy manner. Yet both he and Ernie could be gruff at the track: Any interruption that kept them from producing greatness in their cars was time wasted.

"Ernie is definitely a perfectionist, and it shows," Dan says. "For a driver not to have an ego that's above and beyond anybody else's, I don't think they're going to do well. And for Ernie not to have the attitude that whatever it takes to get the job done—and if anybody wants to carry on a conversation with him, if it's not a conversation that he has any interest in, he's not going to give you the time of day—that's not a bad thing in the business you're in. Given the goals you're trying to achieve, personality-wise, the driver has to have an ego; Ernie would have to have an ego in the sense that his engines are better than everybody else's, and he's out to prove it. If you can't sell yourself, you're not going to sell anybody else."

In 1985, Bill, Ernie, Dan, and company would have no problem selling that point. Some might even argue they sold it too well.

To understand what the Elliotts went through in 1985 means going back to the announcement by R. J. Reynolds Tobacco Company at the 1984 NASCAR Winston Cup Series banquet. NASCAR's biggest sponsors promised that beginning the following year, they would offer up the Winston Million for the first time. Any driver who won three of the circuit's four premier superspeedway events—the Daytona 500, the Coca-Cola World 600, the Southern 500 and the RJR-sponsored Winston 500—would earn a $1 million bonus.

It was a bold PR coup for a sport hungry to increase the breadth of its fan base. Adding a "Triple Crown" contest to the games couldn't help but make things more interesting—and help link NASCAR to other sports boasting a higher national profile. Never mind that the long odds against a driver maintaining that kind of consistency throughout the year made the Million seem pretty unattainable. The point was, the paycheck was there for anybody good enough and lucky enough to claim it, along with the deafening hoopla that would accompany such a run.

Bonus notwithstanding, the Elliotts—who had, up to that point, only won four races in their entire NASCAR Winston Cup Series career—began the year with confidence. They had spent Harry Melling's money wisely and had maintained a typically manic off-season schedule spent getting their Fords just right. The No. 9 could not have been any sounder as the season opened in Daytona, with Bill Elliott nearly lapping the field in his 125-mile qualifier, before winning the pole for the 500 at a blistering 205 mph. Then, for the first hundred miles of NASCAR's biggest show, Elliott posted an unbelievable average speed of over 192 mph. The other drivers in the field struggled to keep up, and before long, many succumbed to engine failure. In the end, it was outside circumstances that nearly did Bill Elliott in. During a green-flag pit stop with 55 laps to go, a NASCAR official noticed that the Thunderbird's right front headlight panel had been jarred loose, and he demanded that Ernie tape it up. Forty-two seconds later, Bill's commanding lead was gone. The fact that it only took him 11 laps of green-flag racing to regain that lead is testament to the power the Elliotts had under the hood that day. After the race, with Bill smiling broadly in victory lane, announcer Chris Economaki wondered aloud if the driver or the car had won the race. Paying tribute to Ernie, Bill admitted it was probably the latter.

Noting the Elliott team's dominance at Daytona, Junior Johnson and other owners grumbled that perhaps some rule changes might be in order to level the playing field and make the going more competitive. However, the Elliotts certainly required no monitoring during the second and third races of the season, where Bill finished 22nd and 29th, respectively. In that third race, the Carolina 500 at Rockingham, Bill's day—and his year, it seemed—was further complicated by a broken leg. He spent the next two weeks trying to rest up for the Coca-Cola 500 in Atlanta, where Jody Ridley would be waiting in the pits to relieve his friend when necessary.

The necessity never came. Elliott, broken leg and all, beat Geoffrey Bodine and the rest of the field for his first win at the closest thing he could come to calling a hometown track. The brothers appeared to have destiny on their side.

The Elliotts confirmed that impression at the spring race at Talladega: the Winston 500, second jewel of the Winston Million. A week after NASCAR revised the rules regarding the height of a car's roof—a move that could easily have slowed down the Elliotts—Bill and his brothers shocked the Alabama crowd with a blistering qualifying speed of over 209 mph. But 48 laps into the race, smoke poured freely from the back of Bill's Ford. Ernie swiftly diagnosed the problem: a broken oil fitting. After a 69-second pit stop, Bill returned to the running in 26th place, nearly two laps down.

What Elliott needed badly was a yellow flag to make up some of the huge distance. He didn't get it. Instead, the crowd watched with a growing sense of awe as he kept running laps well over 200 mph, passing other cars in the process and creeping back into contention.

One hundred laps later, Elliott passed Cale Yarborough to retake the lead, and after dealing with the elusive caution that ultimately came several laps later, Elliott pulled away to victory. With two Winston Million races won, the driver who once had to buy Benny Parson's used tires in order to field his car had to win only one of the two remaining legs to pad his bank account by $1 million.

The fallout from Talladega, however, would be hard to deal with. Not only was there the pressure of such immeasurable success, there were also the testy car owners, and the outcry that perhaps the Elliotts were somehow stacking the deck. After Talladega, the Elliotts were guaranteed their post-race inspections would be more thorough than an airport strip search. The brothers may have felt no tension from within the team, but outside forces were another story.

"Going into it, we weren't even sure what the limits were at that time of car-driver-engine," Dan says of the Talladega. "We were new at that area of the sport—we'd never been that competitive before. And to push the car to the limits Bill pushed it that day was beyond belief. But the worst thing I think it did for us as a team is it showed all the competitors what we were capable of. Were it not for that oil fitting at Talladega, and having to run like we did, I think we would have made it a little bit easier on ourselves through the year."

For Bill's part, the ensuing pressure and public clamoring were difficult by-products of success.

"It was very hard to deal with from my standpoint, especially me being a shy person," he says. "I don't like crowds, and I kind of shy away from that type of deal—being thrown to the lions. The whole sport was changing at that time—whether we were a part of it, or we helped, whatever, you can look at it any different way.

"But we got through it," he adds. "We continued to work and let the other stuff deal with itself, and just try to take it the best we could. We made mistakes along the way, but we still did what we had to do racing, and that's the biggest part. I think adversity like that helps to get you closer together."

Still, the brothers' nerves were frayed by the time the circuit rolled around to Charlotte, North Carolina, for the Coca-Cola 600. A victory there and Bill Elliott would have earned the elusive brass ring. That week, however, the Elliotts were forced the think of everything but racing, with a media frenzy following them everywhere. The pressure showed in their performance as Bill, who'd won the pole, ended the day in 18th position, some 21 laps off the pace of eventual victor Darrell Waltrip.

In the eight races between Charlotte and the Southern 500, the Elliott team continued their exceptional tear, winning four times. They arrived at Darlington with one more chance to make a million bucks, trying desperately to focus on the race. It is often said that Darlington is the one stop where a driver must beat the racetrack, not the competition. The Elliotts tried to keep their eyes on that prize.

To do so, they employed a rather controversial method. The brothers scheduled whatever media time they felt necessary and then brought in a pair of South Carolina Highway Patrolmen to keep everybody else out of their garage. The troopers would earn their keep that weekend, which saw the sport in the midst of the biggest media crush it had ever known.

As had become his pattern that season, Bill Elliott earned the pole at Darlington and jumped out to an early lead. He avoided a couple of incidents that could have sent him home early and remained in the running the entire afternoon. With about 70 laps to go, the action centered on Elliott and Cale Yarborough. The pair traded the lead a number of times until a long stream of smoke began to trail Yarborough's No. 28 Ford. Convinced he'd lost an engine, he pitted and happily discovered he'd only blown a power steering line. Yarborough dashed back into the running to resume the chase. For 40 more laps, he fought to catch Elliott, hoping the latter might slip up just long enough for him to make a pass. Given the kind of year Bill Elliott was having, that didn't seem likely.

When the racing was done, Elliott ended up in front by less than a second, and he coasted to victory lane, to collect the largest check in NASCAR. He had a 206-point lead with eight races remaining and there seemed no way to stop the man newly christened "Awesome Bill from Dawsonville."

In terms of unpredictability, the only thing that rivaled Elliott's million-dollar victory in 1985 was his swift fall to second place in the standings by year's end, more than one hundred points behind champion Darrell Waltrip. The incredible pressures of the season, including the long nights of preparation, had finally taken their toll on Bill, Ernie, Dan, and company.

But no matter how the final championship tally worked out, the year clearly belonged to Elliott, whose eleven superspeedway wins broke David Pearson's record. Not surprisingly, his $2,383,186.30 earnings that year were more than double the previous annual record.

For a family who professed no desire to be in the spotlight, the great glare trained on them in 1985 took an enormous amount of adjustment. Ernie claims he rarely thinks about the year. His baby brother, on the other hand, has a few regrets.

"It was a tough deal, but I learned a lot," Bill admits. "I look back on it and it really helped shape my life. I wish I could have done some things differently, but there isn't anything I did that I'm ashamed of, either."

Of the three brothers, it is Dan who reveled most. Perhaps because he was not as involved in the daily setups of the car, he could almost regard the proceedings with an outsider's gaze. The view, he still maintains, was wondrously sweet.

"It's almost as if you could do no wrong, and that was the fairy-tale part of the whole year," he recalls. "Everything was on a positive note, and that's the only thing that's hard to come down from:

the reality that this won't last forever. You're on such a high, it's like your emotions were intensified. You were so much more in tune with your feelings than any other time in your life."

For loyal fans of Bill Elliott, who keenly felt the surprise of his NASCAR Winston Cup Series loss in 1985, there would be celebration three seasons later, when Bill won his title in a squeaker over Rusty Wallace. One season earlier, he'd notched two other notable triumphs: a second Daytona 500 victory, and the NASCAR version of the land-speed record. Elliott's 212.809 mph qualifying time for a race at Talladega remains the fastest any driver has ever traveled in a stock car.

The team did not, however, keep up so swift a pace after that. From 1989 through 1991, Elliott won only five times. Even with Ernie giving up the crew chief duties and concentrating solely on the engines, things did not improve. In 1991, Bill dropped to eleventh on the annual points list.

Still, it was a shock to most fans when he left Harry Melling and the family operation before the start of the 1992 season, signing instead with Junior Johnson as the senior half of the legend's two-driver team.

But, says Dan, "It never was anything that anybody criticized anybody or blamed anybody about. I think that time in his life you probably gain more knowledge by being away a little bit and regrouping. You kind of lose focus for a little while, or maybe it's just he needed that to see what he did have."

During the 1992 season, Bill found himself in the thick of yet another championship battle that came down to the final weekend. In the closest finish in NASCAR history, Elliott lost the title by ten points to Alan Kulwicki, the owner-driver whose independent style Elliott admired greatly.

After three seasons with Junior, Bill departed and finally fulfilled his long-sought dream of owning his team. He had McDonald's in tow as a sponsor and the family back together in the same garage.

"Sometimes it takes a whole lot more to get it back together than it did to drive it apart," Dan says of his brother's return. "And if you learn anything in your life, I think you learn that trying to keep your family together is the most important thing. I think that was probably my father's number-one goal, that we'd all be together as a family when it was all said and done. When the smoke clears, it'll be family that'll be there anyway."

The going has not been easy for Elliott since the team formed. For two years, beginning in 1994, the Elliott family watched Ernie's son Casey wage his battle with bone cancer; the disease ultimately claimed him in 1996, at age twenty-one. And while the Elliotts could appreciate their triumph as the only owner-driver team to finish 1997 in the top ten in points, 1998 carried with it yet more bad tidings. On May 21st, George Elliott underwent surgery to remove a brain tumor. Four months later, at age seventy-four, the man who sired one of NASCAR's great racing families was gone. His legacy remains intact and continues to thrive.

"I just try to keep a part of him living in me and continue on," says Bill. "That's what we're here for. There'll be another generation and another generation. I just remember what he instilled in me and try to keep believing that."

True to form, Bill Elliott remains competitive on the racetrack, despite the proliferation of teams with much higher budgets. Like in the old days, the Elliott brothers continue to defy the odds. At last count, Bill had tallied forty victories and winnings of $21 million. Dan owns a racing gear business and Ernie a motor business on the side; both remain part of the Elliott family team.

Many would argue that their original rise from poor stock to champions created an unrivaled fan base for the Elliotts. That base remains and helps to explain why Bill Elliott has won the "Most Popular Driver of the Year" award an unprecedented thirteen times.

But few accolades could ever mean more to the brothers than the one that took place at the Rockingham, North Carolina Speedway the last weekend in February 2000. Officials there paid tribute to the many triumphs in the twenty-five NASCAR seasons since Ernie, Dan, and Bill first took to the track at the Rock, seeking fortune and fame and gaining a bit too much of the latter for their blood.

But it is their family tradition that is worth celebrating for the Elliotts. Even though George Elliott reveled in the success his sons earned, their lifelong bond was his paramount desire when he bought his boys their first ride.

"It's happy memories, I can tell you that," Dan said of the Elliott legacy a few weeks before the tribute. "But to do this anniversary at Rockingham, and knowing that my dad won't be there, there's no bigger hurt for me. Still, it's not anything we can control; we just go on and be there and know that we're thinking about him and we miss him. Because, *God*, how proud he would have been to have been there. I could just see his face, and it would have just lit up."

8
The Flock Brothers

Watching the bulky stock cars course and slide their way down the dirt track at North Wilkesboro that afternoon in the spring of 1947, Tim Flock's frustration rose, but there was nothing he could do. It didn't matter what Tim wanted; his mother had laid down the law, and the law was final. Tim would not be a race car driver. It's not that Maudi Flock—"Big Mama," as all the Flocks called her—didn't normally support adventurous pursuits. Her husband Lee, who'd given her nine children before dying of cancer, had counted tightrope-walking among his hobbies. He'd also been a bicycle racer. And each of Big Mama's children had inherited the daredevil gene. But Tim was her baby. She could no longer stop the older boys, Bob and Fonty, from racing; they had already spent years earning their reputations as top Modified drivers throughout Georgia. However, she made them promise that Tim would never give her cause to worry about how he'd fare behind the wheel.

The routine was getting a little old, and Tim wasn't getting any younger. At twenty-three, he was married with one child, and had been supporting his family through a variety of professions: short-order cook and taxi driver among them. Driving was the only thing he really wanted to do. But on that 1947 weekend in North Wilkesboro, he settled for helping his brothers tow their cars to the track.

Tim stood in the pits, watching Bob and Fonty take their practice, when Bruce Thompson, whose son Speedy was just getting his start on the track, walked over with a proposal. Knowing the talents of Tim's brothers, Bruce was ready to offer him a ride in an extra car he'd brought. Tim answered by vaulting over some tires and diving in through the driver's side of the unused car. In seconds, he was away, into the first turn. It would be an instant education in aerodynamics. When the car stopped spinning again and again, Tim straightened out and was off.

He'd timed getting out onto the track perfectly; less than a lap after he'd gone, Bob and Fonty returned to the pits and looked around for their brother. Bruce Thompson walked their way and pointed to a driver going through only the second lap of his stock car racing life. The brothers ran quickly to the side of the track as Thompson's spare car headed their way. They raised their arms above their heads, but it was not to try to force their exuberant little brother back into the pits. It was too late for that anyway.

"They're yelling, 'Go Tim, Go,'" recalls Tim Flock's wife, Frances. "They were just jumping up and down, thrilled to death."

At home again after the race, Bob and Fonty endeavored to quickly school Tim in the art of racing, figuring that if he insisted on driving, he'd have to learn to do it the right way if he hoped to do so without comment from their mother. They took him to Lakewood Speedway, where the brothers typically spent their most grueling days driving against Lee Petty, Buck Baker, and other top competitors. Bob and Fonty brought Tim there ostensibly to help him practice, the hidden motive being to see if his desire was strong enough. There were only two cars; Tim took one and the brothers switched off driving the other, often using it to force their way past Tim. Each time Tim spun out, he righted himself immediately and returned to the pack. Having spent years watching his brothers race, he was acutely aware of their unique moves. In little time, he avoided whatever situations they tried to put him in.

The day ended when the brothers gave up; they were doing little but putting considerable hurt on their cars. Their younger brother, whom they'd once taken care of as a baby, had become someone else they'd have to look out for on the track.

In these early days of stock car racing, most drivers had to look out for one or more of the Flocks, often as not through their windshields. The Flocks drove hard and shared a taste for showmanship, thrilling fans on and off the course. The respect they received came from an uncommon degree of success—especially for Tim, who in a thirteen-year NASCAR career, won better than one out of five of his races, highlighted by a little more than one season of extremely successful, agonizingly pressured driving for legendary taskmaster Carl Kiekhaefer. Given this level of success, Big Mama ended up rather pleased by the way it all turned out.

The Flocks were worth rooting for partly due to their savvy and skill, but also because they were stock history's prime example of siblings' professional competition and respect. "The only thing I can remember all the boys talking about, their biggest thrill was to outrun the other ones," recalls Frances. "All three of them would rather outrun their brothers than anybody else on the racetrack. If Fonty was leading and Tim could pass him, he'd blow him off the track. No matter which one it was, they absolutely got thrilled passing the other one, and taking a spot away from him. Tim used to say brotherly love leaves when you're on the racetrack."

Once the race was over, such passing inspired little more than ribbing; on the track, however, the action between them would always be spirited.

Few career choices seem more preordained than those of stock car drivers Bob, Fonty, and Tim Flock. Given their history, if one of these youngest three Flock brothers had done anything that didn't involve driving or speed, he would have been considered the family rebel.

Their oldest sister, Jackie, ran the family taxi service after their father died. Oldest brother Carl was a champion outboard speedboat racer. Next came Irene, who tended the family garage and took her first airplane flight—in her son's single-engine plane—at age eighty-five. Then came Reo—named after a new make of car by her father—who ran away from home at age nineteen to pursue her unique professional dream: walking on airplane wings. Ethel, born between Bob and Fonty, drove with her three younger brothers in many Modified events around the south.

During the Depression, Carl—who had learned the bootlegging business in Atlanta from his uncle Peachtree Williams, and then inherited it after the latter's untimely death—brought his younger siblings from Alabama to Georgia. In time, the entire Flock clan made it to Atlanta and managed to survive during the hard times. By the late 1930s, Bob and Fonty were making deliveries for their older brother. After returning from the war, they picked up where they'd left off and began their stock car careers the way many of the early racers did, by making runs on dirt roads during the week, and trying to outrun each other on dirt tracks over the weekends.

The complexion of stock car racing changed dramatically in 1947. At that time, the Flocks—including Tim, who, after that fateful run at North Wilkesboro, drove for Bruce Thompson the rest of the season—ran on the National Championship Stock Car Circuit (NCSCC) in races promoted by Bill France. Bob and Fonty achieved memorable levels of success on the circuit and Fonty won the 1947 championship. But the NCSCC was one of several promotional vehicles for drivers that operated independently, making for a lack of any coherent rule system in the sport. In some instances, a promoter would pay winners in goods (meat and wine was a popular choice); other promoters would set up races, collect the gate, and leave the drivers high and dry before the race ended. The sport remained fun and exciting, yet for the participants, it could be an exercise in frustration.

Bill France and company changed all that in the December 1947 meeting that led to the formation of NASCAR. The league began in force in its first instance of strictly stock racing on June 19, 1949. The best Modified drivers of the day showed up to give the Charlotte Speedway a try for two hundred laps. Bob, Tim, and Fonty Flock started the race in first, second, and fifth, respectively. Fonty finished second to Jim Roper and Tim ended up fifth; Bob left early with engine trouble. In the season's second race, Tim, who finished second, was the only Flock brother to best his sister Ethel, who wound up eleventh. Bob had little trouble the rest of the eight-race season, ending up one of two drivers with a pair of victories. He finished the year third in the standings, with Fonty fifth and Tim eighth; Fonty, meanwhile, also won another Modified championship that same year. NASCAR was young, and the Flocks were already the circuit's most successful name.

• • •

By the time they began racing together in strictly stock contests, the Flock brothers each stuck out among their competitors. The trio offered a wide range of manner and temperament. Says Buddy Baker, who watched his father Buck take on the Flocks before starting his own stellar career, "Fonty Flock had almost a Clark Gable look about him and could drive the wheels off a race car. And then Tim was just great, smooth—had more of a David Pearson-type style; always doing the right thing on a racetrack, staying out of conflicts but always there when it counted. And then Bob, I think, was probably the purest driver out of the whole family and he didn't get the notoriety that Tim and Fonty did. But they were great drivers, all of them."

If Bob didn't get the recognition of his siblings, it was because he spent the least amount of time in stock car racing's most public circuit. Often rough and impulsive on the track, Bob was one of the nation's most respected drivers in his prime (he was among the handful of racers to attend NASCAR's founding meeting in 1947), but he preferred the Modified driving circuit, which ran things a little faster than NASCAR.

His brother Fonty, a man with a wild streak, felt at home in strictly stock. "Fonty was what they called a showman," recalls Frances Flock. "He was always acting up—he was more the Earnhardt, daredevil type. Tim and Bob were always very smooth. Fonty took chances where Tim and Bob never did."

If Fonty's hard-charging style earned him his name as a driver, it was the way he laughed—and got laughs—in the face of convention for which he is now most remembered. His large grin would spread easily below his pencil-thin mustache. Fonty often drove wearing Bermuda shorts, and when he won the 1952 Southern 500, he stood on top of his Olds '88 in shorts to lead the 32,400 spectators in singing "Dixie." "He was a clown," recalls one of his earliest opponents, Buck Baker. "He wore his shorts and would always do something that he thought would please the crowd. They called him the clown prince."

Tim Flock could have competed for that title, at least in one instance. In 1953, at the suggestion of his car owner, Ted Chester, Tim ran eight races accompanied by Jocko Flocko, a small rhesus monkey with a tiny custom-made uniform and helmet who sat in a specially designed passenger seat, from which he could wave to fans and stare down opposing drivers. Jocko was clearly more popular with spectators than competitors but the gimmick didn't hurt at the gate. It also didn't hurt Tim's chances behind the wheel: In those eight races, Jocko enjoyed five top-fives and six top-tens, along with a trip to victory lane at Hickory. But the parting was inevitable after Jocko proved himself unable to handle the pressures of big-league driving. Tim was running near the front in a May race at Raleigh when Jocko managed to free himself; he reached down and opened a hatch through which Tim normally checked the wear on his right front tire. For Jocko, the timing was poor: A rock shot up and hit him in the head. The monkey eventually escaped harm by climbing on top of Tim's head. The driver had to make an unscheduled pit stop to hand the monkey to his crew, which cost him a victory in a race Fonty won. Jocko's racing days were over, but Tim, at that time the defending NASCAR Grand National Champion, had made a slew of new fans.

By the early 1950s, Tim surpassed his brothers in terms of racing success. His smooth style on the track made for some fascinating battles in competition against the wilder styles of Buck Baker and Fonty. Like the Pettys, he managed to stay out of trouble, and instead of charging out early, knew when to peak toward the end of a race.

"They were very protective, very thrilled over him," Frances says of her husband's two older racing brothers. "He was their baby brother and they had to take care of him, they wanted the best, but I think as years went on, as Tim blossomed and went forth, I don't know, they might have been just a hair jealous. But they taught him everything, they gave him advice—they always were together, they were very close always. Tim never would take praise away from his brothers. People would ask, how do you rate your brothers and Tim would always say, well, Bob's the best of the three of us. He always gave praise to his brothers; he'd always say, oh, I can't compare to them—knowing good and dadgum well he was the best of the three."

On track, there were plenty of occasions where the brothers would finish first and second, and a number where they all placed in the top ten. Still, no occasion could ever match the thrill of one particular race day in the 1950s when they didn't share the same track, and could revel in one joint achievement that likely won't ever happen again in racing.

"They all three raced in a different state one Sunday: Bob, I believe, was in Alabama, and Tim was I think up here in North Carolina somewhere, and I think Fonty was in Jacksonville, Florida, but they were in three different states and all three of the boys won their race that Sunday afternoon," Frances recalls. "The boys just had a ball over that."

The highlight of Tim's career was the forty-six races he ran for Carl Kiekhaefer in little more than one season. The stretch made him a rich man but the pressure of it also exacerbated a long-standing stomach ulcer condition. Through the time he spent under both the thumb and aegis of the dictator-like Kiekhaefer, he experienced elation and exhaustion; by the time it ended, he had established a record for victory that remained unparalleled until the glory days of Richard Petty.

Tim had won the 1954 Daytona Beach-Road Course race only to find himself stripped of the victory due to a technicality. The event angered him to the point where he gave up racing for the rest of the season, and after a grueling year running an unsuccessful gas station business, he grudgingly returned to Daytona in 1955 to watch the race. He was soon introduced to Kiekhaefer, a short, tyrannical engineer with a big cigar and a quick fuse. Kiekhaefer had invested a chunk of his fortune, made through the outboard motor business, into racing; the investment changed racing history. The first owner to employ the team concept that so dominates NASCAR today, Kiekhaefer hired the most accomplished mechanics and drivers and unleashed the latter in a fleet of spectacular white Chryslers that came to dominate racing as no cars ever had before. Among drivers on the circuit, he was respected as much for his deep pockets as for his even deeper, visible hatred of losing.

Kiekhaefer enlisted Flock to drive one of his cars that day in Daytona and Flock became the first competitor ever to win the beach-road race driving a car with an automatic transmission.

Although Kiekhaefer had several cars and drivers, Flock, with his kind, respectful manner, was clearly his favorite; the driver was even paid his entire winnings from each race. In addition to the winnings, many was the time Tim Flock found an added bonus of several hundred- or thousand-dollar bills in his pocket, placed there by the team owner.

Tim was also able to secure a number of Kiekhaefer rides for Fonty and Bob. And in a show of brotherhood rare in any circle, Tim and Fonty had a pact going to ensure that both their families would prosper from such good fortune.

"Tim and Fonty were so close and we both had such big families, it was hard to make ends meet," says Frances. "When Tim was winning and Fonty wasn't as much—he would finish second or third or maybe fall out or whatever—whatever the boys won on Sunday, they pooled their money and split it down the middle. This is in 1955 and '56. And if Fonty didn't finish at all, he still got half of Tim's winnings. If Fonty had a bad couple of weeks, it made no difference. If Tim made a thousand dollars, we gave Fonty five hundred. If Tim fell out, he always took care of Tim to be sure we had our bills paid and this and that. They took care of each other."

On his own, Tim won eighteen races, the most ever in a season at that time, leading to a 1955 championship. But all was not entirely well in Kiekhaefer's camp. On several occasions, the owner would send a plane to pick Flock up at a moment's notice and fly him to his house in Wisconsin. There, Flock would wait, often for days, for some word from Kiekhaefer about what he wanted. Word would finally come that it had been a false alarm and Tim would be flown home just in time to make another race.

"He used to have Tim fly up there and sleep in that big mansion of his and Tim said he'd have his eyes shut like he was asleep and [Kiekhaefer] would come in and pull up the covers and tuck him in," Frances says. "He treated him like he was a son.

"[Kiekhaefer] was a wonderful guy; he'd send the plane to Atlanta to pick up me and all five of my children to stay at a big hotel at Daytona, got me a maid, anything. But Tim couldn't come up there. Kiekhaefer just didn't believe in a husband being around his wife at the racetrack."

Indeed, on nights before races, Kiekhaefer made sure his drivers and their families stayed in separate quarters, barracks-style. Ultimately, the pressure of driving for Kiekhaefer played havoc with Tim's ulcer. He lost weight and grew miserable, until, a mere eight races into what was already a promising 1956 season, Tim quit Kiekhaefer in memorable fashion. After winning a race at North Wilkesboro, the NASCAR champion walked into the boss's room where a steak was waiting on the table for the two of them to enjoy during a victory dinner. Tim refused the meal, said he wouldn't be driving for the man anymore, and turned on his heel and left. The owner and his driver, once so close, would never speak again, according to Frances Flock. Tim would try to reconcile, but Kiekhaefer's bitterness at the parting was too great. In all, Tim Flock won twenty-one races for Kiekhaefer; Fonty won three and had nine top-fives in the twenty-four contests he pedaled in one of those majestic Chryslers. Tim would never have such success behind the wheel again.

By the late 1950s, the Flocks had pretty much made their run through NASCAR. Bob's most triumphant moment had come several years before in a 1952 comeback that defied expectations. Sidelined by a neck injury in 1951, all indications were that his driving days were over. But nine months later, he made his return at the Asheville-Weaverville Speedway, while still wearing a support around his neck. Through the contest's two hundred laps, Bob made it quite clear that his skills had not diminished and he won the day, besting little brother Tim in an afternoon of family triumph.

He ran his last NASCAR race four years after that and then owned his own garage in Atlanta for several years before succumbing to a heart attack in 1964. Fonty had all but retired before agreeing to race in the 1957 Southern 500, driving a car for veteran racer Herb Thomas. A crash on the 27th lap led him to leave the game for good; he went into the insurance business and also did some work with Bill France before a long bout with cancer claimed him in 1972. Tim, on the other hand, had a more unceremonious leave-taking from the sport. After an attempt to organize the drivers into a union failed in 1961, he remained one of the only holdouts still on the proverbial picket line. He was banned from the sport and officially left the driving business later that year, not long after his thirty-seventh birthday. The profession he had yearned to be a part of while watching his brothers practice the craft had occupied him for only thirteen years, but in that time, he'd earned two championships and thirty-nine victories—

impressive numbers for any length career, and good enough to win him a place on NASCAR's list of 50 Greatest Drivers in 1998.

A couple of years before the union incident, Tim, realizing his most successful days were behind him, prepared to end his involvement with racing altogether. He planned to work for his brother Carl in Florida when his friend Bruton Smith got in touch to offer him a job. A new motor speedway was being built in Charlotte; would Tim come and work there full-time?

Carl Flock's loss was Bruton Smith's gain. Tim accepted the job at the speedway; a house had been set up for the family and he could begin work as a representative of the track. Tim spent the rest of his professional life doing public relations, selling stock, working on race programs, and performing whatever other functions suited his considerable people skills. He also maintained his standing as one of his sport's most influential practitioners.

Tim's death, at age seventy-three in 1998 after a long bout with cancer, closed an important chapter of stock car racing's gloried past. If the racing world had lost a giant, Frances Flock, one of the most prominent and well-known of all racing wives, and still a fixture herself on the racing circuit after more than fifty years, had lost the best dance partner she'd known, going back to the first time they'd met when, as a girl of thirteen, she'd been swung into seventeen-year-old Tim Flock's arms by a soldier at a local ball.

"Our whole life was so much fun," she says. "We played music all the time and I'd be cooking and he'd come in and there'd be something that we'd want to dance to and I'd stop cooking and we'd dance there in the kitchen. We did that right up until four weeks before he died. There was something that came on and he said, 'We've gotta dance this last dance because I don't know when I'll get another one.' And it was literally the last dance. These are the memories that are keeping me going today."

Tim Flock's death forced a decision on Carl Lee Flock, Tim and Frances's forty-eight-year-old youngest son and the only one of their five children to pursue a racing dream. The dirt-track racer, who also worked full-time with two of his brothers for Loews, had sat out the Friday race the week his father died, but ultimately decided to return to the No. 14 car—the same number his Uncle Bob had used—the next week. As Frances Flock confirmed, his father would have wanted him to run.

"He said, 'I have on Daddy's shirt with his picture on it that the speedway made up in his memory, and I have his picture on the dashboard of my car.' And he said, 'I'm gonna go win this race for my daddy tonight.' Well, dang if that phone didn't ring at two o'clock in the morning and he's on the other end saying, 'Mama, I won it, I won it!' He was thrilled to death. He said, 'Daddy rode every inch of it with me. I could just hear Daddy talkin' to me: Do this, do this.' Tim always gave the boy lots of advice," Frances recalls. "He was so proud of him, he didn't know what to do."

9
The Jarrett Family

Gentleman Ned

During a race in Greenville, South Carolina, in June 1965, NASCAR veteran Ned Jarrett's car quit at the worst moment possible. The drivers had just restarted after a caution and Jarrett was leading the race when his engine left him capable only of speeds best suited for a drive in the country. One look in the rearview mirror at the field of cars approaching and Jarrett realized he had little choice but to brace for impact. When all the jostling was finished, Jarrett found himself being rushed off to get treatment for a bad back injury.

He'd been leading in the season point standings, attempting to win his second championship in five years, and there he was, possibly facing the premature end of his year and his career at age thirty-two. In the hospital, he told his wife, Martha, that if he'd broken his back, he'd quit driving.

The doctor's diagnosis, however, was somewhat more hopeful. His back wasn't broken, so Jarrett began to concentrate on his long-range plans: specifically, his chase of the championship, beginning with a race five nights later in Myrtle Beach. After four days of therapy, he slid cautiously behind the wheel the following Thursday night. He was determined to hold off the competition trying to take the standings lead away from him.

It's a tribute to Jarrett's sense of purpose that he was able to

"My grandfather was a visionary and my grandmother made sure that it all stayed right on track," says Lesa France Kennedy about NASCAR founders William and Anne France *(above)*. "They trusted each other's instincts." They extended that trust to Bill Jr. *(below, in car)*, who ran the business beginning in 1972. (DAYTONA RACING ARCHIVES)

Leonard *(left)* and Glen Wood relax with one of their many talented drivers, Donnie Allison *(center)*. Together, the Wood brothers redefined the art of the pit stop, an event that became anything but relaxing *(below)*. (DAYTONA RACING ARCHIVES)

"All three of them would rather outrun their brothers than anybody else on the track," says Frances Flock *(above left)* of the Flocks, the most successful brothers in NASCAR's early run. But off the track, competition turned to camaraderie for Frances's husband, Tim, and siblings Fonty *(below left)* and Bob *(below right).* (DAYTONA RACING ARCHIVES)

Buddy Baker (*above right*) stands with the first man ever to bump him off the track in a race—and the first one to greet him, tearfully, in victory lane after win number one—his dad, Buck. *Below,* Ralph Earnhardt, the dirt-track intimidator and first of three generations of NASCAR title holders. (DAYTONA RACING ARCHIVES)

Ralph Earnhardt

Dale and Teresa Earnhardt relax in victory lane with another future champ, little E *(above, second from left). Left,* father and son—car owner and driver—get used to a familiar pose as Dale Earnhardt Jr. collects his first of two NASCAR Busch Series trophies in 1998.

(ABOVE: PHIL CAVALI, WINSTON CUP SCENE;

LEFT: DAYTONA RACING ARCHIVES)

By the mid-1970s, Alabama Gang members Donnie and Bobby Allison had been blazing a trail through NASCAR for almost 20 years, and had inducted new members such as Neil Bonnett *(above right)*. But for Bobby, nothing in his career would ever match the thrill and wonder of watching his son, Davey *(below left)*, become one of NASCAR's finest. (AP WIDE WORLD PHOTOS)

Above, a portrait of Ned Jarrett and his young family at Daytona. Thirty-odd years later, Ned and the kid above at center would return to Daytona for an afternoon of personal triumph enjoyed by millions of TV watchers. Throughout his career, Dale Jarrett has always counted on the counsel of his chief advisor. (ABOVE: JIM FLUHARTY; LEFT: DAYTONA RACING ARCHIVES)

Under the watchful eye of Lee Petty *(above center)*, sons Maurice *(left)* and Richard learned the family business and created a dynasty. Few drivers ever inspired more talk of great potential—and even greater personal regard—than Adam Petty *(below, second from left)*, grandson of Richard, son of Pattie and Kyle, and the first fourth-generation driver in the history of pro sports. (ABOVE: SOBINA PHOTOS; BELOW: AP WIDE WORLD PHOTOS)

In the mid-1980s, Dan, Bill, and Ernie Elliott became NASCAR's equivalent of pop stars when their relentless efforts in the garage led to their 200-mph qualifying times and the first ever Winston Million. (DAYTONA RACING ARCHIVES)

Brett Bodine (*left*) counted on his big brother Geoffrey's aid early in his career. Now both are lending a hand to the NASCAR Busch Series–driving brother, Todd (*below left, with Geoffrey*). (LEFT: LADON GEORGE; BELOW: DAYTONA RACING ARCHIVES)

In 1999, the only on-track revenge Ward Burton could have on his younger brother, Jeff, was a little tap on the last lap of the Southern 500, which Jeff *(left)* won under caution. Other than that, Ward and his No. 22 came in second to Jeff three times.

Bob Labonte raised his sons Terry *(above left)* and Bobby to be NASCAR racers, and the brothers root for each other harder than any siblings in the sport's history. (ABOVE: TIM WILCOX; BELOW: DAYTONA RACING ARCHIVES)

Mike *(above left)* and Kenny Wallace have achieved great success in the ranks of NASCAR racing, but they both know they'll never run up the kind of numbers gained by brother Rusty *(below left, with Kenny)*. (ABOVE: TIM WILCOX; BELOW: LADON GEORGE)

When he was a kid, Michael Waltrip could only lean against his big brother Darrell's car and dream of speed and glory; he proved his worth to DW when he won the Winston All-Star race and found his brother waiting for him in victory lane. (ABOVE: DAVIE HINSHAW/*CHARLOTTE OBSERVER*; BELOW: DAYTONA RACING ARCHIVES)

Mark Martin, his back healed, began the 2000 campaign at Daytona with the same goal as always: winning a NASCAR Winston Cup Series championship both for himself and to honor his late father, Julian, who helped mold Mark into a great racer. (DAYTONA RACING ARCHIVES, BRIAN CZOBAT)

For the present and future, NASCAR remains a family business, with Bill France Jr.'s children, Lesa France Kennedy *(above left)* and Brian France *(above right)*, helping to create new outlets of popularity for the sport. Meanwhile, brothers Bill *(below, seated)* and Jim France are hardly resting on their laurels. (DAYTONA RACING ARCHIVES)

keep racing. On that June night, there were still some things he wanted to prove to himself. But few people realized how seriously he'd been contemplating shutting his motor down for good. After seeing a rash of accidents and a number of issues involving Ford Motor Company's involvement in the sport, he became increasingly aware that in racing, things could change for you in an instant. As he nursed his sore back, Jarrett thought about fate's all too indiscriminate hand. Racing had earned him a good short-term wage but all things considered, it couldn't provide the security he desired—a notion Martha Jarrett had long been trying to impart to her husband.

Things were swiftly changing in this most mythologized era in motor sports, as the devil-may-care innocence of dirt-track and short-track racing continued to give way to the higher stakes of the superspeedways. Meanwhile, Jarrett was considering the pursuit of a new career, which many would regard as his true calling. The day loomed ahead when he'd experienced enough victory on the track for his appetite. He had no inkling of the triumph that waited once he got off of it.

Ned Jarrett had been a stock car fan as a kid, when his father had taken him to watch the dirt fly at the Charlotte Fairgrounds. There was, by his own admission, very little to do for entertainment growing up in Camden, North Carolina, but all that changed with the building of a brand-new dirt track in nearby Hickory. The timing couldn't have been better and the tall and slender, unassuming, athletic Jarrett immediately embraced the idea of driving. He bought a half interest in a 1939 Ford Coupe, splitting the deal with ex-motorcycle racer John Lentz. Jarrett ran for the first time in 1952, at age nineteen, in the inaugural event at Hickory, where he finished tenth.

That's when his father sat him down for a little talk. This driving thing, he told Ned, would not fly. Ned was a fine young man, a Fundamentalist Christian—smart, nice, and sensible. In other words, according to his father, he didn't fit the typical stock car racing profile. No, Ned could work on cars, even own one if he wanted to, but he couldn't go behind the wheel.

Lentz took over the driving duties for several races until one night when he wasn't feeling well. The pair didn't look very hard to find a replacement. Given that the Hickory Speedway did not have a very good lighting system, Ned and Lentz could change shirts and helmets and nobody would be the wiser. That is, until Ned did something Lentz had not done: He won a race. The triumph brought enough publicity that Ned's father learned of the deception and ultimately told him that if he was that committed to it, he might as well race under his own name and get the credit for it.

The credit would come quickly as Jarrett developed the skills that made him an excellent dirt-track racer. All motor sports are exercises in sheer horsepower, track knowledge, and strategy, but in dirt-track battles, constant shifts in the track surface always led to instant reshuffling in the way a driver might plan to get ahead. With forty cars going over the same ground lap after lap, chances were slim the terrain would remain recognizable by the time you got back to turn four. Given the skidding ordinarily involved in making turns at high speeds, running door-to-door with a fellow driver meant risking the possibility of getting knocked into the infield or onto a high bank on the outside of the track. So any competitor with a hope of a chance would need a method. The flashier drivers might fishtail in the turns and gain the advantage by keeping their speeds up. But Jarrett always reasoned that the race car would run faster going straight than it would sideways. He'd watched drivers such as Junior Johnson take their dramatic fishtailing turns on dirt, slinging the cars with the wheels spinning. Jarrett, the consummate thinking-man's driver, preferred to gain a victory by outsmarting an opponent rather than outrunning him.

During one race in Valdosta, Georgia, where the top cars were lapping him because he couldn't handle the turns well enough, he set about creating a groove for himself on one turn by first running hard into it and then, in each ensuing lap, running over the same exact ground to essentially develop his own lane. After thirty or forty methodical laps, he was able to catch up to the leaders and ultimately win the race.

For years he generally stayed out of harm's way, quietly if aggressively practicing his craft on the track and earning the nickname "Gentleman" Ned Jarrett for his easygoing nature. He rarely went looking for trouble and trouble just as infrequently found him. By 1959, he had gained enough success to win two junior division championships and decided to move up to the Grand National Series, with its higher paychecks and stiffer competition against the likes of Richard Petty, Junior Johnson, Fireball Roberts, and Lee Petty.

By this time, Jarrett began to face some stiff opposition from a different camp. His wife Martha, whom he'd married in 1956, always feared the worst when it came to racing, although, she admits, it was easier for her in the early days of their marriage. "The safety part I was concerned about, but at that time, they didn't drive on the superspeedways," she says. "They were basically short tracks and there were not an awful lot of accidents, so that calmed you down to make you think, well, this is okay." But as the tracks got faster, she began to feel less sanguine about her husband practicing a livelihood with a greater set of risks than faced by the average working man.

Their son Dale was born toward the end of 1956, and their daughter Patti in 1959, the same year of the inaugural Daytona 500. Although the famous race went without a caution, one could not argue with the incredible speeds drivers attained on the longer tracks. At another Daytona race later that season, Fireball Roberts posted an average winning speed of 140.581 mph; no short-track winner came close to 90 mph in a victory the whole season. Races soon got longer and engines got faster as promoters drew up plans to provide more of the action that had once only been offered by open-wheel cars at the famed Indianapolis Motor Speedway. These developments would have a profound affect on everyone involved in stock cars, from drivers to automakers to track owners. In 1956, of the fifty-six races in the Grand National Series, forty-five were on dirt or beach-and-road courses and NASCAR ran only eleven events on fully-paved surfaces. By 1963, only nineteen of fifty-five races were held on dirt.

Jarrett, whose methodical style better fitted the give-and-go racing on short tracks, toiled away at his specialty, and his consistency throughout the schedule earned him a Grand National Championship in 1961. Nine years after first climbing behind the wheel, he'd reached the top of his sport. He was also the perfect champion for the times: He could look as far as possible around a turn on a track and see what loomed ahead, allowing him to plan for the inevitable.

Several years after his first championship run, Jarrett began to grapple with serious issues regarding his chosen field. In 1964, track-related accidents claimed superstar drivers Joe Weatherly and Fireball Roberts. Looking back on the incidents now, Jarrett believes that, though the deaths took their toll, they did not dull his willingness to compete.

"I was concerned about these things but I couldn't let them prey on my mind if I was going to continue driving race cars," he states. "You have to keep it out of your head. If you dwelled on it, you wouldn't be effective. Most race drivers look at it that, yes, it's dangerous and things do happen but they happen to someone else, not me."

Despite maintaining the necessary on-track philosophy, other pressing factors were inspiring him to reassess his career while he was enjoying his prime. On one hand, Jarrett had always been the consummate family man. Some drivers were legendary night crawlers, organizing parties that could last days at a time. Jarrett never even made the guest list. When he wasn't spending time at the track and the garage trying to better feed his family, he could be found at home with them—and there was precious little time for that. Making a good living at racing made the sacrifice worthwhile.

At least it did for a time. But in the mid-1960s, the sport did not have the long-term security it eventually would and Jarrett felt the need to prepare for the day when he'd give up the game. Years earlier, an interviewer had asked him a question about racing and it had frozen him. To guarantee no such repeat performance, he took a public speaking course and had grown into a sought-after radio and television voice among the drivers on the circuit.

In 1965, Jarrett had to deal with serious back problems, but that season may well have been his finest. The groundwork for his success was laid by a controversy raging between NASCAR and the automakers. With so much money at stake, Ford and Chrysler were each developing faster engines. NASCAR president Bill France, in order to create a level playing field, set up some restrictions for each manufacturer, hoping to create the right compro-

mise and appease everybody. In 1965, Chrysler thought the compromise—which included limiting the use of their powerful hemi
engine—unfair. They saw no alternative but to boycott Grand
National racing for the year, leaving Ford the king of the road.

No one used that advantage better than Jarrett, and his cars
were clearly the pick of the field for a good part of the season.
Though Jarrett and fellow Ford driver Junior Johnson tied with
thirteen wins apiece—more than half of the fifty-five races run that
year—Jarrett finished in the top ten a whopping forty-five out of
fifty-four starts. His main competition for the Grand National title
that year, Dick Hutcherson, matched Jarrett's dominating short-
track skills perfectly.

Ironically, the race that would decide the title took place at a
superspeedway: Darlington, site of the venerable Southern 500.
Darlington was the first paved track ever built for NASCAR, and on
Labor Day Weekend 1950, it hosted the first-ever 500-mile race for
Grand National stock car drivers. From that race on, the track
became the proving ground among drivers on the circuit. The
Daytona 500 would eventually surpass it in prestige, but no race
allowed a driver more bragging rights than South Carolina's Labor
Day classic. And Jarrett, who lived nearby in Camden, considered
it the one race he always ached to add to his resume.

In the early going of the 1965 running, a Jarrett victory appeared
out of the question. The two best rides of the day clearly belonged
to Fred Lorenzen and Darel Dieringer in their own Ford factory cars.
Jarrett, meanwhile, was comfortably holding onto third place, but
he had already been lapped once by the leaders and his car was in
danger of overheating.

Two-thirds of the way through, however, mechanical troubles
started to run rampant. Lorenzen's engine, badly overworked in
the lengthy battle with Dieringer, suddenly gave out, and racing's
Golden Boy was unexpectedly done for the day. Amazingly, on the
same lap, Dieringer began to trail a cloud of smoke: The rear end of
his car was on fire. He would finish the race, but at a decidedly
slower pace.

Suddenly, Jarrett found himself alone and on top, needing only
to battle his own engine problems to secure a victory. When he
crossed the finish line, Jarrett had won by a still unthinkable

record margin of fourteen laps. Before 1965, the best finish he'd managed in the Southern 500 was fourth. For Jarrett, the resounding win was his most satisfying.

"That victory pretty much clinched the championship for my dad that year. It was a big day when we got back home," recalls Dale Jarrett, eight years old at the time. "It seemed like the entire town of Camden was in our front yard waiting on us."

In 20/20 hindsight, the timing of Ned Jarrett's Southern 500 victory seems to have been fortuitous. In a way, it served as a fitting last hurrah.

The squabbles between the auto manufacturers continued in 1966, this time adversely affecting Ford. One day, out of the blue, Jarrett got a phone call telling him the company for which he'd won enormous success the year before would be severely limiting its involvement due to new NASCAR regulations they disagreed with. It was another example for Jarrett of how things could change in an instant, with him able to do virtually nothing to stop it. He came home that day, looked at his family and decided to make his own change. Just as he'd done when he carved a groove on the dirt track in Valdosta, Georgia, he set about planning for a future away from the track.

He continued to run a reduced schedule in 1966, and then on October 30th, after finishing third at the fall race in Rockingham, he never drove competitively again. It would also be the last race for Junior Johnson, the man dubbed "The Last American Hero" in Tom Wolfe's famed profile. In a year and a half, the sport had changed dramatically while losing three of its biggest names. To this day, Jarrett remains the only driver to retire as defending Grand National champion. He had turned thirty-four only a couple of weeks earlier.

"I set certain goals for myself and vowed that however far up the ladder I was, I'd quit when I was there and not go down the other side, and I managed to reach those goals," he says. "And back then the sport didn't have the security it has now and I had a family to raise. My children were growing up—Dale was only nine when I retired and I wanted to spend more time with the family and that was probably the biggest thing. I was not financially able to retire.

And we didn't know how long we could go as a driver. We thought like other athletes, you get to your mid-thirties and you start losing your ability and competitive edge, but we've learned since then that race drivers can go much longer than that and continue to get more effective as time goes by. There have been times that I regretted it."

If you ask Dale Jarrett, his father left one factor out of his description.

"Obviously a big reason my dad quit when he did was my mom's [concerns]," he says. "I think if we speak of my mother as 'family,' then family [as a reason for retirement] probably had seventy to seventy-five percent to do with it. The other was my dad had set goals and he was very goal-oriented. He just didn't realize he was going to do it all in that short period of time. There were a lot of things involved, but my mother had a big part. Her wish was that he could be with the family more and she would choose for him to do something else if he could."

That something else turned out to be the career in broadcasting Jarrett had considered. After trying other options—including promoting races at Hickory—broadcasting became the worthy replacement for the competition he'd once embraced so eagerly on the track.

Jarrett honed his skills, growing into one of the sport's most prominent and intelligent voices. Each year, new drivers would rise up to battle older champions; each year, technology made cars safer and swifter. Jarrett's considerable talents at the mike for ESPN, CBS, and TNN have always made the sport easier to grasp and more exciting to watch.

But one particular development has offered him more thrills and greater challenges than all the others—covering races that include one of the sport's premier drivers, his son, Dale.

Dale Jarrett Gets Called to Victory Lane

For years, the Charlotte Motor Speedway has held its popular media tour every January. Reporters the world over converge on the famed North Carolina track for several days and go to the different team shops to get the preseason lowdown from drivers, crew members, and owners.

In addition, promotional events are held. In 1997, Ford arranged an historical demonstration of how NASCAR Winston Cup Series cars and drivers had changed through the years. Luckily, someone at Ford found a 1963 model in a shed in Michigan. The car had not been raced since its glory days—after a tune-up, it drove reasonably like it had when it came off the track—and the company shipped it to Charlotte. Next to it on the track, they put one of the fastest Fords available in the world, from the team of Dale Jarrett, who had finished third in the NASCAR Winston Cup Series standings the season before, behind Terry Labonte and Jeff Gordon.

Jarrett happily agreed to participate, especially since the demonstration provided an opportunity he'd always desired: The chance to race side by side, however briefly, with his father.

"We put on a little show and raced a bit for them," Ned Jarrett recalls. He had started driving in the '63 Ford and then father and son switched, to see how the other half lived. "[Dale] couldn't believe that we could have driven those race cars the way they were back then; I knew the technology had improved tremendously and there was a totally different feel in getting into his car."

From this new perspective, Ned Jarrett remembered a time when he ruled his sport.

"When I got into the old [car], it came back. I had a uniform, one of my old ones; it still fit," he says, laughing. "So that was the thing I was most proud of."

Hickory Motor Speedway in Hickory, North Carolina, has been called "the birthplace of NASCAR stars." Generations of drivers have cut their teeth at the short track, racing in various divisions in search of triumphs and a link to the next step in racing. Ralph Earnhardt practically made the track his home and Dale Earnhardt began his run to NASCAR fortune there.

Few families, however, have as much tradition with the track as the Jarretts. Ned Jarrett's racing career began the night of the dirt track's debut in 1952. And twenty-five years later, Dale Jarrett made his first mad dash for racing glory at Hickory, driving in the Limited Sportsman Division.

"It was just such a thrill," Dale recalls. "I'd been fortunate to be successful in winning in other sports but there was nothing like the feeling I got that night in driving that race car. I knew right then and there that's what I was gonna do. I had no idea how I was gonna go about it because I had no money or anything else, but that was what I wanted to do."

Jarrett had wanted to race since the age of five or six, sitting in the family car, pretending to drive against his father's rivals. He would accompany Ned to a number of short tracks, running around the infield with the other boys whose fathers met each other in the races, boys like Kyle Petty, Davey Allison, and Ricky and Larry Pearson. But when his dad retired from racing in 1966, his thrills came from basketball, baseball, and golf. After high school ended, however, Jarrett felt the same pull his father once had and debuted at Hickory.

"As I got through high school and opportunities for those sports went away, and as I chose not to go to college, racing was still in the back of my mind because it was competition and that's always what's driven me," Dale says. "It became a real priority again when I was about eighteen years old."

Dale ultimately had the support of his parents, even if Ned did sit his son down to explain the facts of life and offer the benefit of his own experience.

"If anything, he was probably trying to steer me away from the sport a little bit because it's a very difficult sport to get to the top, to really make a living at," Dale says. "It has come a long way but he knew how difficult it was."

His father's words proved prescient, even as Dale won Hickory's Limited Sportsman Division Rookie of the Year award in 1977. By then Dale already had a son, Jason, and was dealing with the often frustrating, and expensive, learning curve of the sport. Still, he rose through divisions; he ran NASCAR Busch Series races beginning with the start of the series in 1982, and continued to make strides toward the goal of a NASCAR Winston Cup Series ride, thanks in part to an unquestionable commitment to his craft.

"He has given a lot of thought over the years to how he can improve himself and as a result of being a good athlete, he can put those thoughts to use and become a better race driver," Ned says. "He has trained himself well over the years to handle the circumstances, whatever they might be—one racetrack you drive differently from the other and he sized them all up. He's a thinking-man's driver."

Like his father, Dale was a natural behind the wheel: intelligent, not necessarily flashy, but consistent. Still, Ned's six-foot-two-inch son was the Jarrett for a new generation, one who felt just as comfortable on a superspeedway as he did on the short tracks his father favored. Off the track, he represented the best qualities of the Jarrett style, mastering the art of public speaking that has become a driver prerequisite in NASCAR's modern era. He connected with fans, was open to the press, and, with his wife and family often at the track, seemed as devoted a family man as his father.

He also earned himself a NASCAR Winston Cup Series ride, but what he lacked for years was the perfect one. At first he drove for the Wood Brothers, and won his first NASCAR Winston Cup Series race in 1991, taking the Champion 400 at the Michigan International Speedway. But generally speaking, he remained frustrated, uncomfortably toiling below the top class.

Things improved when Jarrett was tapped to drive for the new team established by Joe Gibbs before the start of the 1992 season. Gibbs, the three-time Super Bowl-winning coach of the Washington Redskins who drag-raced as a kid, had, since the end of his football days, turned his attention to a long-standing interest in racing. Jarrett's consistency, ease under pressure, and deep-rooted devotion to faith made him a perfect match with Gibbs, a born-again Christian wishing to invest in an up-and-comer who could grow with his young team. After a season where the team established itself, Jarrett began 1993 in excellent fashion by qualifying second for the Daytona 500, sharing row one with Kyle Petty. Years earlier, Kyle and Dale had played together on the sidelines as their fathers raced door-to-door on short tracks throughout the country. Now, the sons of the King and Gentleman Ned would get their turns side by side at the sport's premier superspeedway.

The 1993 Daytona 500 started out as a significant one for several reasons. This would mark the first race Richard Petty hadn't driven in since the end of his "farewell tour." At the race, Petty would be publicly splitting his rooting interest between his son and Rick Wilson, who would on that day be driving Petty's familiar red and blue STP car. Meanwhile, Kyle, was in the fifth year of driving for car owner Felix Sabates after having also driven for Petty Enterprises and the Wood Brothers. Kyle was coming off his first two-win season, which helped propel him to his highest season-ending ranking, fifth. A Kyle Petty victory at Daytona—the site of his dad's seven victories in the 500, and his grandfather's triumph in the inaugural race on the new track in 1959—would make for great copy.

The other interesting stories were in row two. Starting third was Dale Earnhardt, the King's most frequent competition for "greatest driver ever" honors, and son of dirt-track legend Ralph Earnhardt. This would be his fifteenth attempt to complete his packed resume with the Daytona 500, the victory that continued to elude him despite his success at all other Daytona races. And he longed to start 1993 off right: In 1992, he'd finished 12th in the rankings, his worst showing in a decade. Qualifying fourth and starting next to Earnhardt—and making only his second NASCAR Winston Cup Series start ever—sat twenty-one-year-old rookie Jeff Gordon, a skinny kid who seemed too young for his odd-looking mustache. During the week, he'd won a 125-mile qualifier, becoming the youngest driver ever to do so.

Before the CBS telecast began, there was a taped segment of Richard Petty and CBS commentator Ned Jarrett, walking the track, talking old times and new possibilities. Soon, Petty would have the honor of waving the green flag to begin the race, and Jarrett would have to take his place in the booth and call a race in front of more than one hundred thousand fans in the stands—not to mention almost thirty million people watching at home—with his son having a legitimate chance of winning the sport's biggest annual event.

"It's a special challenge to be in the booth when he's out there racing and try to keep things in perspective," he admits. "Certainly I'm interested in him and what he's doing and try to keep a corner of an eye on him, but also realize that I have a job to do, and my job is not to report on what Dale Jarrett is doing."

That might normally be the case, but the 1993 Daytona 500 would not be your typical race for the Jarretts.

Very early on, Dale and Kyle settled into the top ten or fifteen as Earnhardt, Gordon, and Geoffrey Bodine traded the lead. For Jarrett, the key was to stay on the lead lap throughout. At one point, after a caution and pit stops, he was several seconds back, but it was obvious from the week's qualifying that his engine was one of the choicest in the field. He caught up and sat in 11th place after 120 of 200 laps.

Forty laps later, Kyle Petty's day ended in awful fashion, thanks to an incident that sums up how lucky you need to be to win at Daytona. On lap 161, Al Unser Jr.—the IndyCar and IROC star making his only NASCAR start in a car borrowed from Rick Hendrick—got together with Earnhardt, and Al Jr. collided with Bobby Hillin. Hillin's car spun into the infield, sliding over the grass in circles. His brakes had quit, and he helplessly rolled back onto the track just as Petty was coming around. Boxed in with nowhere to go but straight into Hillin, a frustrated Kyle ended what had been a superb afternoon.

Several laps later, everyone went in for final pit stops, and the lead cars got into what they hoped would be their best possible drafting positions. With ten laps remaining in the contest, Jarrett was running door-to-door with Geoffrey Bodine behind Earnhardt and Jeff Gordon.

Jarrett's car felt perfect. Earnhardt's car seemed a bit loose coming out of turns; still, Jarrett knew that beating the formidable Intimidator would take a perfect move and significant luck.

In the booth, Ned Jarrett was trying to not let anything personal interfere with his job. But there was the camera, switching at one point to his wife, Martha, nervously watching her son from inside a van on the infield and listening to the account on the radio.

Meanwhile, Dale Jarrett tried to see as far around the turns as his father always did, in order to calculate when he could make the right move on the leaders. If he stood a chance, he'd have to pass both Gordon and Earnhardt as late as possible, and not have to spend too much time trying to keep them behind him.

For the next several laps, he kept threatening: He'd drive up high, judge the lane and throw out a fake; then he'd drive another lap and go low, scanning for an opening. With seven laps left, he looked high again, testing the possibilities of his strategy against Earnhardt's expert drafting.

Two laps later, Jarrett went high off a turn, trying to pass Gordon, but the pass was rebuffed. In the booth above the action, Ned Jarrett had to report on what Dale Jarrett was doing, or on what he needed to do if he wanted to win, which was to get far enough past Geoffrey Bodine so that he could help Gordon draft even with Earnhardt, and then pass them both.

With three laps to go, Dale Jarrett finally put his plan into action, looking high off a turn and then charging to the outside as Gordon, reacting, went to the inside, trying to hold him off. Gordon's block could not keep Jarrett back and when the leaders returned to the start-finish line again, Jarrett had second place with two laps to go.

Meanwhile, to Ned Jarrett, Earnhardt looked passable. In the booth, play-by-play announcer Ken Squier had been asking Earnhardt's friend, racer-turned-commentator Neil Bonnett, if Earnhardt might end up with another disappointment. Cameras caught Martha Jarrett covering her face with her hands.

On the track, Dale Jarrett was on Earnhardt's tail, trying to take some air off the master's spoiler at just over 190 mph. He paused momentarily until, timing the move, he shot out underneath, going down low with one lap to go.

Side by side now, Earnhardt and Jarrett tapped doors and instantly jutted apart, as if magnetically repelled. Jarrett hung low, inching into the lead, with Bodine now behind him, trying to draft with him. In an instant it dawned on anybody watching that Dale Jarrett had, unbelievably, put himself into the right position at the right time, with the best shot at winning.

That's when millions of people at home heard words they probably never expected to hear an announcer say on television: "Come on, Dale—go, baby, go!"

As Ned Jarrett tells it, a call had come in the booth for the announcers. "The producer told Ken Squier and Neil Bonnett to back off: 'We're gonna let Ned call the last lap.' Then he came on my headset as we went into the last lap and he said, 'Okay Ned, call your son home—but be a daddy.' I had no idea what to say, and he wanted a spontaneous reaction."

He got one. "I was telling him how to drive a race car," Ned says. "I said, 'It's a Dale and Dale show at Daytona—you know which Dale I'm pulling for.'"

Dale Jarrett stayed to the inside coming around the last turn, keeping Earnhardt behind him until there was no more room left for the great champion to counter.

"He's gonna make it!" Ned yelled. "Dale Jarrett's gonna win the Daytona 500!"

At age thirty-six, Dale Jarrett had won his second NASCAR Winston Cup Series race ever. Martha Jarrett, still on television, could hardly collect herself.

"When they came out of that turn and they touched, I mean your heart just goes up into your throat," Martha Jarrett says. "Now I stay home or get somewhere where there are no cameras."

Meanwhile, her husband was in the booth, being professionally encouraged to continue his gush of pride in a moment that, despite all his own success, may well define his long career in NASCAR. Conducting the interview with Dale in victory lane, father and son shared their great joy in the moment.

"It wasn't very professional," Ned admits of his call. "A few people criticized it, but the majority of people have been very supportive of it. I run into literally hundreds of fans and it's still very flattering that they would remember that. To have grown men come up—and you can tell that many of them are executive-type people—to say that they had tears in their eyes, and if they watch a replay of it or hear about it again, still get tears in their eyes, it makes me feel good that the human-interest story touched people that much."

"He probably enjoyed it almost as much as I did," echoes Dale. "He said a number of times that he enjoys living through me more than he enjoyed his own racing."

Two Champions . . . and Another Hickory Debut

Ned Jarrett shakes his head and smiles at the idea that he might ever have raced full-time against his son, just as the Pettys and Allisons were able to do.

"I don't know that my wife could have stood that," he says. "I've made the statement jokingly a number of times—there might be some validity to it—but she is more concerned about Dale than she ever was about me, because you can replace husbands but you can't replace sons."

Now, however, Martha Jarrett has a different situation to deal with—the sight of her son occasionally competing against her grandson.

"The first day that I actually drove a race car—I'd been running go-karts in '92, '93, and '94—we had the car built pretty early in the year and went to Hickory Speedway. My dad and grandfather happened to be in town, and it was one of those days where I could tell that's what I wanted to do the rest of my life," recounts Dale Jarrett's twenty-four-year-old son, Jason, telling a familiar tale. "It kinda hit home that day; you could see the gleam in their eyes that they were happy I was gonna try to carry on the family name."

In 1994, seventeen years after his father earned the same honor, Jason Jarrett won Rookie of the Year in the Limited Sportsman division at Hickory. He moved on to Late Model Stocks and ran NASCAR Busch Series races in 1999, toiling in the same division that boasts, as champion, third-generation star Dale Earnhardt Jr. Undoubtedly, the greatest triumph he's had so far in his young career was at the NASCAR Busch Series race in Charlotte in May 1998. Jason qualified 12th and his dad qualified 11th: Father and son would get to start the race in the same row.

"It was almost like a dream," Jason says. "Starting the race brought back a lot of memories of not only how hard he had worked to get there, but how hard he and I had worked together to get me to that point in that short period of time."

The thrill continued after the flag dropped. "I kinda jumped out in front of him and that was pretty exciting to know that I'd gotten a few spots ahead," Jason says. "But I knew my car was not as good as his on long runs, so it was a matter of time till he passed me. Once he did, it all settled in and it was like the race had begun then."

"It was a totally different feeling than I've ever had before," adds Dale. "It was a lot more fun than I anticipated."

Unfortunately, Jason's 1999 NASCAR Busch Series experience ended with a concussion after a race in California. All three racing Jarretts agreed that Jason needed a better ride, and he got one in 2000, driving the NASCAR Busch Series schedule for BACE Motorsports.

"I find myself a little more nervous when he's out there than races that I work when Dale's out there," says Ned of Jason. "I have become comfortable with Dale; I have total confidence in him which makes me comfortable. Jason, with his lack of experience— I'm just more concerned."

With time, that concern will presumably disappear, as Jason attempts to become the third Jarrett making his ascent up the ranks.

Whatever becomes of Jason's racing future, the Jarrett family legacy is secure. In 1999, Dale—who a year earlier had been honored alongside his father as one of NASCAR's 50 Greatest Drivers—enjoyed his finest year ever in his fifth season driving the No. 88 Quality Care Ford for Robert Yates. There were the victories, of course—including the win at Richmond, which gave him the NASCAR Winston Cup Series points lead; his utterly dominant performance at Michigan; his gas-rationing nail-biter in Daytona; and his second Brickyard win—but for Dale, the key to the year was a familiar one: consistency. Along with having a great car, he approached each race with patience and persistence, a formula that finally found him in a position he'd long worked for: way out in front, with his competitors fading back in his rearview for the better part of a championship season. When the yearly totals were tallied, Dale Jarrett had won his first NASCAR Winston Cup Series by 201 points over Bobby Labonte on the strength of 24 top-fives and 29 top-tens in 34 races. At the annual award banquet at the Waldorf-Astoria hotel in New York City, Dale Jarrett won the cheers of his peers, a winner's check of just under $3 million and a hug from his proud father. Together, they are only the second father-and-son NASCAR Winston Cup Series champions, after Lee and Richard Petty.

Meanwhile, Ned continues to add his perspective to races on CBS, TNN, and ESPN; his oldest son, Glen, also a former racer, is a long-time NASCAR television commentator as well. After the 2000 season, Ned plans to retire from life in the booth. Just as he did when he stopped driving, he'll be leaving on top.

"I still stand by the reasons I quit [racing] and certainly appreciate the opportunities that have come along since then to keep me in the sport," he reflects. "Had those opportunities not come along, I think it would have been much more difficult to have accepted. But that's okay; I've been rewarded for the accomplishments that we did have. And once [your] accomplishments are in the record books, then they're there forever."

Also there forever is his son's march to the title—not to mention that 1993 Daytona call, and a moment in NASCAR history that will never happen again.

"A lot of times when I'm introduced, especially if it's one race fan introducing me to another, they'll say, this is Dale's dad," Ned says, smiling. "I say, yeah, he's gonna make me famous one of these days."

10
The Labonte Brothers

With five laps to go in the 1998 Pepsi 400, NASCAR officials saw no alternative but to raise the red flag and pause the race until the rain stopped. For thirty-seven minutes, the action was at a standstill and the cars were covered, leaving the drivers to stand around and chat amongst themselves. Strange ideas can spring up in so tense a time, while you wait patiently for a restart and an intensely mad dash for the finish. And few ideas would ever be as interesting as the one that hit Terry Labonte while he waited in the rain.

Maybe he started off wondering what else could happen in this first-ever night race in NASCAR Winston Cup Series history. The event had earned a reputation for unpredictable results after being postponed three and a half months from its original July 4th running date, due to fires that had swept through Florida, forcing tens of thousands of people to evacuate their homes. Meanwhile, the race itself had already seen its share of incredible moments. Earlier, two separate incidents—at laps 32 and 141 out of 160—had put varying degrees of hurt on nearly half the participants. Then finally the rain, which had always seemed to respect the authority of the France family in Daytona on race days, could wait no longer, and the action slowed to a halt.

The competitors stood around, many huddling together for friendly chats, while in the back of everyone's mind there were persistent thoughts of strategy. Drivers wondered who among the field they might be able to count on for drafting help when the eventual return of green-flag racing came upon them. Every driver felt first and foremost the anticipation of getting back into his car and making a spirited run for it.

That is, everyone except for Labonte. During the delay, the 1996 NASCAR Winston Cup Series champion, and Hendrick Motorsports teammate of race leader Jeff Gordon, scouted out his younger brother, Bobby. Bobby had qualified for the pole earlier in the week at a blistering 193.611 mph, but would unfortunately hit the restart back in seventh place. Terry, meanwhile, was right next to him in eighth.

Seventh, eighth, what difference would it make, the older brother wondered? Who would notice?

"We were sitting there under the caution, he was telling me what his car was doing, I was telling him what my car was doing, and I said, we should just trade, you know?" Terry says. "We started to trade cars. We thought that would have been pretty cool, him finish the race in my car, me finish in his. But it's kind of hard to do it down there at [Daytona]."

The pair had a good laugh about it and eventually got back into their respective cars. Then they proceeded to do what they have so often done on race tracks in this highest level of racing: help each other out.

After two laps of getting up to speed, the race restarted with three laps remaining, but the field up front remained stable until midway through the final lap. Terry Labonte, drafting right behind his brother, forced him forward in a three-wide maneuver on the high side. The push was just what Bobby needed to vault past both Mike Skinner, who was in third, and then Gordon's drafting partner, Jeremy Mayfield. Coming out of turn four, Gordon had only the hard-charging Bobby Labonte on his tail.

At that point, there wasn't nearly enough track space left and the field watched Jeff Gordon claim his eleventh victory—the most in a season since Dale Earnhardt's 1987 campaign—and all but clinch his second championship in three seasons with three races left.

Meanwhile, after the contest, the man who in 1996 had interrupted Gordon's flow of NASCAR Winston Cup Series titles, had a good laugh with his younger brother. The Labonte brothers are unique among siblings in NASCAR. They're a highly competitive, extremely successful pair who rarely let any on-track incident get the better of them, and maintain an unusually high sense of humor in the midst of their weekly drama. There have been several races where they found themselves finishing one-two, and the occasions have led generally to laughs and celebration instead of increased competition. Bobby's recent rise into the top ranks of the NASCAR Winston Cup Series has been greeted by his older brother with only the hope that one day Bobby, too, will get to experience the thrill of winning the annual crown. And some of Terry's NASCAR Winston Cup Series championship success rubbed off on Bobby a bit, when the latter played a huge part in the most memorable day the family has ever had: the race at the end of 1996 that secured Terry's championship, wherein Bobby won the battle and Terry the war.

The Labontes might be on competing racing teams, but every driver on the circuit knows that with them, blood often comes first. And had they switched cars before that restart in Daytona, there's no doubt they'd have each raced as hard as possible to try to secure the best finish for the other.

"We laughed about that later; we said, 'Man, we should have [switched],'" Terry says. "That would've been pretty funny. I told him if it had been anyplace else we might have been able to do it. It would've been pretty cool to pull up to the gas pumps after the race and say, 'Hey!' But he wound up finishing second. I was in sixth. It was probably a good thing we didn't."

When talking individually about specific times they've had together, the Labonte brothers both have a habit of talking in dialogue, as if they're each somehow there in the other's head. They could be talking about growing up and racing quarter midgets, or the best days they've had together in NASCAR Winston Cup Series, or even their ESPN commercial from several years ago, which found them playfully batting the who's-better-at-this-and-that questions back and forth; whatever the story, you can sense the closeness between them, a seven years-plus age difference notwithstanding.

"I know we don't ever get closer in age, but you get older, you get more mature—and [Terry's] been more mature than I have for a lot longer—but I'm getting closer to being more like him," Bobby says. "We have a lot more fun together."

"We're real close," adds Terry. "We've always been that way. I don't know if it's kind of big brother looking after little brother or what, but now it's kind of, you know, the same. I'm a big fan of his."

It started the other way around when Terry raced quarter midgets with some help from his dad. He'd started racing at age seven at tracks near the family's home in Corpus Christi, Texas, and took to it instantly.

"I remember the first big weekend I think we had," he says. "We went up to Dallas racing, and Dallas is a long way from Corpus. They had a track outside of Dallas—it was a state meet or something. We had fast times in two classes and won both races. I won four metal trophies—I still got 'em in my attic. I was seven or eight years old."

Bobby was born when the seven-year-old Terry raced the quarter-midget tracks. With successful racing already such a big part of the family practice, it became natural for Bobby eventually to want to try his hand at it as well. It wasn't long before he, too, drove on the quarter-midget circuit with his brother, though their age split kept them in different race classes.

With as much success as he had during his early days, some of Bobby's favorite early memories involve the other racing impulse he seemed to have been born with: an endless pride in being the younger brother of Terry Labonte. Due to their ages, there was never a real feeling of sibling rivalry; instead, the brothers had a genuine appreciation for each other's talents, without a lot of the jealousy that colors even the most successful sets of brothers toiling in the same business. That impulse in Bobby only increased the more he saw his brother's ascent as a driver.

"The best part I had was actually watching when he was racing stock cars," Bobby says. "We'd travel each weekend in Texas for two nights in a motor home. To me, watching him, that was like 'Yeah, hey, that's my brother, man.' That was exciting to me, because I was his biggest supporter. I guess I could have stayed at home, but I didn't want to. When I was ten years old, I wanted to watch my older brother win."

For fourteen years, Terry did win, in quarter midgets until he was sixteen, and then in stock cars—driving at first in cars owned by his father, Bob—earning fame and victories on tracks in Corpus Christi, Houston, and San Antonio. While running stocks in Texas, his car was sponsored by Billy Hagan, who a few years earlier had begun running a NASCAR Winston Cup Series team. He saw in Terry the development of a quality that would forever be associated with him: consistency. Terry had long subscribed to the racing philosophy that if you couldn't win a race, it at least paid to finish. While he never had anything against the wide-open dash to the finish, he learned early that winning a championship meant finishing races as frequently as possible in as high a position as possible.

The style paid off when, in 1978, Hagan offered the twenty-one-year-old Terry the jump into the NASCAR Winston Cup Series. The move opened up new options for the entire Labonte family. In terms of racing, the Labontes had gained as much success as they could in Texas, and Terry, Bobby, and their parents picked up stakes and moved to North Carolina. Bob Labonte began to work for Terry's NASCAR Winston Cup Series team and Bobby got to drive go-karts.

For Terry, life in the NASCAR Winston Cup Series offered a rude awakening in his first race, the 1978 Southern 500 in Darlington.

"The race lasted forever," he recalls. "The longest race I'd run was two hundred laps on a half-mile track and this is five hundred miles. Man, my neck was about to fall off because I wasn't used to it. Ran, ran, ran, wrecking, wrecking. Coming into the pits, the track can get real sandy down there at Darlington, I spun out coming in. I had never been this tired in my life. I was looking at the scoreboard to see how many laps were left, I think it was like three-hundred-sixty-seven laps, or something like that. This thing must have lasted five hours. I never thought to look at my car number up on the scoreboard, and I finished fourth. It's probably a good thing I didn't see it; I'd have probably wrecked. So I was off to a pretty good start."

It didn't take him long to earn the respect of his competitors. He was in the running for NASCAR Winston Cup Series Rookie of the Year honors in 1979, and though he lost to Dale Earnhardt, he ended up in the top ten in points. He also began to earn a reputation for incredible consistency. Most notable is his streak of running in consecutive NASCAR Winston Cup Series races and never faltering, regardless of injury. There's also his amazing penchant for finishing races in or near the money. Beginning in 1980, the year he won his first race by edging David Pearson in the Southern 500, he has gone only two seasons without at least ten top-ten finishes, and most years the total tops fifteen.

That pattern is probably what encouraged Hagan to tell the press, at the end of the 1980 season, that his driver would win a championship within five years. Considering Labonte would have to contend with Darrell Waltrip, Bobby Allison, and Dale Earnhardt, it seemed a far-fetched notion, even given his talent and perseverance.

Still, it only took him four. In 1984, on the strength of only two wins—Waltrip had seven—but 17 top-fives and a total of 24 top-tens in 30 races, he took the crown by a slim 65 points over Harry Gant, becoming, at twenty-eight, the youngest NASCAR Winston Cup Series champion ever at the time. His calm attitude in the pressure of the season-long hunt would eventually earn him a change in nickname from the hardly colorful "Texas Terry" to one more appropriate: The Iceman.

Terry Labonte drove for Billy Hagan for what would be considered a great length of time by any auto racing standards: sixteen years. It was a fruitful association that produced ten victories and twenty-six top-fives. But his career was not up to the standards Labonte held for himself. Other than his 1984 championship, the closest he came to capturing the crown again was a third-place finish in 1987. From 1989 on, he was languishing in the middle of the pack, dissatisfied with his situation. He went four seasons without a win and the talk in the garage area was that he would never regain the form he once had.

Meanwhile, Bobby Labonte was a rising star in NASCAR's junior divisions. In 1987, he won a Late Model Stocks championship at the Caraway Speedway, and three years later he made his NASCAR Busch Series debut. Now it was Terry's chance to watch his brother's development with pride.

"In whatever he's always done, I've always thought he really did a good job at it," Terry says. "A lot of Winston Cup guys run Busch and always have, and he hadn't run many races and it was Bobby and the Winston Cup guys—he was kind of in a league above the rest of the Busch guys. I remember the first time he went to Daytona with the Busch car, he led the race. I remember he passed Bobby Allison and Darrell Waltrip at the same time, and I went, 'Oh my god, he made it, but don't do that, just stay right there behind them,' and he cut down across the straightaway and he pushes the button on the radio, and he said, 'Yee-hah!' He's quite a competitor. He's very, very intense, a lot like my dad. I got my mother's personality, but Bobby and my dad are the same. When they go off, they go off."

The similarity of personality certainly didn't hurt matters when Bobby's father Bob served as his son's crew chief during the NASCAR Busch Series days. Bobby gained valuable experience in the junior series and enjoyed a reputation as one of the top drivers on the circuit. Even as Jeff Gordon made his awe-inspiring rise through the ranks at the same time, Labonte went about putting up extremely solid numbers. He contended for the NASCAR Busch Series title in 1990, won it the following year, and lost it by three points to Joe Nemechek in 1992 after a late-season battle. It was on the strength of those finishes that he was able to move up to the NASCAR Winston Cup Series himself in 1993.

The Labonte picture in NASCAR began to improve drastically the following season when Rick Hendrick recruited Terry to join his team. It was an offer Terry couldn't refuse, carrying with it the promise of bigger budgets, more testing, and in Terry's mind, a greater commitment to winning. In the past, Hendrick had owned the rides of such proven winners as Tim Richmond, Geoffrey Bodine, and Darrell Waltrip. In 1992, he had orchestrated the signing of NASCAR's prized rookie, Jeff Gordon. In 1994, Labonte would be teamed with Gordon and Hendrick regular Ken Schrader, who had finished in the top ten the year before.

Terry felt the impact of his new arrangement quickly the next year, notching three victories in a season for the first time in his career and improving from 18th to 7th in the annual standings.

Later that year, Joe Gibbs, the former head coach of the NFL Washington Redskins and another owner with the right resources and a reputation for winning, tapped Bobby Labonte to replace

Dale Jarrett on his team for the 1995 season. Finally, each brother had secured a coveted ride on the tour, and they would make the most of their situations. Together, during that season, the brothers finished in the top ten in points, gaining three wins each. Out of 31 races, Terry had 17 top-tens to Bobby's 14. The Labontes were clearly riding the crest in the elite division of the sport.

In two of Bobby's 1995 wins, Terry finished second. "This is getting a little old," he joked after the second time, and he wondered if perhaps the tables might turn the next time. Bobby wouldn't get another chance for a checker until the end of the 1996 campaign, and on that day, his big brother would do no complaining.

Considering the grueling nature of NASCAR Winston Cup Series driving, it may well seem appropriate that the annual championship is awarded to a driver as much for his ability to survive and thrive as to dominate the field. The best drivers, in their greatest years, have been able to do both. In 1996, the title run came down to a battle between two teammates, the dominant one and the consistent one. For Jeff Gordon, who in 1995 had beaten Labonte's record to become the youngest NASCAR Winston Cup Series champion ever at age twenty-four, another championship would signal his ascent to the highest levels of the sport, threatening Dale Earnhardt's long rule throughout the previous decade. For Labonte, twelve years past his first championship, such a victory would seem fitting in a season where he would break Richard Petty's record for consecutive starts and become his sport's greatest Ironman. A title for Labonte would also erase much of the has-been talk that had dogged him for years and vault him back to a place of prominence. But to win, he'd have to overcome Gordon's winning numbers.

The pair would deal with other title-hunters, of course, most notably Earnhardt. The Intimidator, who was running second to Labonte in series points and certainly would have contended for his eighth championship, experienced the worst crash of his life at the DieHard 500 in Talladega. The experience effectively ended his chance of a run for the title, but it didn't stop him from racing—and from winning the pole and leading the most laps during the race at Watkins Glen two weeks later.

But throughout all the drama it was Terry Labonte's No. 5 Kellogg's Chevrolet that kept jockeying for the season lead. Gordon began the year playing catch-up, having wound up near the back of the pack in the first two races; he more than made up for it, however, with a stunning set of victories. Gordon and Labonte passed the lead back and forth, and by the time Labonte won his second and final race of the year—compared to Gordon's circuit-leading ten wins—Labonte held a single-point lead on his young challenger with only three races remaining. The lead was based entirely on his ability to stay near the top in seemingly every race, combined with Gordon's occasional finish in the back of the pack, which constantly ate away at any points lead he established.

Meanwhile, Bobby Labonte was not exactly in the midst of his most memorable year. Going into the last race, the NAPA 500 in Atlanta, he'd won no races, but he earned an advantage when he won the pole in Atlanta; he was also coming off two of his best finishes of the year, and he went into that race feeling a need to end his season on a high note.

Terry would need to do so as well, but the going promised to be rougher. In a practice run for the Phoenix race two weeks before, he'd hit the wall and ended up with a broken bone in his left hand. With the championship on the line, he ran at Phoenix—using a smaller steering wheel, courtesy of Bobby's car owner, Joe Gibbs— and ended up finishing in third, two spots ahead of Gordon, which extended his lead to forty-seven points. The championship was now his to lose: Mathematically, if he finished eighth or better in Atlanta, Gordon could do nothing to beat him. Terry took the first step toward doing that by qualifying third in Atlanta. Driving the 500 miles in pain, however, would make the task that much harder.

With Bobby on the pole, though, it all felt a bit more doable. Having an ally up front certainly wouldn't hurt matters.

What also didn't hurt matters was Gordon's tire trouble early in the race. Gordon had qualified on the outside pole, but he suddenly found himself with some serious catching up to do. Not that Labonte took that as a gimme. There was plenty of racing left and he charged up front to try to earn the valuable five bonus points for leading the race. The only obstacle was his brother Bobby, who moved over and let Terry by for a couple of laps.

"Then I moved back and let him go and 'Thank you,'" he says, waving to mimic the moment. That was lap nine; for the next forty-three turns, Bobby stayed out in front.

There were lead changes throughout the afternoon but control always returned to Bobby. Out of 328 laps, he would eventually lead 146 of them, and when he took the lead for the last time, it was in daring fashion, going three-wide around Gordon and Chad Little coming out of the first turn, and then quickly steaming by them.

His older brother, meanwhile, drove in the enviable position of wondering how safe to play his run. As Gordon kept his relentless pursuit of the lead, Labonte sped cautiously around the track as consistent as always, waiting for the checker to come.

It did, in time, and Bobby Labonte—who'd led the final forty-two laps of the race—took it, with Dale Jarrett in second and Jeff Gordon in third. Terry Labonte finished fifth. Bobby had won the battle, Terry the war. When the tallying was done, Terry Labonte had beaten Jeff Gordon for the title by thirty-seven points, earning himself a $1.5 million prize—as well as the privilege of taking one of the greatest victory laps in NASCAR history.

Driving around the speedway together, Terry and Bobby Labonte accepted the cheers of the crowd, which included their wives and children and their parents. It was a moment that brought the normally reserved, newly crowned NASCAR champion to tears.

"The most memorable time I've ever had in racing, without a doubt," Terry says, still recalling the day with glee. "Nothing else comes close to that."

"Our heads were in a vice because we hadn't won a race," Bobby remembers. "And Terry and I, we talked about, 'Man, it would sure be neat if I won the race and you won the championship.' Then during the race, we had an awesome car, the pit stops were great, and everything we did was right, we led the most laps, and ended up winning the race, Terry got to lead some laps and won the championship. Our mom and dad were there, and to have two sons win on the same day—even though Terry didn't win the race, he won the battle. It was like both of us won."

In the press room after the race, the brothers soaked in the glory of the day and noted that it had to be the greatest day they'd ever had together . . . except one, Terry pointed out. There was that time, years earlier, when they'd shot their dad's pickup truck. The truck had caused nothing but trouble, constantly breaking down at the worst moments. The brothers were in the shop one day, working on one of Bobby's Late Model cars, when their dad called and told them to get the local salvage yard to pick it up. Staring at the truck, Terry and Bobby concluded that it wouldn't be proper to send it off without a fitting payback—which turned out to involve some well-aimed gunfire.

It was just a little mischief—not quite on the same scale as almost switching rides at Daytona, but in the same family.

For NASCAR fans, one of the many pleasant by-products of Bobby Labonte's continued swift rise to the upper levels of his sport is the fact that he and his brother are occasionally pitted against each other in a race to the finish. The 1997 DieHard 500 at Talladega offered just such a spectacle, adding to the drama that normally unfolds in restrictor-plate races at the grand 2.66-mile tri-oval. Earlier in the race, Jeff Gordon's deflated left rear tire caused him to slide over hard into Sterling Marlin. That brought about a great deal of trouble for half the field and ended the day for nearly two dozen drivers. The Labontes and several other competitors were lucky to escape the fray unscathed, and after caution, they went about the business of trying to win on a day which saw the lead change hands sixteen times among thirty-two drivers—and in some cases from lap to lap. With just two laps remaining, Ken Schrader held the lead but was without a drafting partner. More misfortune lay in his rearview mirror: Behind him and charging fast was Terry Labonte, leading his brother Bobby. Ken understood immediately the cold reality of the sight: If Bobby Labonte was looking for a drafting partner, chances are he would choose his brother.

The Labontes powered past Schrader, and once there, Bobby made his valiant attempts to pass Terry and keep alive his streak of leading their one-two finishes. Terry was more than a match on that day, however, and Bobby went home the runner-up.

Even when things don't go perfectly for the brothers, they can eventually deal with it. At the 1998 DieHard 500, with two laps to go and Terry in the lead, Bobby and Jimmy Spencer drafted by him in a spirited outside move. When the passing was ultimately done, Terry had fallen from first to fourth. Between them, the brothers had led 148 of the race's 188 laps and the disappointment of finishing as low as he did pushed Terry to leave the speedway without comment at day's end. Bobby joked that he'd have to call his father first to see how mad his older brother was before calling and broaching the matter, which was quickly settled.

As long as the pair remain in the NASCAR Winston Cup Series and competitive, chances are pretty good such a scene may arise again. But an equally interesting question is whether or not the family's next joint project will turn out to be as successful as their current ones. Justin Labonte, Terry's eighteen-year-old son, now shares a NASCAR Busch Series ride with his father and is attempting to rise to the bigs. He won two mini-stock division championships on his way to his 1999 Grand National debut. His driving is, according to his father, smooth, impressive, and, not surprisingly, consistent. And Justin gets the added influence of his grandfather Bob, who works on the crew for the Terry/Justin Labonte NASCAR Busch Series team; Justin's grandmother, Martha, works in the office for the team.

But the 1999 focus was on the present generation, not the future, and as the campaign was drawing to a close, one of a handful of drivers who seemed to have the greatest shot at interrupting Dale Jarrett's date with destiny was Bobby Labonte. From his older brother, who twice experienced the wonder of that moment, there was no jealousy, only excitement and encouragement.

"I hope he wins the championship this year," Terry said midway through last season, and then he smiled at the idea and added, "C'mon, he's gotta win his championship."

Nothing in his racing life would give him more pride and joy at this point than to see that happen for his brother. You get the feeling that's one ride he wouldn't try to switch for anything.

11
Mark and Julian Martin

Through three-fifths of the 1998 NASCAR season, a seemingly unstoppable Jeff Gordon appeared on his way to winning a second-straight NASCAR Winston Cup Series title, his third in four years. While many at the time believed Gordon could only lose if he managed to beat himself, Gordon knew better. All he had to do was look in the rearview mirror, which is where Mark Martin, regarded by his peers as one of the finest stock car drivers alive, normally sat.

August 9, 1998, ended somewhat typically for the pair. Martin ran second to Gordon at The Bud at the Glen in Watkins Glen, New York. The race may have been Gordon's third victory in a row, but it was also Martin's fourth consecutive second-place finish, an all-time record distinctive, perhaps, for its futility, but also for its consistency. At that point in the season, twenty races had been run, with Gordon finishing on top in seven and Martin winning four. The gap between the rivals could be explained by saying that Gordon seemed to be having a better career year than Martin. That Martin ended this August afternoon a highly reachable eighty-two points off Gordon's proverbial back bumper spoke volumes for Martin's endless effort and skill, not to mention his drive. And no one could question his courage, either—while fighting for the title, he also battled the painful effects of a herniated disc.

Still, Martin, who was thirty-nine years old at the time, had to face reality: There were thirteen races left to pursue his dream of winning a NASCAR Winston Cup Series championship. Being in second place was an all-too familiar spot for a driver who'd ended up the bridesmaid in the title hunt in 1990 and 1994.

Martin is legendary in NASCAR circles for his unflappable nature, the intensity of his focus, and his strenuous exercise regimen. It has kept him sound and successful for the past decade—since 1989, he is the only driver to finish in the top six in the point standings every year.

On that August day in Watkins Glen, Martin, forever the realist, knew it would take his single-minded work ethic to succeed. He'd grown up with that focus thanks to his father, Julian Martin, the hardworking businessman who had forged his successful trucking company as solidly as he'd built his son's first stock car when Mark was fifteen. "I was born with a gift that said if I wanted something, there wasn't any problem to excel. All I had to do was work harder than anybody else around," Mark says. "If you take two people with equal skills, the guy that gets ahead the fastest is the one that works harder at it and thinks the most about it. I grew up seeing that."

Julian had given Mark time, money, encouragement, and the benefit of his experience necessary to help launch a career. He was father, mentor, friend, confidante, and example, and he wanted a Mark Martin NASCAR Winston Cup Series championship in the worst way. As Martin looked ahead to the August 16th race in Brooklyn, Michigan, where he'd start the afternoon as defending champion of the Pepsi 400, he felt equal to the challenge of that goal. It was what he'd been working for since the day he first gripped the steering wheel of his father's car when he was five years old.

But Martin was utterly unprepared for the news that would greet him when he returned home from the race in Watkins Glen: Earlier that evening, sixty-two-year-old Julian Martin, his wife Shelley, and their eleven-year-old daughter Sarah, were killed when the twin-engine Piper Julian was piloting crashed in Nevada, near the Utah border.

For Martin, the devastation was shattering. He'd always been a private person, preferring to do his job and focus on effort and results, on the things you have a chance to control, week in and week out. There would, however, be no way to change what happened in Nevada, no quick fix or easy answers.

His main inspiration was gone. Dealing with that would be a challenge to dwarf any NASCAR Winston Cup Series dream.

The following Wednesday, Martin attended the funeral for his father, stepmother, and stepsister. He also said he planned to be on track days later for both Saturday's 200-mile Busch Grand National race and Sunday's Pepsi 400. It was, he knew, what his father would have wanted, and Martin planned on trying to win a race, and a championship, for his hero.

In the days following the accident, Mark Martin made hesitant but open statements on his father's influence in his life, saying, "This is not a typical son-lost-his-father deal. I lost the man who made me who I am." But months later, it became clear that discussing his father's death is something that will never get easier for him.

"Well, I lost my hero," he begins, and pauses a moment. "There's a piece of my life that was missing and still is. I had a close relationship with my dad. He was instrumental in my racing, and I live to make him proud."

Indeed, even in NASCAR circles, where fathers routinely help carve careers for their sons, the Martins were different. Julian wasn't a racer; he was a businessman who saw in his son the same goal-oriented commitment to hard work that he'd seen in himself and then had the foresight to cultivate it.

It is easy for Martin, even comforting now, to see himself as a kid standing on the seat of his father's car, with Julian pushing the pedal to the metal, going as fast as eighty mph, as the pair raced through the local dirt roads near their house in Batesville, Arkansas.

"I wasn't older than five," Mark says. "I was standing in my dad's lap, steering the car while he was running fast and coming up on one of those one-lane wooden bridges that were very narrow." Martin was afraid to drive across it, but his father would have none of it. "I started to cry and my dad was saying, 'You have to, or we're gonna wreck.'" Martin chuckles at the thought. "That'll teach you to do it," he says.

A decade later, Mark nagged his father to build him a race car a few years before he was old enough for a driver's license. That first car, which the pair built along with some friends, was heavy with all the protective bracing Julian insisted on putting in, and with the driving apparatus in the middle, a place Julian hoped Mark—who was hardly big enough to see over the steering wheel—would be safest. Over time they built more cars; the pair always believed they had less skills than enthusiasm, but they made up for the former by working long into the night, trying to complete the right car for competition.

Whatever the combination, it worked. Father and son went through all these rites of passage together. Martin won a great many races through several seasons on local tracks, routinely beating a roster of opponents who were a great deal older than him. And then he and his dad would go back to the garage and build still faster cars for each season or new driving circuit. All the while, Julian Martin invested his resources and time to help shape Mark Martin, the driver and the man.

Julian claimed he always either tested his son or gave him plenty of latitude in order to lay down the proper foundation so that Mark would be prepared for any troublesome situation. That may have been true, but Mark recognized his father's other agenda: He liked to have fun and the wilder the fun—and the greater the chances taken—the better. Julian had gone to work at his father's feed business and was driving a truck at ten. In 1959, the year Mark was born, Julian started his trucking business, which he ran with the help of his wife Jackie, an attractive Arkansas woman with a daughter from a previous marriage and a wild streak to equal his own. Julian and Jackie eventually parted ways; in time, they would marry again and part a second time. He loved to fly, loved to ride motorcycles; he had a passion for speed and a disdain for limits.

"He was definitely a cowboy; he lived by his rules and no one else's," Martin recalls with admiration. "He was an extremely unique person. Laws, in his opinion, were made to be broken. He followed his own code of things and was a very high-strung, intense, hardworking, passionate man."

Perhaps as a consequence, Mark grew up serious. "Some things about my dad, the way he acted and reacted to things, embarrassed me," he says. "It made me want to be a little less visible because he was typically very visible, and in some cases not possible to overlook. He was extreme to some degree, and sometimes I personally would have rather gone unnoticed."

But in terms of recognition for success, Martin didn't mind being noticed; indeed, he had no choice. Four years after he started his first race at the Locust Grove, Arkansas, track in 1974, he became, at nineteen, the youngest American Speed Association (ASA) circuit champion ever, driving a car primarily built by father and son. And later, during his hard first years in NASCAR, the years that tested Mark's commitment financially and emotionally, Julian Martin was there to help.

"He was prouder of me than anything in the world and I knew that," Martin remembers. "There never was any question of that in my mind."

The week after the accident, it wasn't going to be easy for Martin to simply sit and grieve and collect himself. At first there were the endless details involved in the funeral, and in dealing with his father's business. That Wednesday, the funeral attracted seven hundred supportive family members and friends, where Julian Martin was remembered as a generous, loving man who lived as fast as his son drove. Then it was on to Michigan for testing and qualifying—and facing the understandable media barrage. There were the inevitable questions about why Martin chose to race, even as an honor to his father. Later on he would reveal that three weeks prior to the accident, his father had left some strangely prescient instructions with his right-hand man at the trucking company: *If anything ever happened to me, keep things going, and make sure Mark never misses a race on account of me,* the note read; priority one was winning a championship.

The idea of Mark Martin driving with even more single-minded focus than usual seemed far-fetched, but that Sunday, he got onto the track at the Pepsi 400 with the notion that winning the race was his responsibility, even his destiny.

He had qualified fifth, behind pole-sitter Ernie Irvan, Bobby Labonte, Jeff Gordon, and Dale Jarrett. He led for a good part of the race, holding back the tide of challengers, Irvan chief among them. At times, they were close enough to reach out and shake hands; at other times, Irvan raced bumper-to-bumper at 180 mph with the man who was one of his best friends on the circuit. In Brooklyn, Irvan battled Martin and himself, the instinct to win going up against his desire to see to it that Mark would be in a position to own the day as he deserved, in the best spirit of camaraderie.

With twenty-two laps to go, Martin appeared to have command of the race, owning a five-second lead. He was running well as usual on one of his favorite tracks. Had the green flag been out for the rest of the race, chances are no one would have had a ride strong enough to beat him.

Everything began to quickly unravel the moment smoke poured from the back of Ward Burton's car, which brought out a yellow flag on lap 178. Martin's margin was erased; the leaders pitted, and when they emerged, Martin continued to be in front with Jarrett a close second. Gordon had gone into the pits in sixth, having run inconsistently all day, but the 24 team sent him out in third place.

The green flag flew again with sixteen laps to go, and suddenly, for the first time all afternoon, Gordon's car started running the way it had all year, like a prize thoroughbred getting the whip at the top of the stretch. By lap 188, he had overtaken Jarrett for second place.

This left only Martin, who planned on doing everything in his power to block a race car that was now clearly faster than his own. As Irvan would say after the race, this jockeying was the easy part for Martin, easier than dealing with a week's worth of troubles.

But Martin quickly learned that sometimes the best intentions and the greatest determination can't prevent what seems like fate. Gordon pulled up on Martin's rear bumper on lap 191, but Martin kept him at bay; it would be his last hurrah of the contest. When the rivals had raced through turn two on the next lap, Gordon made the pass and took his first lead of the day. He would not give it up, not to Labonte or Jarrett, who ended up second and third, and not to Martin, who faded to fourth. It was Gordon's fourth win in a row, a distinction only six other drivers had managed to achieve since 1976, the last one being Mark Martin in 1993.

Fans and opponents were in a state of disbelief—few more so than Gordon, who'd been shocked to suddenly find himself with a car worthy enough for the win. He knew what it would have meant to Martin, and even acknowledged that he hated being the spoiler. "He deserved to be in victory lane," Gordon said.

It was hardly solace. "I wanted it real bad," Martin said afterward. "I did what I could. I had a motivation but I didn't have the stuff to do it today."

After the intensity of Brooklyn, it was time to regain a measure of control: Winning was not about grieving or honoring, winning was about winning, and adding victories on the road leading to a championship. He promised himself he'd come to the next race, the Goody's 500 in Bristol, Tennessee, and give the effort necessary to start closing the gap with Gordon in the title chase.

It appeared early on in the race that Gordon did not have the kind of car which could make a serious run at the record fifth-straight win—not that anyone was counting him out. The .533-mile oval track—the shortest on the circuit—did, however, take its predictable toll on a number of competitors. On lap 215, Brett Bodine got tapped from behind, and when the spinning was done, seven other cars had damage to deal with.

Meanwhile, Martin moved into the lead on lap 320, running well and comfortably. For a time, it appeared Rusty Wallace might give him a run for his money. Wallace had been as far back as 39th thanks to a loose screw on a brake caliper. He was a lap down, but the short-track expert regained it after a caution and by the time Martin took the lead, Wallace was in seventh, well within striking distance. He had moved up to third when another caution sent the leaders into the pits. They emerged with Martin in front and Wallace second. Wallace, who hadn't won in fifty straight tries, was overdue; despite an old friendship with Martin, business was business.

He threatened the leader for a few laps but Martin eventually began to pull away; by the time lap 430 came around, Martin's teammate, Jeff Burton, had moved into second.

Jeremy Mayfield made contact with Bobby Labonte on lap 435, bringing out another caution and resurrecting the possibility that, two weeks running, someone was going to ruin Mark Martin's day. Gordon was in fifth now, and anything could happen.

But for the next seventy laps, Martin raced with himself alone; no one made a serious challenge. When he took the checkered flag, to the delight of the jubilant crowd, he had led the final 181 laps.

Martin wasn't exactly sure how to feel. His emotions from the week before had been potent enough to drown his perspective; now, the victory almost seemed anticlimactic. He was once again absorbed in the effort and the chase, addressing the business at hand as his father would have wanted. With the win, he'd gained thirty points on Gordon, putting him only sixty-seven out of the lead with eleven contests left—and it was going to be a race.

"I cried last week because I didn't get to dedicate a victory to my dad, Shelley, and Sarah. This one is for them tonight," he said after the race, adding, "This helps me because I was so devastated. But to me, this just feels like a win. It feels like we're moving on."

Despite Martin's best efforts, 1998 ended the way many predicted. Mark Martin ran extremely well, but Jeff Gordon had a season for the ages. Gordon won five of the last eleven races, finishing second four other times. With the exception of subpar showings in the Southern 500 (40th place) and the Winston 500 (34th), and an all-too-human finish in the Pepsi 400 (16th), Martin finished in the top four every time. At season's end, Gordon had notched a modern record-setting thirteen wins; Martin counted his blessings, complained that the media kept asking when he was going to win a championship, and ended up the bridesmaid for the third time.

In 1999, he had another year that tested his courage and added to the lore of how committed he is to his ride. After bypassing back surgery before the start of the season, he drove in a barely tolerable level of pain, but managed to find himself, as usual, in the title hunt. His chances were dulled considerably, however, after leg and wrist injuries suffered during a happy-hour practice run before the July race at Daytona. For weeks, he had to be carried in and out of his car just to get to the green flag, but that didn't prevent him from giving chase to eventual champion Dale Jarrett. Martin finished the season in third, behind Bobby Labonte. Right after the final race in Atlanta, he checked himself in for surgery and rested in preparation for the 2000 campaign. Once the year began, he was ready for another go-round.

Now forty-one, with a back that might still cause him problems down the road, some question if Martin is considering retirement, but he appears more determined than ever to join the ranks of the honored few. The events of 1998 took their toll, of course, but it all seemed to mature Martin, providing him greater insight into how quickly things can change, for better or worse, and how you can only do so much to stem the tide.

They also added an even greater sense of responsibility to his life, in terms of how to honor the memory of his father. Julian Martin's company, J-Mar Express, is now Mark Martin's J-Mar Express. Days after the funeral, Mark showed up at the company's offices, and with 125 employees looking for an indication of what to do, Mark assumed the reins. Now chairman and CEO, he's kept the company prosperous, and tribute photos of Julian and Shelly adorn the walls in the lobby, a constant reminder of the family legacy.

In the sport, Martin enjoys an extremely supportive relationship with his team owner, Jack Roush, whom he has been with since he first broke into NASCAR Winston Cup Series racing. Beginning in 2000, owner and driver went in together on the team of Rookie of the Year hopeful Matt Kenseth. Martin and his wife Arlene have five children, four girls from her previous marriage, and their one son together, Matt, who's now eight, and races quarter midgets.

Unlike the intense relationship Martin enjoyed with his father, he finds he cannot spend as much time as he might like with Matt. "My relationship with Matt is very different," he says. Part of that has to do with how much his life has changed from the more laid-back days of Batesville in the 1960s, although Martin admits, "My drawn-back personality also comes in." What isn't different is the unmatched pride Martin feels for his son.

And nothing has changed his commitment to winning a championship. Every driver understands the sacrifices necessary to mount a successful run in NASCAR; given the events of 1998, few drivers are as open about them as Martin.

"I deal with realism a lot," he says. "The reality is that in order to do what I do now, I have to make the compromises it takes to do it. It can't be different from the way it is. Believe me, the money that you make doesn't fix everything for you; it doesn't get you back your family. No matter how much is there, how big the trophy is—you can't go back and relive your children's childhood.

"There's not any way to change the commitment I have unless I quit, and I can't quit so I just have to do the best I can with it. We're at a point right now where, the next five or ten years, I have to make the most of what I've built over the last twenty-five years— that's another one of those reality checks. That's what I have to do. I can't let up now. I'm too close to the end of the marathon."

When it comes to legacy, Mark Martin is set: In 1997, he was honored as one of NASCAR history's 50 Greatest Drivers. The past, good and bad, may contribute to why he wins and succeeds, but it really explains why he endures. You can never count Mark Martin out of a title hunt, under any circumstances; even given the injuries, the surgery, and the tragedy, that is truer now than ever.

12
The Petty Family

Lee Petty and Sons

In time, Richard Petty became the acknowledged, beloved King of stock car racing, winner of seven NASCAR titles, seven Daytona 500s, 200 races and nine most popular driver awards—in time. It did not all come to him overnight. He had to start somewhere and there would be lessons to learn before he could run with the best and win. For Petty, the learning curve began on July 18, 1958, two weeks after his twenty-first birthday, when he drove up to Toronto for his first NASCAR Grand National race. The day ended for him when he was unceremoniously pushed aside by the man who eventually won. The victor, one of stock car racing's premier drivers, went on to win his second Grand National title at the end of that 1958 season: Richard's father, Lee Petty.

"Daddy and Cotton Owens were racing, they were lapping me," Richard begins. "I thought I was trying to get out of the way, but they must not have thought so. I didn't feel I was in anybody's way, but I didn't have the experience."

The experience would come and in 1960, a year and a half after his inauspicious debut, Petty finished second in the running for the annual title and began developing the most famous of his many trademarks: winning races. His first win had come in that 1960 season in Charlotte—and it, too, had the stamp of Lee Petty on it. With eighteen laps remaining and Richard in front of a charging Rex

White, Richard's dad—perhaps to maintain his own position—tangled with White for a few seconds, just long enough for his son to build an insurmountable lead. When asked after the race if the maneuver hadn't helped Richard a bit, Lee reportedly smiled and said that it sure hadn't hurt him any.

That Richard Petty succeeded brilliantly in his career has to do, first and foremost, with his father. Richard claims Lee didn't realize he was knocking his own son's car into the wall during Richard's first race in Toronto. Had he known, Lee might have tried a different tactic; along with trying to protect his son, few things were more important to Lee Petty than keeping as many dents as possible from being put into one of his cars. As the most successful driver-owner in the first days of NASCAR, victories and accidents were credits and debits that, when equaled out, determined how well the family ate that evening.

That attitude inspired the work ethic passed down through the family from Lee—the gruff, strong-willed patriarch whose word was never questioned—to his two boys: Richard, the older, more confident son with curly hair, a wide smile, and an outgoing nature that made him an instant hit with fans; and Maurice, one year younger, quieter and more reserved, much like his father. For the boys, it's wasn't a question of if they would go into the family business, only when. For them, the wonder of stock car racing started in 1949, when their father drove at the inaugural event in NASCAR's history, continued as they trailed him from race to race, and reached its height with Lee Petty's controversial photo-finish victory in one of the sport's greatest races: the first-ever Daytona 500 in 1959. Two years later, after an accident prematurely ended Lee's career, his sons had to take the reins of the business and put their father's example to good use. Though Maurice also followed driving dreams of his own, the business thrived after the brothers settled into their destined careers: Maurice as the greatest engine builder in stock cars, Richard as the winningest driver. What started with Lee Petty's idea for a better way of life turned into a sports dynasty now more than fifty years old and still running.

If the American dream preaches that hard work and business savvy can earn you a fruitful slice of the American pie, then Lee

Petty symbolized that effort in the postwar world of NASCAR. He was that rare driver who combined business acumen—in time, he'd build his business up to a team of several cars—and a field general's instincts on the track. To his sons, his word was law. Looking back, Maurice Petty sums up his father's influence with a simple, "He told me what to do and I did it." With Lee calling the shots, the system worked.

During NASCAR's earliest periods, the vast majority of stock car racers drove for independent owners who supplied cars and offered a percentage to a winning driver—a situation that hasn't changed drastically since then. But at this time, decades before the days of million-dollar sponsorship deals—and paydays—an owner-driver like Petty had to be responsible for every part of the car himself.

"We drove over there in the race car," says Richard, remembering the first NASCAR race ever run, on a three-quarter-mile dirt track in Charlotte, North Carolina. "Daddy borrowed a '46 or '47 Buick from some of his buddies over at the service station—a real fast car on the road. They pulled the car in the Texaco station, put it up on the rack, changed the oil, greased it, checked the air in the tires—I mean, after driving *it* to the race, we're getting ready *for* the race. I think they took the mufflers off, taped up the headlights, put a number on it, and it was ready." It raced well until the sway bar came off and Lee rolled the car over four times. He escaped with bruises; the car, not quite as lucky, had to be picked up the next day on a flatbed. Lee then realized that in order to have a serious shot at winning, he had to have a serious car. He got a 1949 Plymouth Coupe; "That was the lightest, cheapest thing he could buy," Richard says. "That got us in the racing business. And the next race we ran was Hillsboro, North Carolina, and me and my brother and my mother and Daddy got in the car and drove it to the race, and when the race was over we got in it and drove it home."

When school was out, the Petty boys got to travel with their parents from race to race, gaining some necessary on-the-job training during their father's early, halcyon days in NASCAR racing.

"We started when I was about eleven years old, and we got to go all over the United States," recalls Richard fondly. "We went everywhere. We'd just get in the car and away we'd go. We'd get hungry and we'd stop, fix some peanut butter sandwiches—we took Mother along to fix supper. Daddy never had a pit crew or any of that kind of stuff. He just went. You know, we'd help him change the oil in the car and all that. And in those hundred-mile races, as soon as you start the race, if you didn't have trouble you didn't stop. You'd make it on the gas and tires and everything. But he was his own crew chief, chief mechanic, and owner and driver; he did it all."

The pay at the track normally wouldn't make one wealthy, but Lee was starting what would turn into a Hall of Fame career that planted the seeds for decades of growth and family business expansion. What began with Lee tooling his cars underneath an open-air reaper shed next to a family home with no running water in it, slowly turned into the precursor of the modern NASCAR race team. Recalls Richard, "First thing you know you got a pickup truck, then we got a trailer, then we got a truck, and then you know all that stuff, it just *grew*."

Lee Petty had turned to racing after stints as a farmer and owner of a trucking business, among several other vocations near the family home in Level Cross, North Carolina. On the track, he learned early on that winning championships—and earning a good living—depended a great deal upon staying near the front and having good enough equipment to finish races. He won his share of them—fifty-four, which is good enough for seventh on the all-time list—and also posted, arguably, the greatest record of consistency in stock car history: During his career, he finished in the top ten in a whopping seventy-eight percent of his races. And since he ran every race the circuit offered, he remained in the running for the Grand National title each season.

A big part of his success story came from bringing Richard and Maurice into the business. When the boys were still in high school, they began helping out on their father's cars when classes ended— or after practice for one of the sports they played. In time, they began their long study of engines, painstakingly learning through trial and error the ways to get the most out of the family cars. "It's not like it is now. Years ago, you couldn't go out and buy every piece for a race car," says Maurice. "We'd work out of a junkyard a lot. You'd develop it to [suit] your own car."

Throughout his years in high school, Richard was content to do nothing more than build the cars and engines; when high school ended, and he began working on the cars full-time, he was taken with the idea that he might want to get behind the wheel himself. So at eighteen, after much nervous hesitation, he worked up the courage to ask his father if he could take a crack at it. Lee knew exactly what was on his boy's mind but he wanted him to wait a few years, until he was twenty-one. There were no questions asked; Richard kept working on the cars, building the engines and learning the business along with Maurice. Part of the reason for the hesitation was that Lee wanted Richard and Maurice to take business classes at the local college, as he had.

Meanwhile, Lee enjoyed continued driving success. During the first eleven years of the sport, beginning in 1949, he never placed lower than fourth in annual points. And his 1958 Grand National championship was the first of two consecutive titles; having also won in 1954, he became NASCAR's first three-time winner. By the time Richard turned twenty-one and asked his father for another shot, Lee Petty was prospering to the point where he could afford to pay for the inevitable training period his son would need to go through.

Richard's stock car racing experience would soon come well earned, through the necessary period of crashing and rebuilding cars, learning the ways around a track and the right and wrong time to go into a turn. After some experience, he moved up through the pack, finishing better and better each race and then obsessively analyzing his strengths and faults.

In time, Richard Petty perfected the art of pursuit; he became the man stalking you relentlessly in the rearview mirror. He had excellent equipment, which he knew inside and out, and an uncanny ability to be within striking distance when the race came toward its end. Being the smart, observant kid he was, he had followed his father's lead in terms of driving style and then came to master it. To honor his father, who drove the No. 42 car, Richard—after stints with 142 and 42A—settled on No. 43: "So we could be like a team," he says.

To his peers, Lee Petty was a relentless, ultra-serious competitor when it came to his livelihood. Richard learned this firsthand at the start of his career, after a 1959 dirt-track race in Atlanta. It was a race Richard had won—after taking the checkered flag, he stood proudly in victory lane holding his trophy, until he learned a protest had been filed by one of the other drivers. Lee Petty, convinced the flag had come down on the ninety-ninth lap, kept running one more set of turns. Race officials soon realized the elder Petty was right. Richard came away with second place.

Lee also had his share of clashes with drivers whose more fun-loving, free-wheeling style differed greatly from his own. A man who spent most of his free time with his family, Petty's struggles with some of his fellow competitors dominated an occasional early NASCAR race, and often ended with some trading of paint. Says Maurice, "Even though that was his livelihood more so than theirs—they were driving for somebody else—Mr. Lee still stood toe-to-toe with 'em."

Which goes a long way toward explaining why Petty earned the respect of the majority of his fellow drivers—quite a few of whom eventually drove for him. He also earned the admiration of fans who thought enough of him that he was voted the most popular driver award in 1953 and 1954.

"It's a people business—you got people working for you, you meet people, you got fans, you got sponsors, and so his big deal was, you got to sell yourself before you can sell your product. That was always his big saying," says Richard of his father. "Even though I learned mechanical ability and a bunch of this driving deal from him, the biggest thing that's lasted throughout life probably is you gotta get along with people. That makes everything else work."

So Richard Petty always won with a disarming smile and a nod of respect. His favorite course at business school had been penmanship; it was there that he learned the flowery signature that became another of his trademarks. Before and after races, he would greet fans who came out to the track, talk to them, and give autographs for the asking without hesitation. He was new to the game and already on his way to being its first true ambassador.

On February 20, 1959, the Daytona International Speedway debuted. For the inaugural 500, Lee Petty, even with a fast '59 Oldsmobile beneath him, qualified fifteenth. Richard qualified sixth.

The younger Petty didn't last long after they dropped the flag, however. A victim of a blown engine, he had to retire after eight laps of the two hundred set for the race. His father had better luck. It took him awhile but by the three-quarter point, Lee Petty had finally worked his way through the dense pack to take the lead. With ten laps remaining, there were two front-runners way ahead of the rest of the field: Petty and Johnny Beauchamp, a veteran of a different stock circuit who was making only his sixth NASCAR start. As the race wound down off turn four on the final lap, Petty, Beauchamp and Joe Weatherly—driving one lap down—ran three wide toward the finish. When the trio took the checkered flag, it appeared Beauchamp was the victor.

The only problem was, Lee Petty knew he had won, and he wasn't alone. Many fans, competitors and people in the press agreed with him, even as Beauchamp was being feted, garnering the winner's trophy and a kiss from the beautiful presenter. After the ceremony, Petty filed a formal complaint with Bill France. But France hadn't installed a photo-finish camera at the track. Petty didn't care; he wasn't going anywhere until someone came forward with proof. So he camped there in Daytona with his family in tow.

The subsequent investigation lasted three days, as France sifted through mounds of photos and movies taken by the press and people in the stands. In the end, France announced that Petty indeed had won the race. "It took 'em till Wednesday before they made a final decision," recalls Richard. "That was a big deal, you know, kind of an emotional deal. We knew we won the race and weren't getting it. But it worked its way out."

The win also turned out to be a sign of good things to come. After having won the championship in 1958 on the strength of seven victories and twenty-eight top-fives in fifty races, Lee outdid himself in 1959, having a historic year. With eleven wins—including his lucrative Daytona payday—and twenty-seven top-fives, he won his second championship and record earnings of almost $50,000. The next year, Richard came into his own, finishing second in the points chase to his father's sixth. And Richard's kid brother Maurice, then twenty-one, got his shot to move from the garage to the driver's seat. Maurice made two starts that produced two top-ten finishes. All in all, Petty Enterprises had become one of NASCAR's thriving success stories.

Two days before the start of the 1961 Daytona 500, NASCAR held a pair of hundred-mile qualifying races to determine who would make up the field. The roster for the first race included Richard Petty; his father ended up in the second. By day's end, the fact that neither driver made the final grid would be the least of the family's troubles.

The day started poorly when Richard got a nudge from Junior Johnson toward the conclusion of the first qualifier. The tap was enough to make him lose control of the car, sending it over a wall.

Lee Petty still had an opportunity to make the race, and toward the end of the second qualifier, he found himself in the midst of an impressive run. His closest competitor, ironically enough, was his Daytona challenger from two years earlier, Johnny Beauchamp.

It looked like the pair might be set for another last-lap duel on the superspeedway, this time with driver-owner Banjo Matthews in fast pursuit. As Petty and Beauchamp headed toward turn four, Petty saw Matthews beginning to swerve into a spin and tried to clear out of the way as he approached the high banking; unfortunately, Beauchamp didn't see Matthews spin, and he and Petty connected.

Momentum carried the two cars swiftly up the 31-degree banking where they scaled the wall and vaulted over.

By the time Lee Petty eventually landed, his No. 42 automobile had journeyed almost to the parking lot. Rescue crews freed him from the wreck and rushed him to the hospital.

"All of a sudden here I was, what, twenty-three years old, maybe twenty-four, and my brother was a year younger than I was, and we'd always done what he said to," remembers Richard. "We had two brand-new cars and we went to Daytona. I crashed in one race and totalled it out, and he crashed in the other race, and there was no sponsorship, so there was no money. And we go in and talk to him and he says, 'Go on up to the dealership and get another car; start getting it ready.'"

The brothers did so, but during their father's long recovery Richard and Maurice were faced with the sudden realization that they were now the business; there would be no relying on their father for all the day-to-day answers.

"We were having to do the business part of it, all the mechanical part, all the thinking, the strategy, whatever it was," Richard says. "All of a sudden, you were running the family business, and there was no money."

"At the time it was, 'How are we gonna do this? Can we survive? Can we stay in racing?'" recalls Maurice. "You know, it was just always a question, a doubt, in your mind, 'Can we survive this deal?'"

The boys discovered they needed very little motivation to work together and follow their father's business instincts. True, they had lost some money, but they still had their chief assets: an excellent young driver and a talented mechanic.

"From my standpoint, and from my brother's standpoint, here's these boys running a business, so they had to learn," says Richard. "And you picked that stuff up real dang quick when your family depends on you. By that time, I'd already married and had Kyle, and then Sharon came along just a year behind. So I had a family of my own. And my brother was married and he had a daughter. So, you know, we were looking after a lot of people all at one time who had always depended on Daddy to do it. I grew up real quick. But I look back on it and though it was bad on Daddy, it was good on my brother and myself, because we were able to cope with business and problems at a very young age."

Richard won two races in 1961, and although he didn't post the numbers he had the season before, he did end up with eighteen top-fives in forty-two races, good enough for eighth on the annual points list. Five other drivers drove for Petty Enterprises that year, including Maurice, who, in his second year of trying to learn the ropes, came away with four top-tens in nine races, to go along with a few instructive mishaps. The Petty brothers were staying afloat.

Lee, testing to see if he could pick up where he left off, attempted a comeback. He started a few races each of the next several years, but the urge and competitive desire were no longer there. Meanwhile, his sons continued to handle general operations at Petty Enterprises, having come into their own as businessmen in his absence. It was a bitter pill for the proud patriarch to swallow and matters inevitably came to a head between father and sons.

"When he came back, he stepped in and started trying to help and all this stuff," Richard says. "And we were in Martinsville, and me and him and my brother got in an argument over something. And he come in the next day and said, 'It's y'alls. Y'all take care of it.' He said, 'I'm outta here.' Grabbed his golf clubs and took off. And he's been basically out of the business ever since."

Another matter that came to a head involved Maurice Petty's driving aspirations. Publicly, Maurice and Richard have always been polar opposites: Richard is an outgoing driving legend who never refuses an interview; his clothes—jeans, cowboy hat, and sunglasses—are a trademark; and he has one of the world's most recognizable, eye-catching signatures, punctuated by a "43." Maurice, uncomfortable in the spotlight, is reserved about his many accomplishments (which include building the engines for cars that have won a record 198 times in NASCAR history), rarely gives interviews, and makes much less use of his signature. But for a time in the early 1960s, Maurice got his chance to follow his father and brother to driving fame.

"I was sort of doing it in between, mostly after Lee got hurt," he recalls. "Richard and myself, we were running the business, gettin' started and racin'. I would just run every now and then. I'd pick and choose my races. And it was just a fun time, you know. My best deal was when we used to run on a lot of dirt tracks, somewhere you could broad slide one and get back on it."

Maurice was good enough behind the wheel to record sixteen top-tens in twenty-six Grand National races throughout the early 1960s. He did, however, also experience his share of crashes, and at some point, it was decided that he would concentrate solely on building engines. It may well have been a simple matter of timing: Richard could work full-time on developing his driving because he started when there was more money around to devote to it. When it came time for Maurice to start racing, Richard was the only bona fide meal ticket behind the wheel at Petty Enterprises, and there were more family members to feed. Had Lee been healthy and driving as well, chances are Maurice would have had a longer shot.

Instead, a practical choice was made to keep the brothers doing what they each did best. Exactly how the decision was made is still up for debate.

Richard claims his brother made this choice himself. "He got a chance, and he didn't run as much as I did, but once we were able to run him, we'd run him. Yeah, that was his decision. Daddy didn't make it and I didn't make it; he made it himself. Being he made that decision, it made it easy for him to always live with it. There was never any conflict of me getting to be in the limelight or whatever it was, you know. There was never any jealousy or any of that stuff."

Maurice doesn't remember it exactly the same way, but he'd also be the first to admit it doesn't matter: It all turned out pretty well in the long run.

"At that time I missed it, very much, absolutely," he says of his driving days. "But I was using up money that could have been put toward Richard. He was doing good, and at that time it wasn't the right thing to do. And as time went on [driving] got less and less meaningful to me."

Beginning in 1962, Richard and Maurice Petty got down to the business at hand. In 1964, Richard won his first NASCAR Grand National (now NASCAR Winston Cup Series) championship after finishing second two years running. In those three years, Petty won 31 races and finished in the top ten 121 times in 167 contests. In his championship season, he won over $100,000 for the first time and claimed his first Daytona 500 victory.

Part of that success no doubt had to do with superior equipment. In 1964, Chrysler developed their powerful hemi engine. With that under the hood—and Maurice preparing the ride—the No. 43 car squashed the competition.

As they continued to work together to build their business through the mid-1960s, the brothers Petty went through their disagreements. They were stubborn perfectionists, each believing they knew the best way to build the perfect ride. But in the garage, as in business, they compromised. As the decade progressed, they helped shape their sport.

"Oh, we used to fight all the time about something," recalls Richard. "I got scars here, I got scars right there. We fought when we were little. About '56, '57 was the last time I remember us having a fight. I think we finally decided we were big enough then to hurt each other. We had a lot of arguments, now, ain't no doubt about that. But with the arguments, we were after the same thing: We wanted to win. He had his ideas and I had my ideas. We'd usually settle on somewhere between me and him, and we got pretty good at it. Look, he built more winning engines than anyone. Take two or three of the best ones that's ever been and they ain't even close to him."

Adds Maurice, "We had a good driver, you know, and luckily we were fortunate enough to keep all our pieces together. A lot of credit goes to Richard and his driving style. Here again, we didn't know anything else. It was our livelihood. We ran the business a lot like Lee ran it. It put bread on the table, and you had to do it. You *had* to do it."

Richard and Maurice Petty—Petty's Enterprises

Two-thirds of the way through Richard Petty's 1967 season, he joined the other NASCAR regulars in Tennessee for the Nashville 400, run on a half-mile paved track. At the time, Petty was in the midst of a season for the ages, one that seemed to defy all conventional logic in terms of his ability to win. Considering that Ford Motor Company had returned to NASCAR racing at the end of 1966 with the introduction of an engine that could compete with Chrysler's famed hemi, Petty and his hemi should have run into trouble early on in 1967. Instead, he outmuscled the field on most occasions—when he wasn't out-strategizing them. And while it was true he had excellent equipment, Petty's 1967 Plymouth had been prepared essentially the same way as the '66 had. In 1966 he'd won only eight times. But with the circuit heading to Nashville and thirty-four races on the books for 1967, Petty had already won an astonishing sixteen times. Up to that time, the most races ever won in a full season were Tim Flock's eighteen in 1955. In 1967, Flock's record didn't seem to have a chance.

Once the race started that Sunday in Nashville, however, it became obvious that Petty would probably not be adding it to his victory total. In the early going, the car wasn't running well, and he found himself way behind and fading. His day didn't improve when he scraped a wall and tore off part of the rear of his car.

Not surprisingly, everything about the Plymouth felt out of line as he drove it into the pits. Petty's cousin—and crew chief—Dale Inman, Maurice, and the rest of the crew lined everything up in the car as best they could and sent their driver on his way, where he joined the pack more than ten laps behind. That deficit made Petty really mad, which made him run faster.

He had no real thoughts of catching the field that day, however, even though his damaged car seemed to respond much better after the stop. More than half the four hundred laps were still left to run; perhaps, thought Petty, he could move up enough to get a top-five finish.

But then strange things began to happen throughout the rest of the field. As Petty recalls, "Whoever was leading the race had trouble, then the next guy, he had trouble." The "trouble" soon began to take on the quality of an epidemic. At the front of the pack, Bobby Allison developed engine problems. The same fate hit Dick Hutcherson. Two more top drivers went out with the same difficulty. Earlier in the race, one driver had developed engine trouble and the race leader, trying to get around him, went into a wall, knocking them both out of the running. Leading the race seemed to carry with it some kind of punishment.

Meanwhile, Petty's car felt better and better as the day wore on. He kept moving through the pack, making up laps on the diminishing field.

With the race far from over, he made a pass on Friday Hassler and suddenly found only daylight in front of him. Eventually, Hassler would retire with, not surprisingly, engine problems. Petty stayed in front, overcoming, among other things, a late-race 360-degree spin. When he took the checkered flag in front, he had an astonishing five-lap lead over James Hylton.

"Stuff like that is beyond your control," he says, still a bit mystified by the event. "It's supernatural. We didn't outrun 'em, they eliminated themselves."

Richard Petty had found another way to win.

The week after Nashville, Dick Hutcherson won the race in Atlanta. It was the only race all season Petty wouldn't finish. Beginning with the next race, he did something that wouldn't ever be done again in NASCAR history—he won ten races in a row.

The streak made headlines all over the country. For Petty's fans, it was proof of his exceptional talent and prowess; others cried foul. His car was analyzed, studied, and inspected by NASCAR officials after races, and revealed nothing out of the ordinary. As each contest ended the same way, Ford executives shifted from concern to frustration to anger, especially since it had been proven that a stock car's Sunday victory affected the sale of the car the following week. They searched for solutions, trying to stay competitive.

All of a sudden, NASCAR had a bona fide curiosity on its hands, one that brought consumer interest in the sport to greater heights and added a legion of new fans. Before the streak—and the 1967 season itself—the sport had already developed a rich lore, with tales of triumph and tragedy, and of old-time champions who tested their mettle and metal in dirt-track matches. But in 1967, thanks to Richard Petty, NASCAR suddenly seemed to gain a mythology.

The affable Petty rode his success well. It had always been easy to like Richard Petty; in 1967, it became easier. At racetracks, he spoke to anybody who approached him, signed autograph after autograph, and flashed his winning smile. Even competitors acknowledged that it was easy to respect him. And as the streak continued, someone came up with an idea that quickly caught on, one that no one could dispute. Suddenly, Richard Petty was King of stock car racing.

Meanwhile, Richard and Maurice simply went about their business as if nothing had really changed, trying not to think too much about their good fortune. At season's end, the Petty brothers had amassed a total of twenty-seven wins; Richard ran in the top ten in forty out of forty-eight races.

Says Richard with a laugh, "Every time we started a season, we felt like we were gonna win all the races. We got pretty close that year."

That pivotal year would be a boon for Petty Enterprises. While Richard was always the public face for the company, he would not have achieved his success or status without the quiet vigilance and talent of his younger sibling. Together they argued, compromised, and built a dynasty.

● ● ●

Richard Petty built his career on the solid foundation of his father's success. But Petty's superstardom came courtesy of his and his brother's incredible 1967 season. Seventeen races into that year, Richard Petty became, at twenty-nine, the winningest driver in the history of his sport. His fifty-five career wins were one more than the previous career champion, his father, Lee. Two weeks before, when Richard had tied the record with a win in Richmond, his father reportedly said, "I've enjoyed having that record. I'm just glad that it's staying in the family."

Through the younger Petty's first seven wins of the 1967 season, five had come by at least a lap; one was by as much as three.

"After we'd won a few, that helped us win more, because the competition looked at us as, 'They can't be beat,'" remembers Richard. "And they didn't even race with you. I mean, they did, but they were psychologically beat before they started. And that helped us, too: Psychologically, we knew we were gonna win when we started. That helped me and the crew."

A few years earlier, Maurice Petty had given up his own driving dreams and devoted himself full-time to building his brother's engines. By the time the 1967 season arrived, the brothers had been running the business together for six years. The partnership's success could be attributed to the fact that each brother had had experience at the other's profession, making communication easier. Of course, it could also have had to do with a work ethic that kept Maurice at the shop endlessly, and once inspired Richard to famously inform his wife Linda that she would always come second to racing.

"I think we paid a lot more attention to detail," Maurice says. "Whatever you had a problem with, you would just work on it to make it better." And even if working with his brother wasn't always easy, their points of view always inspired the other.

"I can't say there's any rivalry," Maurice says of their relationship. "He got out and did his best at drivin' and I did my best preparing the cars, although sometimes, you know, you could do a little better.

"There would be a discussion or a compromise. And not to say we didn't have arguments, so to speak—we'd work it out."

• • •

Richard Petty's streak began on August 12th in Winston-Salem, at Bowman Gray Stadium; he started on the pole and led all 250 laps around the quarter-mile track, besting fellow Chrysler driver Jim Paschal by three. Fifty-one days later, at North Wilkesboro Speedway, he beat short-track master Dick Hutcherson by two.

What happened in between was, according to Petty, no big deal.

"Not when I was doing it," he says. "Our deal was, we'd run a race, and our next objective was winning the next one. We didn't sit around and think about how good we'd done. We'd make mistakes and we'd say, we're gonna fix them. I remember we left Greenville, South Carolina, and we were going to Martinsville, Virginia, and as we started home we were talking about Martinsville. That's the way we looked at it."

But as the wins piled up, the wonder of it wasn't lost on Richard's little brother. "Back then," he begins, "you raced and you drove back and forth; there was no such thing as flying as far as we were concerned, and they didn't have it on radios or TVs. You'd come home and it would be the middle of the night, and the folks at home would say, how'd you do? 'We won another one.' You know? 'Won again.' It was like it was supposed to happen. But I don't care who is on top today or yesterday or the day before, everybody in any sport gets to the top and they have one place to go: down the other side. How long can you stay on top?"

For the Pettys, the ride continued to the point where finally the national press began to take more notice. With each successive win, more reporters and fans approached the lanky driver with the toothy grin.

Meanwhile, Ford executives groused terribly. The company had reentered racing the year before, after a season-long hiatus due to NASCAR rulings that limited the use of some of their better equipment, claiming it gave some drivers an unfair advantage. Since the earliest days of NASCAR, President Bill France had successfully lured dealers and manufacturers to pledge their support by exploiting the direct link between a car's victories and how well it sold. Ford had won a slew of big races at the start of the season, but had failed since then. The streak was a thorn in the company's side.

Various Ford executives held a meeting in Dearborn, Michigan, to discuss ways they could possibly outdo Petty. A few drivers were brought in from competing racing circuits to be put into Fords to try their luck. Some races were stacked with Ford drivers. There was even speculation that regular Ford drivers would be fired for not performing.

"You heard rumors of it, and you know it went on—just listening to the fellow competitors in the Fords, you know," says Maurice of the company's tactics.

Meanwhile, Richard Petty had won four races in a row from the pole, including his first Darlington Southern 500 victory, which he'd captured by five laps after leading all but nineteen of them. Then came Hickory and Richmond, two short tracks, the former paved, the latter dirt. He didn't get the pole on either race, which, perhaps, was progress for other drivers. He did win both, though.

Automakers weren't the only people who tried different methods to change Petty's luck. Some rabid fans of various competitors tried almost anything to stop him.

"You got a lot of the hexes that they tried to put on you," recalls Maurice. "Witchcraft, you know, all kinds of stuff. People doing their thing, hollering, you know. If you don't believe in it, it ain't gonna happen. You believe in anything enough, you'll let it happen to you."

Meanwhile, Petty continued to go about his business. He won the pole for a 150-mile race in Beltsville, Maryland, and on September 15th, after a race-long battle with Bobby Allison, he took the lead two-thirds of the way and bested Allison by two laps. Two days later, racing again from the pole, he overcame an unscheduled pit stop (to clean excess mud off his windshield) that put him one lap down early to beat Dick Hutcherson in Hillsboro, North Carolina. Richard Petty had won eight races in a row.

The more he won, the more accessible Petty was to the public. Unlike other drivers, he always made a point of greeting fans and posing for pictures. "He really worked the crowds good, you know, and nobody showed him the way to do it," says Maurice. "It was his nature, and that's what he did."

Richard rarely got into tussles on the track and always made sure to leave the conflict there and not have it follow him to the next stop. With very few exceptions, competitors regarded him as a fair driver out to make a living like anybody else. He had some of the best equipment money could buy, to be sure, but it was hard to be jealous of someone who never seemed to brag about his good fortune. As NASCAR Hall-of-Famer and fellow second-generation driver Buddy Baker puts it, "Richard Petty and I were, I feel, great friends all the way through my entire racing career. He's the only one I know of that I never had a run-in with—and I drove for him for a couple of years. And my dad drove for [Richard and Maurice]."

The week after Hillsboro, the tour went to Martinsville where, on a half-mile track, Petty beat Hutcherson by four laps. ("Doesn't anything ever go wrong with him?" Hutcherson reportedly asked afterward.) Then the circuit returned to North Wilkesboro. The Ford presence was especially strong there, both in terms of drivers and executives. At the start of the race, Petty found a crowd of drivers in front of him, and as per his style, waited a little for traffic to open up so he could forge ahead. By the end of the race, he had led 256 out of 400 laps; once again, Hutcherson ran second, this time two laps shy. After the checkered flag fell, King Richard pulled into victory lane for the tenth time in a row, where he was show-ered with cheers by the crowd.

The press reception to the streak had grown huge. With two weeks till the next race, the Pettys headed east.

"Chrysler took us to New York City and had a big press confer-ence, because it got to be a big deal over the whole country," Richard recalls. "We were in our own little world doing our thing, and we weren't paying that much attention. They took us up there and they had all the press and all this stuff—first time we'd ever done anything quite like that."

The next race would be a more prominent one, the National 500 at the Charlotte Motor Speedway. Of his ten consecutive wins, Petty had won only one superspeedway race, the Southern 500. Charlotte was guaranteed to attract some lead-foot veterans who skipped many of the short-track races, preferring the big stage and bigger payout of the more prestigious stops. Ford planned on run-ning nine cars.

No Ford driver won the race, though. And for Petty, the streak came to an untimely end very early on. He fell a number of laps down, but unlike in Nashville, this time there would be no magic.

His engine blew not long after and he retired the car to the garage. Buddy Baker captured the day, the first win of his career.

Petty didn't win either of the last two races. In the season finale, he got a glimpse of his future when he tussled with eventual rival Bobby Allison and finished second, with David Pearson close behind. The season ended with Petty owning twenty-seven wins. He demolished the rest of the field on the way to his second championship.

Throughout the campaign, Petty gave much of the credit to Maurice and the rest of the crew. He knew he was coming in with great equipment; winning should be expected. Petty could be as self-effacing as he wanted to, but as the other NASCAR drivers understood, the King's feats in 1967 would never be duplicated— unless he himself did it again.

"It was one of those deals where if you won that much, these guys come and they weren't looking to win the race, they were just looking to run second," he says. "You know the same guy didn't run second all the time—might have run second in a couple of races, but it wasn't like I was outrunning one person. I was outrunning the whole field. It just made it phenomenal. It ain't supposed to happen like that but it did. We weren't doing anything different. We were just winning races."

One of the advantages Plymouth enjoyed in their association with Petty Enterprises was that before a big race in a particular city, Richard could be brought into a local dealership to meet and greet prospective customers. A Petty automobile would be set up nearby and Richard, accommodating and friendly as always, would greet the fans lined up around the block. Such priceless publicity made it even easier for Chrysler to provide the Petty brothers with some of the means to make their business run.

When major automakers decided to pull their direct support after a dispute with NASCAR in the early 1970s, all race teams were left to scramble for ways to make up the deficit. Several owners, such as the highly successful Holman-Moody team, were forced to close shop.

The Pettys were, of course, the hottest commodity in stock car racing, a proven public relations machine and now one greatly in need of extra capital. Luckily, the departure of the factories—who always frowned on having other company decals on their cars—created a huge opportunity for new sponsors.

Andy Granatelli, president of STP Corporation, had always wanted to get into NASCAR racing. Already a sponsor on the IndyCar circuit, he was looking for a way to expand further.

"Granatelli had been spot-checking into Winston Cup at that time," Richard recalls. "My brother and myself swung by the [STP] office in Chicago, stopped to talk to him one day, and sat down to work out a deal."

Coming to financial terms was no problem for all concerned. However, one huge sticking point nearly killed the deal. During negotiations, Richard actually stood up and prepared to leave unless Granatelli came to his senses on it.

"It was just—he wanted a red car, because he's always had red cars; that was his deal," Petty remembers. "I had no dang red car, mine was always blue."

The No. 43 car had always been "Petty Blue," and Richard had no intention of losing that. Finally, he suggested a compromise: half red and half blue. From such important agreements, successful long-term deals are sometimes born.

"I guess we were probably the first ones to have a national sponsor," Richard continues. "Other people then saw that it could be advantageous. Before, you had mom-and-pop local deals or a used car lot or something like that. And it was okay for a local deal but that wasn't enough money to make it work."

STP had gotten the most famous spokesman available for their products, Maurice hired a few more people and bought new equipment, and the Petty team had "The Racer's Edge." On January 23, 1972, Petty unveiled his STP/No. 43 red and Petty blue Plymouth for the season-opening race at Riverside, California, and won. By season's end, he had captured his second consecutive championship. Twenty-eight years later, NASCAR automobiles are billboards on wheels, covered with decals from national sponsors lured by the sport's appeal for selling everything from breakfast cereal to electronic equipment to fast food. The Pettys' pioneer relationship with STP would also be the sport's longest running. Until the middle of the 2000 season, the car still had the STP logo on it, front and center . . . and it's never lost the blue.

Kyle Petty Makes His Mark and the King Bids Farewell

In 1979, eighteen-year-old Kyle Petty swore he had never been behind the wheel of a stock car competitively before making preparations to do so in his first-ever contest, an ARCA race. Yet Kyle qualified second for the race, a preliminary feature run the day before the first Daytona 500 ever televised flag-to-flag. With all the hoopla surrounding the main event, the press was having a field day with the son of the King, and his unpredictable showing. Not that Kyle was a stranger to speed, but his experience had been, up to then, "unofficial" on the back roads back home.

During the race, when it counted, the younger Petty drove with unexpected skill. Holding the lead off turn four, a hard-charging challenger moving to his inside, Kyle ducked down low expertly to prevent the pass. From there it was a quick straightaway drive to a stunning victory. Even though he was a Petty, no one figured the teenager had a chance to win, but the many interested race fans gathered to honor stock's newest prince. Said Richard Petty afterward, "You know what it's like to win, son. Now all you got to do is learn how to drive."

Like his father, Kyle had spent a great deal of time learning the family business at the home garage and through pit-crew training in preparation for just such a debut, and to win the race using so mature a defensive strategy pleased many a racing historian.

What was good enough for the son soon turned out to work wonders for the father. The next day, in that most auspicious Daytona 500, leader Donnie Allison and challenger Cale Yarborough would knock each other right off the track on the last lap, generously leaving the race for the next two drivers, Richard Petty and Darrell Waltrip. Waltrip went low for the pass and Petty moved down to prevent it. No matter how far down Waltrip went, Petty was there, and seconds later, Petty secured another Daytona 500 victory in grand style, gaining a wondrous weekend double with Kyle. After years of working with his own father, and then establishing himself as a driver of even greater renown, Richard now had a son to bring along.

The only difference was, the son did not fit the typical driver profile. The handsome and outgoing Kyle, who shared his father's broad smile, lived life at a more relaxed pace than most other young drivers out to prove themselves on every step up the ranks.

There was always something of the dreamer about him. "I remember Kyle, when Richard used to buy him a brand-new pair of tennis shoes and he'd take them over and paint them in the fab shop," recalls Buddy Baker of a boyhood Kyle. "He'd have big red stars and half moons on 'em. Kyle always did hear a different drummer."

After finding instant success, Kyle Petty's testing ground would be a challenge, to say the least: Richard turned his boy loose on the NASCAR Winston Cup Series circuit, where he made his debut six months after his ARCA win, at the Talladega 500. At this, the fastest track on the circuit, he finished a better-than-respectable ninth, which only added fuel to the idea that Kyle was a natural who would compete with other highly regarded rookies such as Dale Earnhardt, Ricky Rudd, and Terry Labonte. To the press and public, he seemed the true can't-miss property and a marketing boon for the sport: Personable like his father, he, too, signed autographs for countless fans. In time, he'd master the Richard Petty trademark driving approach: staying near the front, waiting patiently for an opportunity, and then seizing the lead at the right moment. No one had the same aura and clout in racing circles as the King; everyone expected his son to add to the legacy.

That Kyle didn't rise to become racing's second coming in the face of such overwhelming expectations does not, in 20/20 hindsight, seem surprising. For decades, insiders have speculated about just why Kyle has only eight wins and as many poles to his credit, numbers which pale in comparison to his father's two hundred victories. Some maintain that while Kyle might have learned early on everything there is to know about setting up a car, going back to his days of working the pits for his father while still in his teens, driving was not as much of an obsession to him. Richard Petty always viewed driving as a game, something primarily to enjoy, but he was also deadly serious about winning, having learned under the tutelage of his father, who viewed racing as the necessary method of putting food on the table. Many others say Kyle's mixed fortunes were mainly financial, that for the first six years of his career, he drove for his dad's Petty Enterprises team, where the pair occasionally tussled due partly to the fact that budgets were tight.

On this point, Richard sadly concurs. "We tried to start Kyle off in Winston Cup, without enough money to run two cars," he says. "That hurt me *and* him."

Still, few people could ever regard Richard Petty with as much reverence as his son. The man Kyle still calls King was mentor, teacher, and inspiration, along with being the unattainable example of stock car greatness.

"There wasn't any competition, [between us] 'cause he was so much better than I was," Kyle says. "That's like Michael Jordan shooting basketball in the backyard with his eighteen-year-old. Even though we were racing on the same speedway, I was in a totally different league—in a totally different division, it seemed like. And it took a couple of years before we ever got a chance to run competitive. But by that time, I was coming up one side of the mountain, and he was going down the backside of his mountain."

After decades of success, things began to shift for Petty Enterprises in 1979. Richard won his seventh driving championship that year, but it would be his last. In the ensuing years, with Richard winning fewer races and Kyle learning how to win, there was less money that could be devoted to running both drivers. At the same time, the company switched from Chrysler cars to General Motors to try to get a better edge. Dealing with unfamiliar equipment was difficult, to say the least, for Maurice.

In 1983, Richard and Maurice clashed in the biggest crisis of their partnership. After a couple of early-season wins, Richard began a frustrating drought; tensions built between the brothers as Richard demanded that Maurice somehow find a way to get him more horsepower. He got it, but not the way either brother wanted it.

Three-quarters through the late-season fall race in Charlotte, Petty was running near the lead, but not close enough to be a threat, when a caution sent the drivers into the pits. Petty emerged and after the green-flag racing started again, his car suddenly began to perform as if it had woken from a slumber. In quick time, he effortlessly passed leader Darrell Waltrip and cruised to career win number 198. He was celebrating in victory lane when he was summoned to the garage area. In a post-race inspection, NASCAR officials discovered two infractions on his car. During the pit stop, Petty's crew had equipped him with four left-side tires; the tires, with their increased grip, had allowed him to power ahead. His other advantage came under the hood: NASCAR permitted only 358.1 cubic-inch engines. Petty's was almost 24 cubic inches bigger.

Although NASCAR let his victory stand, Petty was fined a whopping $35,000, not to mention a considerable amount of NASCAR Winston Cup Series points.

Petty insisted he knew nothing of the unapproved changes to the car; Maurice accepted all fault. In fact, the brothers had a clear delineation of responsibilities; Richard had long since stopped being involved in engine-building. His call for greater horsepower had, in his crew's interpretation, meant maybe he could use a little extra playing with the rules.

To have his image tarnished angered Richard tremendously. After the race, he promised that changes in the business would be coming. Still, nobody could have predicted his announcement a few days later that, for the 1984 season, he'd leave Petty Enterprises with STP sponsorship in tow, and drive instead for a Los Angeles record executive named Mike Curb. Then a year later, Kyle, frustrated with the lack of a competitive financial situation, decided to leave as well. With no drivers in the stable for 1985, Petty Enterprises seemed doomed.

Maurice refused to let that happen to his family business. In 1985, on a virtual shoestring, he managed to field cars in four races. In 1984, with Kyle driving, the company had made $329,920; in 1985, they pulled in less than $24,000.

To some, it must have seemed like little more than a symbolic gesture. In fact, the gesture worked. In 1984, Richard earned two wins—his only two NASCAR Winston Cup Series triumphs using engines not built by Maurice—to bring the total up to two hundred. Then, after the 1985 season, he looked back at all his family had built in thirty-five years of racing and saw it falling apart. Kyle had gone, something which upset him greatly. But there would be no chance of Kyle ever returning unless there was something to return to. In 1986, Richard reunited with his brother.

• • •

Seeking better stock car racing fortunes elsewhere, Kyle, who never won a race for Petty Enterprises, joined up with one of the best teams on the circuit, that of the Wood Brothers; it was for the Woods that he earned his first victory in 1986, and began a four-year working relationship that immediately improved his annual standing in NASCAR Winston Cup Series points.

By then, Kyle had developed an appeal among fans as, in a way, the anti-Richard. His father was NASCAR's name above the title, arguably the only driver whose appeal superseded that of his sport. Kyle seemed something of a racing anomaly. Unlike many on the circuit, whose reputations started and stopped with their on-track record and behavior, Kyle was a guitar-strumming, would-be country singer who did some recording and talked about balancing two careers. Kyle's politics are liberal. The conservative Richard Petty counted President Ronald Reagan among his friends.

Kyle's driving career took an even more positive turn when he signed to race in 1989 for Felix Sabates, the millionaire who'd escaped Castro's Cuba and made a fortune in electronics, only to channel his funds into his passion for racing. Under Sabates, Petty gave up thoughts of music and brought his racing performance up to new levels, which included two fifth-place NASCAR Winston Cup Series points finishes. His total number of wins and poles increased and people stopped claiming that Kyle Petty wasn't "hungry" enough.

Still, nobody started thinking he would give up his status as NASCAR's Harley-riding, long-haired free spirit, and an instant favorite among younger racing fans. Before the May 1991 race at Talladega, he'd gotten his first haircut in about a year. It was, he'd say later, a big mistake. At one point in the race, the competitors pitted during a caution and reemerged with Ernie Irvan in front. The problem was, Irvan found himself without a drafting partner. He was driving down the center of the track with two speedy multi-car convoys gaining ground on either side of him. In short order, Irvan fell from first to tenth.

While trying to merge into one of the competing lines of cars, Irvan's right front fender hit Petty's rear quarter panel. The move sent Kyle spinning down toward the bottom of the track, where his car now lay directly in the pathway of Irvan, who sent him into Mark Martin. The damage left Petty with a broken leg that forced him to the sidelines for half a season—and kept the now-superstitious racer out of a barber's chair for much longer.

Kyle enjoyed several quality seasons with Sabates, but beginning in 1994, things took a turn in the wrong direction. Through three seasons, Petty came away with only one win and no poles, a reversal of fortune that put a chill on the warm relationship between driver and owner. They agreed to part ways after the 1996 season.

After Kyle's stint with Sabates, the timing seemed right for his return to the home garage—a situation his father had long hoped for. While Kyle had been driving for other teams, Richard and Maurice had done their best to keep Petty Enterprises competitive. While Maurice did not build any more winning NASCAR Winston Cup Series engines and Richard never made it back to victory lane as a driver, there were still some top-tens and money coming in. And Richard's reputations as a competitor and a towering figure in his sport remained intact.

In 1992, Richard ended his career behind the wheel at age fifty-five with an appropriately named, season-long Fan Appreciation Tour. Ironically enough, the King's last race, in Atlanta in 1992, was also the first race for the Kid, the then twenty-one-year-old Jeff Gordon.

For the next season, Petty Enterprises hired Rick Wilson as their primary driver and the company began their trek to return to the real business at hand—winning races. But with Richard Petty devoting himself exclusively to the business of team ownership, he wanted Kyle back to drive one of the family cars. It took some time, but father and son eventually forged a deal that had Kyle splintering off and running pe2, an additional arm of Petty Enterprises, beginning in 1997.

"I think working with your family in any way has its moments," Kyle admits. "Because you gotta realize that whatever you do at work, you're gonna take it home, no matter what. So I think that's a hard balancing act. You appreciate being a part of a family business a little bit more when you've stepped outside the family. So I think looking at it from that perspective, we have a lot closer business relationship, working relationship, and family relationship now than we've had in the past."

Kyle hopes that this second go-round at the family shop will lead him back to more positive results. Despite closing in on age forty, no one seems a more fitting driver for his No. 44 Hot Wheels Car, with its wild colors representing a sponsor devoted to the kid-like enjoyment of racing. As his father's STP sunglasses and cowboy hat were trademarks, Kyle's own trademark ponytail and earrings set him apart. There is a restlessness about him which has surfaced of late, while dressing down the press for their tendency to hype the proverbial "next big thing," and pining loudly for the sport to return to what he believes was a more exciting past. And he remains a strong conscience in NASCAR: In 1999, he marked the fifth year of leading his annual Kyle Petty's Hot Wheels Racing Charity Ride Across America, a seven-day slice of hog heaven wherein Harley riders—along with a number of NASCAR's top names, including Richard Petty, Kenny Schrader, Steve Park, and Joe Nemechek—journeyed from Ontario, California, to Trinity, North Carolina, in an effort to raise money for children's hospitals and the NASCAR Winston Cup Series Racing Wives Auxiliary Trust.

In 1999, Kyle's eyes were trained on the future in terms of racing, with an inspired, pointed set of goals. "When we talk about racing," he once said of conversations with his father and grandfather, "we don't tell old stories. We're trying to figure out how to make new stories." The only use of the past is as prologue. "If you don't learn from the past, then you're gonna repeat it at some point in time," he says, but then admits, "You know, as good as our past has been, we wouldn't mind repeating it a few times, as far as that goes."

There was no denying that the best chance for the right repetition came with a new young driver winding his way through the NASCAR Busch Series Grand National Division. That's where Adam Petty was learning his chops the same way his father Kyle and grandfather Richard once did.

The fourth-generation driver's bright life and potential perished in a pratice accident at New Hampsire International Speedway on May 12, 2000. And oh, what potential . . .

NASCAR's First Four-Generation Family

Three-quarters of the way through his first-ever ARCA-circuit stock car event, on September 30, 1998, Adam Petty did something he wasn't supposed to. While running second to Bobby Hamilton Jr. in the EasyCare Certified 100, Petty took his Spree-Prepaid Pontiac to the outside of the leader and passed him in turn four. Even though it worked, the high-speed maneuver frightened the eighteen-year-old Petty. This was the Charlotte Motor Speedway and you don't try to make a pass on turn four. That's what Adam had been told by two people he'd most often sought out for advice: his father, Kyle, and his grandfather. Didn't his elders, with their countless trips around Charlotte's 1.5-mile oval, know best?

Perhaps, but they weren't driving Adam's car. With fifteen laps to go, Adam sensed that this could be his night. His car certainly felt strong: Earlier, on lap twenty-nine, he'd bolted past pole-sitter Darrell Lanigan in a three-wide pass off turn two to take the lead. Now he was starting to put some distance between himself and Hamilton.

It was already a special night to begin with: His parents were there, as were his grandparents and several aunts and uncles. For Petty, who lived nearby in Thomasville, North Carolina, this race had the makings of a great family homecoming. Also in attendance were several NASCAR Winston Cup Series owners, there to scout out future talent.

The importance of the evening was also not lost on Mike Wallace, Rusty and Kenny Wallace's middle brother. Wallace, who for a number of years had driven his way through several racing circuits, including the NASCAR Winston Cup Series, passed Hamilton for second and then began to gain considerable ground on the leader. As the race was nearing its conclusion, he caught up with Petty.

With a lap to go, Wallace was on Petty's bumper, contemplating the move. He nudged Petty a little, but the young leader kept his poise and control. Wallace would have only one more shot: a fast duel coming out of turn four. He went up high, putting his car almost alongside Petty's. Wallace was fast inching up toward the lead. But Petty looked to his side and realized the challenger was going to run out of racetrack. He kept his foot on the floorboard, and with the thousand-watt smile that made him a favorite among fans and competitiors alike, took the most significant checkered flag of his young life, winning by less than the length of a car.

The crowd was jubilant as he navigated his way to victory lane, and as he did, he thought of all the efforts that had been made to get him to his great celebration. He had almost missed the race: During practice earlier in the week, he'd put some hurt on the car in a mishap in turn four. But his father helped him with the repairs and the team brought it back up to speed. It was only the latest case of Kyle Petty's aid to his son. Without Kyle's advice, help in setting up sponsors, and presence as a living example of the way of racing, Adam would never have made it to victory lane on that September night.

Emerging from the car to the cheers of the stomping crowd, Adam saw his father sprinting toward him, his long ponytail and earrings bobbing. The clean-cut, handsome young victor fought back tears as he hugged his father and his mother, Pattie. At eighteen years and three months old, he had just broken a twenty-year-old record, becoming the youngest driver ever to win an ARCA event. The man whose record he'd beaten by five months, Kyle Petty, stood in awe as he watched his son accept the trophy, and the same adulation that had been his in 1979 when he, too, captured his first-ever ARCA race. Next to Kyle stood his father, Richard Petty, the man Kyle still admires more than any other. But the night would belong to Adam. Richard would say later on that Adam's win meant more to him than any of his own.

For Kyle, long considered the most free-spirited and liberal-thinking driver in NASCAR, this was a different kind of triumph. After dealing with varying degrees of success in his own career in the face of great expectations, he had helped channel his son's enthusiasm to this moment.

"When you win a race, there's a satisfaction that you've done something and that the team has done something," Kyle began, less than a year after Adam's win. "But when your son does something, you're extremely proud of how they've grown and what they've done. And you look at him standing in victory lane, and you see him as a three-year-old, and as an eight-year-old, and as a ten-year-old. So it's better for me to remember things my father did and things that Adam did, than it is for me to be emotional about things that I've done."

The story goes that when Adam Petty was about ten, he came home after finishing first in a go-kart race and showed his father the winnings. Having been given the option of taking the money or a trophy, the boy chose the former. That's when Kyle laid out some realities to his son: At that young age, racing was about having fun, not making a living. It was about building memories instead of a bank account. There'd be plenty of time for the money later on if he wanted it. The next day, Adam went back and made the exchange. "You'll always remember the trophy," his father told him.

Eight years later, Kyle related that "my main advice to him, when he started playing with go-karts, and then legends cars, and then moved on to Late Model cars: Have fun doing it. Treat it like you're a kid. Drive like you're a kid, act like you're a kid. You're eighteen years old; you're still able to be a kid. It's gotta be fun. You have to love it. And that's what he's always been able to do. That's why I told him [then that] the money doesn't make any difference. Because when you're eighty years old you'll remember the trophies, but the money has been long spent."

Whether it's winnings or trophies, Adam's desire to start collecting began early. He was running go-karts at age six, and when he hit his teens, he'd had enough success and experience to think about moving up to stocks.

"I loved to wake up every Friday and Saturday, 'cause I knew Friday night I'd be at some go-kart track, and Saturday night I'd be at another go-kart track," he said of those days. "And I think my dad realized then, too, that I was really dedicated." So much so that Kyle bought his boy a Late Model Stock car chassis for his fourteenth birthday and then, in that tried-and-true method of testing a young driver's seriousness, told him to get the parts and put the car together himself. After some starts and stops, Adam finally made the commitment, put the car in shape, and didn't look back.

For years, Adam learned on and off the track what it would take to succeed in racing. He started driving Late Model stocks at fifteen, his father guiding his progress. In time, he built his strength by taking on his dad's personal trainer, losing seventy pounds, and changing to a more fruits and vegetables-based diet. Unlike his grandfather and his father, he never even tried to play high school sports, intent instead on spending more time in the garage. That was also his motivation to finish high school a semester early, which he did thanks to an increased course load and a private tutor. Then in 1998, he moved to Grand Rapids, Michigan, to start driving on the ASA circuit. It was there, competing in the circuit's longer races, that such NASCAR Winston Cup Series stars as Mark Martin and Rusty Wallace had cut their teeth, getting a better grasp of the physical strain one must endure in a race car. Twenty years after Kyle Petty began his career in a NASCAR Winston Cup Series ride, he made sure his son was continuing the steady climb up the ranks, away from the brightest part of the NASCAR spotlight.

It did not take Adam Petty long to attract attention. He finished his first ASA race running in 19th place, although he'd run as well as seventh for a time. He won a pole in his fifth race, surprising a great many people, including his father.

With that the case, nobody expected the result of Adam's seventh race, the Kansas City Excitement 300 at Odessa, Missouri's I-70 Speedway. It was a hard race to call to begin with, thanks to twelve cautions that would end the day for fifteen of the field's twenty-six teams before the checkered flag came out. Winning the race would take a quality car, a lot of luck, and the strategy of a veteran. Early on, Petty was running two laps down, but his car responded well as the going continued—so well, in fact, that in time, he began running with the leaders. When a caution came out in lap 225 out of 300, he went into the pits in first place. He decided to change tires and when he got back out, he'd dropped down to sixth. But by lap 234, Adam had moved back up to second behind ASA veteran Scott Hansen.

Another caution on lap 258 sent Petty to the pits again—this time, he and crew chief Chris Bradley decided to put on two fresh tires. Petty reemerged running behind leaders Hansen and Rick Beebe, who'd decided not to pit during the caution.

Petty's somewhat risky strategy proved to be an excellent one.

At one point, he shot from fourth to second in a lap. The near-sellout crowd, aware that they could be witnessing auto racing history, leapt to cheer for the seventeen-year-old rookie. Another caution forced a restart on lap 280. Two laps later, Petty took the lead. He'd be challenged over the last twenty laps, but nobody would be strong enough. As he crossed the finish line in front, looking behind him, Petty seemed more surprised than anybody. With this victory, he'd have to get used to being measured by history: He became the youngest winner ever for an ASA-sanctioned event, beating Mark Martin by four months. He was about a month shy of his eighteenth birthday.

When the celebrating began, the first thing Adam did was ask for a cell phone. On the other end of the line, Kyle Petty could hear the jubilant cries of the crowd. "Where are you?" he asked his son.

"In victory lane," Adam yelled.

After the race, Adam solidified his link to his grandfather by picking up another of the King's trademark gestures—he stayed around the track for an hour and half to sign autographs for anyone who wanted one.

In 1999, Adam ran full-time on the NASCAR Busch Series Grand National Division, earning respectable numbers in the first of a planned two-year stint. In addition to the experience, he enjoyed a terrific fringe benefit—the chance to spend a great deal more time with his dad. And for Kyle, who traveled the NASCAR Winston Cup Series circuit through much of Adam's youth, it was a rarely-afforded opportunity to play catch-up with his son. Not surprisingly, the pair rediscovered a great deal of common ground.

Prior to Adam's death in May, the two discussed their relationship. "I'm thirty-eight and he's eighteen, but, you know, we're driving race cars, having fun, travelling around the country; living in a camper about ninety percent of the time," Kyle said. "When we're on the road, most of the time it's just he and I. [My wife] Pattie goes a lot, but not as much as Adam and I go. So, you know, it's more we go out to dinner together, we stay on the bus together, and we talk racing. I watch his race on Saturdays—and he tells me what he thinks he did wrong, and I tell him what I think he did wrong. And then he watches me on Sunday and tells me what I do wrong. We've always been father and son, but, I think, at some point in time, it's evolved a bit deeper."

"We have a cool relationship," Adam concurred. "It's a father-and-son relationship Monday to Wednesday, but I think Wednesday to Sunday we're more brothers or best friends than we are anything. We share a whole lot of information together at the racetrack, and he helps me more than anybody in the whole world. We room together. I have a bus that I take to the track that's mine, and he has his own bus. But half the time I just room with him in his."

"I'm so close with my dad that if I ever left and went to drive for somebody else, I don't know what I'd do," Adam once said. "Hopefully one day I'll come home and get in the 43 car or the 44 car. But, you know, having my dad there means more to me than anything in the world. I could never say how much he helps me. Some people say, you know, you've got to talk to little Earnhardt or some of the Wallace brothers. And they ask about their brother's or their father's racing. And they'll say it's a double-edged sword. I have yet to find the sharp side of that sword—it's been nothing but dull for me. So it's been pretty easy so far, having the last name Petty and being with him."

Adam ran just one NASCAR Winston Cup Series race, finishing 40th in the race in Fort Worth in the spring of 2000. Yet in doing so he made history, becoming pro sports' first fourth-generation athlete, creating a link back to his great-grandfather, Lee. Three days after that debut, the Petty family patriarch succumbed to complications after surgery for a stomach aneurysm; he was eighty-six.

There was grief, but also a sense of optimism. Adam's early successes were supposed to be only a proud prelude. But his passing on May 12, 2000, cut short his burgeoning career.

And yet the one overriding truth about Adam is that he was committed to his sport. Kyle understood that, even as he once summed up the risks of the business. "Everybody worries about their kids, whether they're driving a racecar or whether you send them down to the corner store," he said. "But at some point you just have to put your trust in the Lord and say, 'I'm giving him to You, and You're gonna have to take care of him.'"

It is the family's faith that continues to sustain them now. This event can't help but change the picture of a family, but if anything, it has brought the Pettys closer together, and made them still more aware of how deeply they are revered. One wondered for a time if Adam's passing would dull their taste for the sport he loved, but Kyle returned to the track and picked up where his family left off, knowing Adam would have wanted it that way.

A day after the accident, Adam's fellow NASCAR Busch Series drivers lined up for the Busch 200. Pole-sitter Tim Fedewa let some distance fall between himself and the pace car—in the symbolic missing pole-sitter formation—and then the green flag waved. Tim and the others then took off and went wide open. They drove as fast and as hard as they could, doing what Adam Petty loved best.

13
The Wallace Brothers

Russ Wallace held a number of jobs throughout his professional life, auto mechanic in a car dealership and newspaper deliveryman among them. For a time he worked in the family business, his brother's vacuum and janitorial supply company. No vocation of his, however, would match the thrill of what he chose to do on many a Saturday and Sunday during the 1960s. On local dirt and asphalt tracks near his St. Louis home, Wallace went about winning races. Driving the stock cars he'd build in the backyard as a hobby and a passion, Wallace, always aggressive behind the wheel, compiled a memorable record in his career—especially according to his sons. Watching their dad race, following him to the tracks, and eventually helping him build winning automobiles, the impressionable youths were struck with a hankering to begin a different sort of family business. And after tasting varying degrees of success, the trio—Rusty, Kenny, and Mike Wallace—would become, in 1991, the first set of three brothers in thirty years to race together in a NASCAR Winston Cup Series event. And it all came from ambition born at the local tracks around their St. Louis home, thanks to a father with an inspiring hobby.

"He used to run a couple of little racetracks in Missouri," recalls Russ's middle son, Mike. "I was a little kid and I used to be able to sell Sno-Kones. I watched my dad race and I made a nickel a Sno-Kone, and I'd end the night with five bucks. I thought I was big-time rich—king of the world. That's probably one of my first fond memories of racing. My dad knew how to win races."

It would take years for Mike—whom his younger brother Kenny calls the natural driver among the three siblings—to fully embrace the profession after also working other jobs, but he, too, would learn how to win races in one of the highest levels of his sport: The NASCAR Craftsman Truck Series.

Kenny, Mike's junior by four years, still looks back and revels in the camaraderie and "the excitement of knowing how good my dad was and that we always had a shot at winning the race. That and the memory of after the race going to a truck stop or something like that; eating and just being in the atmosphere of racing with the family made us really close. I just cherish that time of all of us being together and racing." Kenny, the most accommodating of the brothers, suffered from always being too young to be a part of his dad's crew. His desire to learn whatever he could about the sport on the way to becoming a NASCAR driver meant putting up with some financial hardships, while at other times he enjoyed the generosity of his oldest brother, who financed Kenny's NASCAR Busch Series ride for several years. Kenny is now growing into a more threatening presence on the NASCAR Winston Cup Series circuit.

But of the Wallaces, it is the oldest brother, Rusty—the charismatic one, the exceptionally focused one, the brash short-track specialist with a winning-is-everything attitude—who has risen to heights seen by very few drivers in his sport's history. The NASCAR Rookie of the Year in 1984; NASCAR Winston Cup Series and IROC champion in 1989—a year wherein he earned $2,247,950; winner of fifty races who was named one of NASCAR's 50 Greatest Drivers in 1998; Rusty, three years older than Mike, has made the Wallace name a successful one even beyond stock car circles. He did it by always being in touch with the slightest behavioral cues of his car, keeping aware of the automobile's maneuverability and getting the most out of his ride—tricks he'd started to learn during his apprenticeship with his father.

"My brothers and myself, we just kinda helped Dad along," Rusty says. "When we came home from school everyday, and Dad and some of his friends were working on that race car, we couldn't help but get out there and help him. We grew up in the sport; that's all I knew. I never did get involved in baseball, football, stick-and-ball sports probably like most kids do, I was always in that doggone race car, messing around. In fact, one of those fellas who used to help Dad on his car, I ended up marrying his daughter. So that was a pretty in-house deal. I was always in the backyard of the house, there in the garage working on the cars, and it always stayed that way."

In his years of racing, Rusty has been consistent—as an outspoken voice, a strategic master, and an undeniable talent. His success has served as inspiration, a source of pride and motivation for his brothers. It is, however, their particular challenge to garner attention for themselves when their brother has made such a big impact.

Mike and Kenny Wallace understand the amount of work Rusty put into his career—especially Kenny, who, always the admiring younger sibling, spent much of his early career contributing to Rusty's rise while on his crew. More to the point, they've seen how Rusty's name opened doors for the Wallace family in NASCAR; it has always been up to Kenny and Mike to keep them ajar, and try to add their own names to the roster of champions.

The two younger brothers, with their strikingly different temperaments and considerable talents, have taken divergent paths in racing, leading often to success and sometimes to frustration. Yet both brothers remain committed to grabbing their fair share of the family spotlight—a situation Rusty would relish, especially in regards to Kenny, given the closeness of their relationship. As Mike Wallace says of himself and Kenny, "I think the main recognition, as far as Rusty [goes], along the way opened opportunities for me, not so much paved [the road]. Now it's strictly on our own. Our own performance is gonna get it done."

After he'd put some dents into one of his cars, Russ Wallace gave his oldest boy a chance to get into the racing game by making his sons a promise: If they could get the car fixed up just right, then when Rusty turned sixteen in 1973, he'd get the chance to take it on the track. That car became the first of what would be many projects for the young Wallace trio.

"Me and my brothers worked hard, got it put back together,

while we were working on Dad's car, too, getting it ready," Rusty remembers. "But then when I turned sixteen, I brought it out for my first race at a little racetrack called Lakehill Speedway in St. Louis, Missouri. Dad would take me out two weeks before that and let me practice a little bit at the racetrack, so he got me up to speed. I brought it out and had a semi-feature event and I won the race." The victory allowed him entry into that night's feature event but, says Rusty, "I was so excited about winning that damn thing that I forgot to put gas in the damn car to run the big race and I ran out of gas. So it was pretty wild."

Rusty's success continued that season; eventually he won Central Auto Racing Association's Rookie of the Year. Two years later, with the older Wallace brother winning at a fairly constant rate on the circuit, Mike began racing in the local sportsman division, while younger brother Kenny worked on the cars in the background. Rusty, having seen enough of racing to know he wanted to make it his profession, enlisted his brothers in a new business he and a friend started to help finance his road to bigger and better things. The company name, Poor Boy Chassis, turned out to be a fitting one.

"Rusty had some chassis knowledge and had built a few race cars and was like, 'Okay we're gonna do all this racing but we can't afford to do it without some help,'" Mike says. "The type of racing they were doing back then, it was hard to get a sponsor. You had a bunch of kids running up and down the interstate, and one night you're in Springfield, Missouri, and the next night you're in Portsmouth, Arkansas, and you know there were no TV packages or anything like that, so the chassis business derived by necessity. It was just a motivation to finance Rusty's racing."

Adds Kenny, "We would put roll cages in drag cars, anything around the Midwest where people needed things done to any of their racing hotrods—whether it was building trailers or anything. Don't get me wrong, we didn't make money at it; all we did was make the merry-go-round go around. A dollar came in, a dollar went out."

It did keep Rusty in gear, however—and winning races. In addition to his skills at building and tuning the car right, he'd already honed his own aggressive style, becoming especially proficient at short-track racing. He joined the USAC circuit in 1979, winning yet another Rookie of the Year distinction. A year later, he made a significant mark in his NASCAR Winston Cup Series debut, finishing an improbable second in Atlanta to another new driver with whom he would share a career-long friendly rivalry, Dale Earnhardt. He would run sporadically in the senior circuit while continuing his productive, steady climb through the sport's ranks. The ASA circuit turned out to be yet another positive proving ground; in 1983, he won the series championship, which helped him vault into the NASCAR Winston Cup Series full-time. Then in 1984, he finished fourteenth in points with two top-fives and four top-tens, garnering Rookie of the Year honors. In all, he'd won hundreds of features and short-track events. His rise had been methodical and brilliant.

In 1982, two years before Rusty's NASCAR Winston Cup Series rookie season, his eighteen-year-old brother Kenny stepped into a stock car to try racing for the first time. He had spent years practicing the car-building trade and working on Rusty's pit crews. While his middle brother Mike raced on and off, and worked for a time in his uncle's janitorial supply company, Kenny remained dedicated to the idea of making a career in the stock car business. Like Rusty, Kenny made the most of his first contest.

"It was Springfield, Illinois, a mile dirt track, the Illinois Street Stock State Championship, and I won," he states proudly of the ride that Mike had helped arrange for him. "A friend of our family had won a lot of the street stock races around home and this was an invitational race, meaning they only invited the champions. They talked this guy into letting me drive his race car 'cause he was already successful and had already accomplished everything. So I worked on the car, got it prepared, and when I won, I thought, 'Well, that's it, I'm the next Richard Petty. Nobody is ever gonna be better than me.'

"But to be honest, I got really wrapped up in my brothers' careers. I really got wrapped up in wanting Rusty to make it. Although Mike loved racing, he never showed that he wanted to do it for a living. Rusty tried to make a living out of it."

Kenny served Rusty, as a crew member, mechanic, and fabricator through his years leading to the NASCAR Winston Cup Series. He'd also go back to St. Louis and run some dirt track races near home along with Mike, who was still driving part-time. It wasn't until 1985 that Kenny began to put all his pieces in place for a start to a serious career behind the wheel. He would often wonder what took him so long to do so and his 1986 premiere season in ASA proved it was worth the wait: The twenty-two-year-old driver finished eleventh in points and gained the familiar Wallace family distinction of Rookie of the Year.

That same year, Rusty vaulted into the NASCAR Winston Cup Series top ranks for the first time, finishing sixth in year-end points, and on the short track at Bristol in the spring race, he won his first Cup race—one of two victories he'd gain that season.

Over the next two years, Rusty would climb up the NASCAR Winston Cup Series points ladder, finishing the 1988 season with six victories and a second-place finish in the annual standings, losing out in a squeaker to Bill Elliott. Kenny, meanwhile, toiled in the ASA circuit, learning his craft while he and his wife, Kim, barely managed to make ends meet. Although the experience meant living week to week, it no doubt served him well in the long run.

"Through all those ASA years, when I started racing, I learned how to race," Kenny says. "Nobody can come into a race car, jump in, and know what they're doing. And if they do, it's by mistake. You gotta learn what to do. It's like playing golf. You gotta grab the right club. And if you don't grab the right club, you gotta figure out how to make the hit and make it land where you want to. I learned to drive a race car. And then I had to learn how to keep the fenders on it. And then I had to learn how to go three hundred laps. Up until that point, I was always listening to Rusty or Mike get out of the car and say what it was doing. Now I'm driving and I'm thinking, 'Okay, the car's doing this. Oh yeah, and when it did this, this is what we did.' It was like going to college."

Yet he makes it clear that much of what he's grown into professionally comes from what has rubbed off on him from Rusty— beginning while he served on his oldest brother's crew—and Mike, starting with their short-track days. It is their influence, their strong, vastly different personalities, that helped Kenny see the way to make a successful run in racing, and aided him during the toughest parts of his three years in ASA. It is obvious their examples continue to affect him to this day.

"My whole life has come from my family," he admits. "If it weren't for Rusty, I would not be what I call worldly. I would not have known all the people I know. From travelling with Rusty I got to meet so many people. We traveled and we raced so much that it opened the door for my career. That's what I got from Rusty. And he definitely taught me how to win. He taught me how to understand a race and understand a race car. Anybody can get in a car and go around in circles, but at a controlled state—and knowing when you're in the lead—how to focus and just keep winning, Rusty taught me all those things.

"I hope this doesn't sound corny, but my brother Mike taught me the true meaning of a close relationship with your brother," he continues. "Me and Rusty were so wrapped up in going and doing and we knew we cared for each other but we never said it or anything, and Mike was the one that taught me to really take care of family. If it snowed eight inches in St. Louis and it was midnight, my brother Mike was over shoveling my mom and dad's driveway. He just showed up—nobody asked him to do it. My brother Mike truly taught me the meaning of doing something when somebody doesn't tell you to do it. And Mike has always been the money man of our family. You never find my brother Mike without a dollar."

In 1989, Kenny once again enjoyed the confidence of his oldest brother when he graduated to the NASCAR Busch Series, with Rusty tapping him to drive for the team he'd formed. Kenny returned the favor by quickly winning a race for his new car owner. After a successful first season, it was hardly a surprise, given family history, that Kenny also took home the circuit's Rookie of the Year honors.

For Rusty, the year would be memorable for other reasons as well, namely its peaks and valleys in his points championship chase. The season-long battle with Dale Earnhardt was a vintage study in competition as two of Cup's most aggressive drivers bounced the lead back and forth. At the finale in Atlanta, on the strength of a good points lead—not to mention six wins and thirteen top-fives through the year—Wallace needed to finish eighteenth or better to earn the annual prize. By race's end, Earnhardt had taken the checkered flag, and it had to be the most satisfying fifteenth-place finish of Rusty Wallace's career. His twelve-point NASCAR Winston Cup Series championship remains one of the closest finishes ever. Five years after his first full season, he had elevated himself to the top tier of his sport.

In 1990, his older and younger brothers having long set out on the path toward NASCAR success, Mike Wallace, still a part-time driver at thirty-one, found himself with something to prove; luckily, he also had the forum to do so in what he calls "the most phenomenal season of racing I've ever had."

It's unlikely that either of his brothers ever achieved the dominance Mike enjoyed in 1990, on his way to winning the NASCAR Weekly Racing Series Mid-America Region championship. Of the twenty-nine races he ran that season, Mike ended up in victory lane after twenty-one of them; on five other occasions, he finished second.

"We wanted to go racing for a living; I thought I did," he says. "You know, my brothers were doing it, and I thought if they could do it, I could. And it was just one of those years where we couldn't do much wrong. We'd be behind and we'd catch a break and win a race. You were the guy every week; a certain amount of people liked you, the other part hated you because you won every week, but it did exactly what we were hoping it was going to do. It opened the door to a tie to NASCAR. The name was recognizable then, not just Rusty Wallace but Mike Wallace now. I got the opportunity that year to go to Martinsville, Virginia, to run the first Busch Grand National race I'd ever run, and I ended up finishing seventh. And that was another one of those things [where you thought], 'Wow, this is really easy,' but then you find later on it's not really easy."

Mike's education continued with some success in the NASCAR Busch Series and ARCA series—in the latter, he won six out of eighteen races he entered, adding twelve top-fives to the total. But his chief goal was always a NASCAR Winston Cup Series ride. He made his debut with Jimmy Means in 1991, joining his brothers on the track at Phoenix in the second to last race of the season. A quick three years later, he got his opportunity to show what he could do, gaining a full-time NASCAR Winston Cup Series ride with venerable long-time owner Junie Donlavey. Unfortunately, the experience would turn out to be less than satisfying: In fifty-nine races through only three years, Mike accumulated only two top-tens, driving an underfinanced ride.

"Back when I drove that Winston Cup car, everybody came up to me, telling me how great a job I was doing: 'Man, you're doing a heck of a job in that car, you know, it's not a very good piece of equipment. You're really running well.' Then all of a sudden you haven't won in two years, [and] it's like, 'Well, he can't drive.' You know, the equipment hasn't changed one bit, nor have our finishes, but all of a sudden you're supposed to be able to take that thing to a higher level. We did take it to a higher level, but you can only take it so far."

For Mike, the path led back to a NASCAR Busch Series ride, driving a car with better equipment and solid sponsorship. Although he had some success, it was clearly not where he wanted to be.

His brothers were also learning different kinds of hard lessons; for Rusty, the challenge was about trying to repeat as NASCAR Winston Cup Series champion. In 1993, two years after going in with open-wheel legend Roger Penske on a NASCAR team, Rusty had one of his best seasons, winning ten times with nineteen top-fives, numbers good enough for a second-place finish, eighty points off Dale Earnhardt's pace. A year later, he won eight more times and finished third, behind Earnhardt and Mark Martin. Kenny, meanwhile, drove NASCAR Busch Series during 1992, this time with Felix Sabates. He began driving in the NASCAR Winston Cup Series full-time for SABCO in 1993 and gained three top-tens, but there was some dissension and Kenny returned to Busch in 1994 for FILMAR Racing, winning most popular driver honors on the circuit.

A year later, Kenny and FILMAR ran a half Busch/half Cup season in preparation for a full-time ride in the bigs. For years, he'd run in the long shadow of his oldest brother, gaining a reputation as a competitor who would maintain a sense of fairness on the track and a sense of humor off of it. But by the time his new NASCAR Winston Cup Series opportunity arrived, he had carved a very distinct racing life apart from Rusty's.

"There was definitely a time where there were people in our

sport who didn't care for Rusty because of his brash attitude—his need to win," Kenny recalls. "And everybody would always try to draw a parallel between me and Rusty, and one of the biggest statements Rusty has made to me about my professional career, I'll never forget: He looked me right in the face and said, 'Kenny, don't change, because I can tick off people a helluva lot easier than you can.' And at that point, it told me he doesn't really mean to tick people off; he's just much better at getting stuff than I was. I'm more of the person to go, 'Please,' and Rusty was more the person to say, 'Give me.' But that's the way I needed to be and now I'm more like [Rusty]. This sport requires the element of misery whether you like it or not. It took me a long time to realize that and Rusty had it figured out from the day he jumped into a race car. I did not realize in competition how some people, if they don't win at all, they feel like they're failures. I feel like if I'm a player, and I get a chance to win every time, that's what makes me happy."

Chances are, however, few moments on a track made Kenny happier than the ending of one particular race he knew he was going to lose.

At the start of the 1998 season, the Bud Pole winners from the previous year got the opportunity to compete in the non-points Bud Shootout in Daytona, run during the week leading up to the Daytona 500. With one lap to go in this twenty-five-lap race, a caution came out and the lead cars—Jeff Gordon's in first, Rusty Wallace's lined up next to him in second—headed back to the start-finish line. Rusty, winless in sixteen seasons at Daytona, dashed out in front quickly and found himself in a door-to-door struggle with Jimmy Spencer as the pair headed around the track. Running behind them in third, driving an exceptionally fast car, sat Kenny Wallace, who looked ahead and sized up the reality of the situation: Whoever he chose to drive behind and draft with would win the Shootout. He would dictate who won the race. For years, he'd sat by watching with envy as Terry and Bobby Labonte shared such memorable joint victories as the 1996 season-ending NAPA 500, where Bobby won the race and Terry the championship. Now he'd finally get his chance to show a little brotherly love.

"I thought, 'Holy Toledo, that's Rusty. And I have a choice here and it's an easy one,'" Kenny recalls of his brother's victory in the

Shootout. "I was going so much faster right in the middle of the corner, so I had to easily take my front bumper and put it on the rear of Rusty's bumper, and I literally had to go on and off the gas in the middle of the corner. If I could have had this run three hundred feet farther away, I could have won the race, I could have passed him. But it was right in the middle of the corner. After the race, Rusty said he had never been pushed so hard. I had to keep modulating my throttle because I was literally lifting the rear of his car up. And I pushed him past Spencer.

"It was a great day but I think the most meaningful part of it was later that night. We were in an Italian restaurant—me and Rusty and my mom and dad—and they had a TV there and CNN news. I looked up, and they reported on the pair of brothers finishing one-two in the Bud Shootout and it just sent chills up me; it was great."

While there has always been, between the Wallaces, a sense of familial pride, the brothers also share a sense of professional balance nowadays. Kenny and Mike agree they will never match their older brother's record—at last count, fifty wins, one NASCAR Winston Cup Series, two IROC championships, and earnings of more than $20 million—and trying to do so is not an ambition. Rather, they'd each like to parlay their successes into greater opportunities. Kenny, who earned his career-best finish in 1999 with a second-place result in the July race at New Hampshire, would like to find his way to victory lane in the NASCAR Winston Cup Series and at the very least remain consistent. Middle brother Mike is simply looking for a ticket back to the senior circuit, even though he is enjoying his successes in the NASCAR Craftsman Truck Series, which included a win at Mesa Martin Speedway in March 2000, hours after Rusty notched win number fifty at Bristol. Like many drivers forced to sound more like politicians when rides come up for grabs by season's end, Mike talks about his track record and hopes he will get the chance to prove to the people—in this case, the NASCAR Winston Cup Series car owners—that he can get the job done.

The Wallace brothers continue to make a tremendous mark on their sport, one they never could have anticipated when they first followed their dad to dirt tracks on weekends. Nowadays, their parents trail them by attending some races throughout the schedule. Even given how competitive drivers need to be to succeed in NASCAR, the brothers maintain a rich family history, and the positives of having a sibling nearby far outweigh the negatives. As Kenny Wallace puts it, "The worst part of being a sibling is wanting to do what your older brother has done—and you really want to do it in your heart. When you're the youngest, you have that desire to be as good as your brothers. I think that's the hardest part of when your other siblings are doing what you do. You don't necessarily want to outrun them, but you know you've got to because you're racing them. But the easiest part is knowing you have family, and that you're being looked out for."

14
The Waltrip Brothers

In his stellar twenty-nine-year career, Darrell Waltrip has gone to victory lane as a winner eighty-four times. On one other occasion, though, he got there after finishing a race dead last. It remains one of the happiest trips he ever made.

It came on May 18, 1996, at Charlotte, site of the Winston, an annual all-star race. The contest featured the winning drivers from the previous year's races, along with "preliminary" entrants: additional drivers who had finished in the top five at Talladega's Winston 500 three weeks before. The fifth-place finisher at the Winston 500 was Darrell's younger brother, Michael Waltrip, who had made it into the All-Star field by the skin of his teeth.

"I was running sixth [in the Winston 500] and didn't really see how I was going to be able to pass anybody because my car was handling terrible," Michael remembers. "And one of the five guys ahead of me broke [down]. So now I'm fifth and the guy running sixth is trying to pass me and is all over me and eventually I shake away from him and finish fifth. If you had asked me the chances of my winning the Winston [All-Star race] as soon as I finished fifth in the Open, I'd have told you they would be zero."

But in the weeks leading up to the all-star event—run in a unique format, featuring segments of thirty, thirty, and ten laps and an inverted starting order from one heat to the next—Waltrip and his Wood Brothers crew improved the odds by making some necessary changes, and once he got the car onto the track at the Charlotte Motor Speedway, he could feel an immediate improvement in the way it handled.

He started last in the first thirty-lap segment and passed half the field, including Darrell. The second leg ended with him in fourth place, putting him in an excellent position in his attempt to become the first preliminary driver to win The Winston.

Says Michael, "They threw the green [in the last segment] and we ran one lap and Terry [Labonte] and Dale [Earnhardt] got together and kind of bobbled around there a little bit and I shot underneath them, and passing them was big. It looked good on TV, but the most important thing to me was when I got to the end of the back straightaway and dove down into three and come up off of four, the way my car turned that turn and the way the thing handled, I said, 'Well, they ain't gonna catch me, I can promise you that.' It was just perfect and it handled that same way for the next eight laps."

Michael Waltrip's charge into victory lane shocked the crowd, especially given its irony: He had won the all-star exhibition race, but he still hadn't notched an official NASCAR Winston Cup Series victory in his career.

The news caught his older brother quite unaware.

"I'm pretty sure he didn't expect to win it, and I never thought about him winning it," Darrell says. "The next thing I know, the race is over and I said, 'Who won the race?' and they say, 'Michael' and I say, 'Oh, Okay. . . Michael! He won the race?!' I couldn't wait to get out there and congratulate him."

"He came there and he was real excited and then Dale Earnhardt also came—he kind of stood off to the side—to congratulate me," Michael remembers. "It was neat to see people that are happy when you have success."

It's a feeling his brother knows very well, being one of the winningest drivers in the history of the sport. Darrell Waltrip's eighty-four victories (which tie him for third with Bobby Allison on the all-time list) and three championships, however, tell only part of the tale. By attracting attention as much for his wit as his accomplishments, Waltrip helped pave the way for the modern era of NASCAR, with its greater emphasis on media relations. He was as comfortable—and successful—in front of the camera as behind the wheel.

For Michael, there is an advantage and a burden to racing under such a looming shadow. It has been a long road for Michael to achieve his present level of validation among NASCAR racing's elite. Although now still winless in his NASCAR Winston Cup Series career, his longevity and competitiveness speak for a talent level that could match up well with several of the top drivers.

With sixteen years between them, the Waltrips might almost be from different generations. Once upon a time, the pair hardly communicated because of their age gap; later on, they were in different leagues in terms of performance. Now, with Darrell as elder statesman of the sport and Michael making greater strides, the pair are closer than ever.

"I worry, I guess, being older," Darrell says. "I worry if he's hurt, or if he's running well I want him to do good. You have different emotions about your brother than you would a friend. More compassion for a brother than you would a friend."

Every significant step in Darrell Waltrip's early career development has the seal of family on it. Even before he made it onto a track for the first time, his interest was permanently piqued thanks to a grandfather, a sheriff whose responsibilities included working traffic at the racetracks in Owensboro, Kentucky, and a grandmother who didn't like to sit in the grandstands by herself.

"I was six years old [when I started going] to races with my grandmother," Darrell recalls. "They would race on Friday and Saturday nights and of course, like any kid, I loved noise and cars and speed and I tore up every tricycle or bicycle or whatever I had. I'd pretty well burn the tires off of it playing like I was a race car driver. It had a profound impact on me."

All the drivers knew his grandfather and were more than willing to let the kid run through the pits after the races. In time, he began to speak of his desire to one day follow in the footsteps of heroes such as NASCAR Winston Cup Series veteran G. C. Spencer. "He raced at those tracks in Owensboro; he had a car called the 'Flying Saucer' and it was a GMC flat six, and it made a real odd sound—different than anybody else's," Darrell says. "I was drawn to him like a deer."

Darrell's talking fell on the deaf ears of his father, who drove trucks for Pepsi-Cola. But Darrell rode with his dad in the summer and one of their stops was a hardware store that sold go-karts; the twelve-year-old Waltrip kept sitting in one of the karts at every visit, and the store owner, smelling a sale, suggested maybe the kid should try the thing out for a test run. That led to Darrell entering a race at a track laid out in a mall parking lot in Owensboro.

"We took that thing up there and I won my class right off," he says. "That was the start of my racing career, and of course Dad was along all the time; he was a mechanic, he liked to work on his car, and he was always tinkering around in his garage and it kind of caught his fancy as well. We pretty much were partners in crime, my dad and I. There were five of us kids, and so obviously there wasn't a lot of extra cash to be spending money on a go-kart, but we raked and scraped enough to keep it going there for four, five years and it got me a little reputation for being pretty good. Then we got enough money to buy a half completed '36 Chevrolet Coupe that raced on dirt tracks and we dragged that thing out of a junkyard, took it home, and finished it up."

Within ten years, Waltrip had won a significant number of races on local dirt and asphalt short tracks throughout the neighboring states. At the fairgrounds track in Nashville, Tennessee, he also earned some extra dollars from the track promoter for giving brash, outspoken interviews, and having the talent to back up his claims on the track.

In 1972, he made his NASCAR Winston Cup Series debut at Talladega, this time with financial help from his father-in-law, who was president of Texas Gas. As was the case with his father, Waltrip had convinced the other most important family in his life—and, most notably, his wife, Stevie—that his commitment to the craft of racing would eventually pay off.

"They saw my dedication and my desire," he says of his wife's family. "I told her dad when I asked him if I could marry Stevie, I said, 'I'm going to be a professional race car driver someday,' and he said, 'You mean, you can make a living driving a car?' He wasn't a big fan at the time; all he knew was the local stuff, and local racetracks are not always the most glamorous. But [Stevie and I] got married and as time went by they got behind me and that really helped.

"In this business, with all the ups and downs, and the time and everything . . . it's hard on marriages and the only way you can make your marriage last is to make your wife a part of [the business]. Stevie was the first woman to get a garage pass to get in the pits to work; she kept laps, calculated gas mileage. They wouldn't let women in the pits back in the early '70s, so I made her the car owner and got her a car owner's license. And then she worked in the pits and has done that for most of our married life."

When Waltrip did finally put down some full-time NASCAR Winston Cup Series roots, he actually found the neighborhood a little less than inviting. During the mid-1970s, the circuit was dominated by some names that remain in the top tier of the all-time wins list in NASCAR history: Richard Petty, David Pearson, Cale Yarborough, and Bobby Allison. These elite drivers won most of the races and planned on doing so for a long time.

That Waltrip had other plans seemed moot until 1977, when he began to make serious noise on the track and off. Always a successful short-track driver, Waltrip had a dominant season on superspeedways in 1977, capturing four of his six victories in these majors. One of the most prominent races he didn't win was the Southern 500.

Throughout the afternoon of the Southern 500, he locked horns with Cale Yarborough, who was hoping to add a Darlington victory to his tally on the way to a second consecutive NASCAR Winston Cup Series title. The pair traded the lead back and forth for much of the race—at one point as frequently as every other lap. But Waltrip, by his own admission, grew impatient and caused a mishap for both drivers which, while it didn't knock them out of the running, kept both from threatening to stop David Pearson's trip to victory lane. At race's end, Cale bestowed the nickname "Jaws" on his young rival, as much for the way he ran his mouth as for the aggressive methods he used on the track. Waltrip, of course, fought back, and later in the season, when Yarborough complained about the physical and mental toll some races took on a driver, Waltrip began rating an event's particular challenges through his own "Cale Scale."

"They had this fraternity; there were four of them who won all the races, they raced against each other, they knew what each other was going to do and so they kept it all to themselves," Waltrip remembers. "And there hadn't been anybody that had broken into the circle up to that point, so I felt like I was always odd man out. And really, it was the best thing because it motivated me to do that much better. And I had to be outspoken and I had to do things that were not always popular . . . I was aggressive on the racetrack and it's kind of like if you bat against the same pitcher all the time, you know what his curve looks like, and his fastball, and when he's going to throw it. Well, all of a sudden I'm competing with these guys and they don't know anything about me—they don't know whether they can trust me, they don't know if they want me up there racing with them or not. I had to earn their respect, but looking back, I didn't give them any respect so I probably didn't deserve any. It took awhile for that to change. And it did change."

Part of that shift would have far-reaching effects throughout the sport. At a post-season press conference in New York City that included several members of the national media, Waltrip spoke eloquently about the appeal of NASCAR in a refreshing way that surprised a number of journalists. Stock car racing, he argued presciently, had a cross-country appeal worth being explored and exploited by the press. In a few years' time, he would rise to become a prominent name on the circuit, and in the early days of NASCAR's modern era, his was a clear voice of the next generation of drivers, and one with tremendous talent and potential.

In 1975, when twenty-eight-year-old Darrell Waltrip drove his first full-time season in the NASCAR Winston Cup Series, he got a phone call from his twelve-year-old brother, Michael. Having seen his big brother race, Michael forged his own driving dreams and felt ready to get behind the wheel himself. With his parents outspokenly against the idea, Michael asked his hero for his blessing, support, and whatever advice he could get. He didn't get much.

"My mom and dad had been through it with Darrell and I don't think they saw that I had much of a chance to be successful," Michael recalls. "I think they mainly looked at it as a waste of time. I asked Darrell if there was any way he could help me get started because I had nothing—and he said that it was just so hard to ever hope to make anything out of it, I'd wind up just wasting a lot of time and money. And I thought if that's the way you feel about it, that's fine. I wasn't mad at him; that was his opinion. I was only twelve, but I didn't share that opinion; I thought I could do it. Some people don't know how bad someone wants something. And when you're twelve, you don't really listen to many grown-ups anyway."

"You gotta realize something—there's sixteen years difference in our ages; most people think I'm his father and that happens all the time," Darrell says of Michael's phone call. "When he wanted to start racing, I was in the middle of my career. And I was more focused on what I was doing and where I was going and trying to be successful; and I never thought that he was that committed; I just thought he was doing it 'cause I did it. And I think he wanted to prove to me and to the family as well that he didn't have to have his brother do things for him, he could do it on his own. I think it was a good motivation for him."

Whatever the impetus, Michael began his own methodical pursuit of a driving career. In the late 1970s, he raced go-karts, switching to Mini-Modified cars toward the end of high school. That's when he drove at the Kentucky Motor Speedway track where his older brother had found his own first burst of success. That Michael echoed some of Darrell's triumphs remains a highlight for him.

"Darrell always came once a year to run a special night, and the night he came, I won the feature," Michael recalls. "I was running in a different division and I won that night with him watching and that meant a lot to me.

"The whole summer out there was great. I won the opening night—my first race ever in a car, I won the feature. I never will forget that feeling, running around the corner after I took the checker and just the crowd of people that were standing there, wanting to congratulate me."

Meanwhile, Darrell was earning kudos on a much grander scale. After a couple of highly publicized attempts, he managed to free himself from a long-term deal with the DiGard team he drove for, and hooked up with legendary driver-turned-owner Junior Johnson. In 1981 and 1982, his first two seasons with Johnson, Waltrip won consecutive NASCAR Winston Cup Series championships, gaining each title on the strength of twelve victories. In both seasons, he bested longtime rival Bobby Allison, coming back each time from seemingly insurmountable deficits and then domi-nating Allison in late-season runs. In 1983, Waltrip returned the favor and finished second in Allison's title run.

Darrell had found the perfect ride with Johnson, and Johnson achieved a level of success to match the run he'd enjoyed with Cale Yarborough in the 1970s. In their six seasons together, Johnson and Waltrip posted dominating numbers, highlighted by three championships and forty-three wins. Darrell finally had a ride more than worthy of his talent and attitude—and he always seemed ready with a biting comment to shake up the competition. After one particular victory, he joked that by the end of the race, he had all his competitors right where he wanted them: "Behind me."

However, even success can't guarantee continued contentment, especially between two such strong personalities as Johnson and Waltrip. Johnson had brought Neil Bonnett into the fold in 1984, to Waltrip's displeasure, creating a two-car team. So he left for the greener pastures of Rick Hendrick's organization before the start of the 1987 campaign.

While Darrell enjoyed these glory years, his younger brother made it through the formative events that would lead, ultimately, to a NASCAR Winston Cup Series ride. In 1983, at age twenty, he captured the Goody's Dash Series title, overwhelming the compe-tition.

"I think there were fourteen races; I sat on thirteen poles, won six races, and won the championship my first full season on the series," he recalls. "And if you had told me at the end of '83 that I wasn't going to be the next Richard Petty, I would have told you you'd lost your mind. Everything had gone perfect and I had a lot of momentum."

For the first time, Darrell began to take notice. The siblings now seemed to have some common ground, despite the age difference.

"As I [watched] him race, he reminded me a lot of myself," Darrell states. "And nobody really encouraged him to do what he wanted to do, but he kept right on at it anyway. He never yielded, just kept right on digging. When somebody slammed the door, he went and found another one [to] open."

Seeking advice on what to do next, Michael eventually went to the top. Having become close friends with Kyle Petty, he spent several months in 1984 living in the Petty home in Randleman, North Carolina, where he'd sit up and talk racing into the wee hours with Richard Petty, soaking in the King's wisdom.

"It was really cool because everything I knew about NASCAR was centered around my brother," Michael recalls. "To me there wasn't anyone else. Then I got to meet Richard Petty and just to hear his philosophy on the sport and how he went about things was one hundred-and eighty degrees in the other direction. It really broadened my thinking.

"[Darrell] and I never spent a lot of time together [then]," he continues. "I didn't have the opportunity to sit down on the couch and talk a lot about racing with him. Richard treated me like I was his kid, wanting to help me out. His philosophy was, if you can get a Winston Cup ride, get one right now; it doesn't matter what else you've done. Get in these cars and learn how to drive them because Winston Cup is going to be your goal. That's what he did with Kyle, and that opened my eyes. It wasn't long after that until I made my first start in May of '85; I ran the World 600 at Charlotte in a Winston Cup car."

Eschewing the proving grounds of ARCA and Busch, Michael hooked up with Dick Bahre and began racing; in 1987, when Bahre joined forces with Chuck Rider to form Bahari, Michael went along for the ride and spent nine seasons there. During that time, he also did double duty by driving a NASCAR Busch Series car, winning for the first time in that circuit in 1988.

If Michael was clearly cutting his teeth, Darrell had other mountains to conquer. The most important one remained the Daytona 500; before Dale Earnhardt gained infamy for his long winless string at the speedway, the elusive Daytona win remained, for seventeen years, "the only thing Darrell felt he was lacking," according to his younger brother. His opportunity came in 1989, thanks to an exciting gas gamble. Race leader Ken Schrader pitted with eleven laps remaining and Darrell took the chance that he'd have just enough fuel to make it to the checkered flag. The gamble just barely paid off: Waltrip ran out of gas on the way to victory lane, but he'd earned his trip there for a tearful celebration.

Four years later, Darrell's brother won the race that understandably represents his emotional zenith, although the occasion was about as bittersweet as it gets. Michael captured the 1993 NASCAR Busch Series contest in Bristol, run a few days after the April 1st death of defending NASCAR Winston Cup Series champ Alan Kulwicki, to whom Michael had finished second in NASCAR Winston Cup Series Rookie of the Year voting in 1986. To honor his friend, Michael celebrated by driving Kulwicki's trademark "Polish Victory Lap." Once in the winner's circle, he had one more surprise: an engagement ring for the future Buffy Waltrip.

"It was definitely not rehearsed," he says of the lap. "I didn't know if it was appropriate or not. Everybody was so impressed with what Alan accomplished and how he did it that people were really down that weekend we lost him. And after him being the reigning champion—I don't know, I just did it. It came upon me that he should be honored.

"And then when I got to victory lane, I got engaged. That was not rehearsed, either. I had the ring with me, and I didn't really know when I was going to do it, but victory lane seemed like a good deal. If you get all excited, you're liable to say anything. It was emotional, you know? I wanted to cry for Alan, and then I wanted to be happy."

As Brett Bodine, Ricky Rudd, and Bill Elliott will admit with a shrug, it's harder to be a driver/owner in NASCAR than just about anything else. Darrell Waltrip probably knows the pros and cons of that better than most. In the days since he brought his own team to the track starting in 1991, he's enjoyed several victories and a measure of control to counterbalance the enormous increase in responsibility and the economic hardships of trying to stay current with NASCAR's highly successful multi-car teams. He experienced more than his share of the negative as his tenure went on, and he hasn't visited victory lane since his Southern 500 win in 1992.

Of course, his intention was to change that fact during the Year 2000 Victory Tour, his final season in NASCAR Winston Cup Series racing. As part of the Travis Carter Motorsports team that also features teammate Jimmy Spencer, Waltrip enjoys a considerable boost of ammunition in 2000, thanks to some Robert Yates engines under the hood.

One thing Waltrip can be assured of, regardless of the final season's outcome, is his exalted place in NASCAR—only Richard Petty and David Pearson have posted more career wins. But his role off the track as a spokesman continues to carry even greater significance. Waltrip became a humorous, popular media pundit way before it was fashionable, and his influence may be most keenly visible when one watches Michael cohosting his weekly NASCAR roundup on Speedvision.

"Darrell had all this stuff to say and things he wanted to do— then he'd go out and win the race where everybody wanted to hear what he had to say anyway," Michael points out. "He was the total package. He knew he needed to wear dress slacks and penny loafers to the track, and be able to stand in front of a camera and tell a story about what happened on the track and make it understandable, not only to people in the sport but to people watching in New York City or boardrooms anywhere across the country."

"I believe success in sports is based on timing," Darrell adds. "And I was the right guy at the right time in this situation. The sport was becoming less and less a regional sport and more a national sport. It needed a mouthpiece, and fortunately for me, I fit that role."

Like his brother, Michael Waltrip's goals are centered on a visit to victory lane. Unfortunately, at the start of the 2000 season, he was still saddled with the ignominious distinction of holding the longest current winless streak in NASCAR Winston Cup Series racing, at 428. He has, however, won several Busch contests, including one in 1999, and the streak does not haunt him. "No matter what anyone says, I'm proud of my career," he states. "I think the consistency of my performances, and the fact that I've always been right there—I don't know what to say about [the streak] other than I know I'm good enough to win. And the people I race with every Sunday, they know I'm good enough to win."

One of those true believers is his older sibling. In the years since Darrell first tried to dampen Michael's desire to race, he has come to respect the level of perseverance and skill his kid brother has always shown. On weekends at the track, one will often find the brothers hanging out together.

"Competition does interesting things—whether it's your family or your friends or whatever it is, if your goal is to win, then you'll beat your brother," Darrell says. "Obviously you wouldn't wreck your brother, but nonetheless you're out there to beat him and he's somebody that you've got to compete against. And so your relationships are sometimes strained or sometimes there's no relationship at all because you're just so busy doing what you do. But [Michael] showed me that, like myself, he was committed to what he was doing and he was going to make it happen one way or another. We're closer now than we've ever been."

That's not likely to change when Darrell trades the day-to-day thrills of racing for the dual challenges of helping Stevie raise their two daughters and being a prominent on-air personality once the new NASCAR television contract takes effect. Come 2001, he'll still do his commercials and continue to be a witty public voice and recognizable face to the NASCAR faithful.

Michael Waltrip, on the other hand, has more goals to meet. He may always race in a looming shadow, but it is perhaps a fitting tribute to the Waltrip racing legacy that he can't afford to be too sentimental about his brother's departure.

"If it makes him happy, then I'm happy with it," he says of Darrell's retirement. "But whether he's there or not [won't] affect my day; I have to be a professional and do my job and I don't foresee it being a whole lot different. I'll miss the companionship, having my brother there every weekend, but that won't change what happens at the racetrack."

15
The Wood Brothers

To Leonard Wood, it felt like a government secret.

In the early 1960s, long before the days when a large budget meant you could afford a piece of competitive machinery in NASCAR Winston Cup Series racing, getting the best car on any given Sunday had a great deal to do with small but significant innovations developed in the best teams' garages. The top mechanic-engineers of the day earned that distinction by inventing plenty of products you won't necessarily find listed in the patent office, but ones that won their race teams a lot of money nonetheless. Like opposing factions, they maintained their edge by protecting their inventions, or even denying they existed. Often, a team's success depended upon how long it could keep everybody else guessing about just what its advantage was.

Leonard Wood hid one particular development as best he could for as long as he could. For a time, it escaped view, back when television cameramen weren't recording pit crews leaning on the wall during races, seemingly poised in a constant state of anticipation.

Inevitably, it was discovered, after a photographer took a shot of it as it helped propel another NASCAR driver to victory. It was just a simple little invention that would revolutionize the sport: a jack constructed to raise a car in about three pumps. Up to that time, car jacks used in pits weren't a great deal more sophisticated than the average jack in the trunk of the family car. Fourteen pumps, fifteen pumps, and a stock car in the middle of a competitive race was lifted high enough to change left-side tires. Then down with the pump, on over to the right side. Another fourteen pumps. Meanwhile, the car being fielded by Leonard and his brother Glen—the legendary Wood Brothers Racing Team—was in gear, racing out of pit row.

In NASCAR's early days, a pit stop would sometimes be a thing of leisure, a respite during a tiring day of racing, an occasion even for a driver to start a sandwich. Thinking back on that now, in the days of 500-mile events, constant tire changes, setup adjustments, and race-long strategies that take a grand total of about 16.6 seconds, the old-fashioned idea seems ludicrous. In modern racing, a driver can't win on the tracks unless he can also win in the pits.

Everybody knows that now because the Wood Brothers helped make them see it—much to the chagrin of the many other teams on pit row. Beginning in 1950, when Glen Wood started running Sportsman and Modified events throughout Virginia and the Carolinas, with his little brother Leonard, ten years his junior, in tow as mechanic, the siblings achieved short-track success, finding particular fortune on the quarter-mile paved track at Bowman-Gray Stadium in Winston-Salem. And as NASCAR came of age on superspeedways, the Wood Brothers, with Glen handling the business, and Leonard running the garage, gained the highest stature as a race team any racer would want to drive for. In their prime, their cars were driven by some of history's best: Cale Yarborough, Marvin Panch, Tiny Lund, A.J. Foyt, Neil Bonnett, Buddy Baker, Kyle Petty, Dale Jarrett, and most notably David Pearson, with whom the Woods gained nearly half of their career's 97 Grand National/NASCAR Winston Cup Series wins. Some of NASCAR's top drivers have offered testament to the unbelievably smooth setups that Leonard provided, the fair and honest perspective Glen lent, and the overall class of the Wood Brothers team.

In the pits, the Woods' operation was a successful family affair that included assorted friends and relatives, and their brothers Delano, Ray Lee, and Clay. As races grew longer and pit stops more frequent and lengthy, it was the Woods who first discovered that a quick stop could be a thing of art as beautiful to watch as a driver hitting a turn just so at Darlington. Their strategy helped complete one of the most fabled of all NASCAR tales, the popular Tiny Lund victory in the 1963 Daytona 500. It was their swift pit work that had some executives luring them to try their hand at running a crew for the Indianapolis 500 in the mid-1960s, with exceptional results. They were eagerly manning the radio during David Pearson's extraordinary bump-and-run finish with Richard Petty at the Daytona 500 in 1976. And in the best NASCAR family tradition, they brought Glen's sons Len and Eddie into the business beginning in the late 1960s, when they were teenagers.

But the Wood Brothers' enduring influence is still chiefly felt—and seen—week in and week out; as pit crews race from side to side of race cars, doing their best to beat the clock and win their own races when seconds truly count.

For Glen Wood, becoming a stock car driver was all about competition from the beginning—even if it didn't start on the track.

"He had a friend that was running a car in a race close by here, and was doing quite well, and Glen always felt he was a better driver on the road than him," recalls Leonard Wood. "So Glen goes down and takes his personal car and keeps up with the other guy's race car. And he figured if he could do that, he could make a race car and do all right. That's kind of how it started."

To do that, the twenty-five-year-old Glen quickly realized he'd need Leonard's help, so the Virginia-born brothers began their partnership. Leonard, fifteen at the time, had always been considered the mechanic of the family, having begun to tinker with cars from age seven on. Glen saw racing as a potentially easier way to make a living than the sawmill business he'd been involved with. With that many years between him and Leonard, there was no sibling rivalry from the start; just an excited younger brother eager to showcase his abilities and a respectful older brother who knew a chief mechanic when he saw one.

Great careers are sometimes born from extremely inauspicious beginnings; in the case of the Wood Brothers, their fifty-year odyssey in stock racing almost ended on day one. In his first race, driving a 1938 Ford numbered 50 after the amount Glen and his partner Chris Williams had paid for it, Glen met with a mishap: A car spun out in front of him and the other driver's bumper caught hold of Glen's rear housing and bent it. While they were towing Glen's car home after the race, the bent housing caused the axle to break and the wheel came off. "And in a '38 Ford, the gas spout comes out and up through the fender," Leonard points out. "So when the wheel came off, it jerked the gas spout off and the gas ran out on the pavement, and as the housing hit the pavement, well, naturally, the sparks flying, it didn't take long; it was on fire."

Leonard, who'd just gotten out of the hospital after having his appendix removed, was riding in the trailing car, watching the brothers' future going up in flames. Then things almost went from bad to worse. "[The car] sat there and burned up right in the middle of the road—and while it's burning, all of a sudden the starter started turning over; the motor started, and would you believe it fired and hit a lick or two? Then that was [all].

"And of course we brought the car home and sanded it off, cleaned it up, painted, put number sixteen on it, and then [Glen] finished third the next—actually the first race he really run. Yeah, it was about to end before it started."

It took off then with Glen behind the wheel and Leonard preparing the cars, and in time the operation became a bona fide success on the short-track circuit. Their father, wary and skeptical at first, quickly became a convert as Glen began to tear up the Modified and Sportsman circuits. And if Ralph Earnhardt and Ned Jarrett had Hickory Motor Speedway, their racing home away from home, Glen Wood had Bowman-Gray Stadium, a paved half-mile track where he built his reputation.

"He was extremely smooth, and there again he was quick," Leonard says of his brother's style. "Quick reacting and quick thinking. I remember over at Bowman-Gray one time, Glen and Lee Petty were racing, and Lee was leading and he pulled over to the outside, ran outside of a slow car; Glen tapped that slow car on the back, he shot him ahead enough that he kept between the slow car and Lee, and then passed him, took the lead and won the race. Of course, Lee tried to catch him coming back in the next corner but he didn't catch up to him. It's just little techniques you use."

The same could be said for Leonard, who had already developed into one of the game's best setup men. Ford had been looking to man another NASCAR team in 1956, and the company agreed to back the Woods, giving Leonard the best equipment to work with. His engine designs were so successful, they stood the test of time, especially during the two years he spent in the service stationed in Germany.

"I built Glen a motor before I went to Germany in 1957," he says. "It ran real good down there in Daytona. I believe he finished second or third overall. Then he went back in '58 while I was in Germany with that same engine and put it in another car and sat on pole in the Modified. It was a sportsman-type car, but he sat on pole over everything. That same motor, you know? That made you feel good when you were in Germany, ship you some clippings of the newspapers that he was on pole."

From day one, the brothers understood their responsibilities and played their roles with an uncommon degree of cooperation and a lack of ego.

"A lot of people don't know it, but Glen was the owner and always has been," Leonard says. "I was busy trying to make it run fast, and I wasn't worried about anything else. And then as it went on, you know, he mentioned us being partners or something or other, but like I said, I was just concentrating on it running and didn't care, so I never did become an owner of it. It's called Wood Brothers Racing Team, but I never did own any of it, and I still don't.

"I've been Glen's chief mechanic ever since I started. Glen was the driver and I was the mechanic. He let me do it like I wanted; he supported me one hundred percent. And we'd go to Bowman-Gray and he'd win, like, three in a row sometimes and stuff like that. You know, there's nothing more gratifying than to see your brother win."

Through 1959, in the first eleven seasons of NASCAR's history, a total of 425 races were run. Of those, only forty-seven were longer than two hundred miles. The majority were swift, busy affairs on short-paved or dirt tracks, with the drivers racing and bumping and sliding. Often, during the shortest races, fifty to one hundred miles at times, crew members had little to do, unless some bent metal had to be hammered out. Missing from the pit stop was a sense of real urgency.

Then two things happened. Superspeedways began to more

than simply dot the landscape, and strictly stock cars became a little less strict. Suddenly, there were miles to go before the checkered flag; for crew members there were parts to adjust, and therefore parts to perform. An adjustment here, a tweak there, and a car could rise from worst to first in a matter of laps.

The Wood Brothers might not have been the first team to make this assumption, but when the idea hit them, they ran with it in ways that no other team did or could. Leonard invented the three-pump jack. The crew made pit stops into clockwork affairs that were the envy of other teams. Glen, familiar with driving in the draft of a superspeedway, and Leonard, acutely knowledgeable about gas conservation, spent a great deal of time thinking through the ways to find the edge that creates winners.

"Everybody was doing it but we had a little bit better success at it," Glen Wood concedes. "We concentrated possibly a little more on trying to make quick stops because it was obvious that when you got to run on the bigger tracks, if you came in and you gained five seconds in the pits, that was five seconds out on the track and that was a straightaway. We won a lot of pit races; back then they'd have a series of competitions for the fastest pit crew and we won a lot of them."

And in the garage, Leonard Wood was among the very best at using creative engineering to improve a car's performance. Engineer/mechanics such as Smokey Yunick, Maurice Petty, and Wood were the tops of their day; their cars simply drove better and faster, thanks to skilled tinkering with an engine, changing a setup, or the development of things that had never been made before.

"You had to do all of it yourself back then," Leonard Wood says. "You had your own ideas and you might share something a little bit with some other teams, but if you shared something, you got something in return. But what really made it go, you didn't dare tell it."

By 1964, Glen Wood had stopped racing, having put together an exceptional career. He didn't spend a great deal of time on the Grand National tour, but he produced some significant results. In 1960, Glen, who'd earned the nickname Old Woodchopper, won all three races at his beloved Bowman-Gray Stadium track in spectacular fashion: He started from the pole in each and proceeded to lead every single lap of each race, 600 laps in all. Nearly forty years later, such exploits—along with his stellar career in Modifieds and Sportsman events—would land him on the list of NASCAR's 50 greatest all-time drivers. But he gave up the road and took the reins of his business exclusively, giving seat time to a variety of drivers, many of whom would eventually join him on that list.

For one of those drivers, Tiny Lund, the Woods engineered a victory considered to be among the most significant in NASCAR history.

Given the circumstances, Tiny no doubt would have preferred the ride had not come his way. In the days leading up to the 1963 Daytona 500, the regular driver for the Woods' team, Marvin Panch, was testing a new Maserati engine for car owner Briggs Cunningham. While coming toward the third turn on the track at Daytona, he lost control and the Maserati skidded, fell over onto its side, and caught fire.

Seeing the accident, Lund and four others ran over and lifted the car up enough for Panch to begin to free himself. When the gas tank blew, they continued their efforts, and Lund was finally able to pull Panch to safety by his ankle. The rescue would eventually earn Lund the Carnegie Medal for Heroism.

But first it helped earn him the greatest ride of his life: the chance to substitute for Panch in the race.

Many have come to believe that Panch himself told the Wood brothers to give Lund the ride from his hospital bed, but, says Leonard Wood, "We had already picked Tiny as the choice to have anyway, because we had seen him run at Charlotte Fairgrounds, on a dirt track, I mean, really competitive, you know. You didn't want him on your back bumper." The hardly diminutive Lund—at six feet five, 265 pounds, Wood calls him, "The quickest big man I've ever seen, and strong"—was a more than agreeable replacement to Panch, and so owners and new driver, without a great deal of time, set about getting ready for the prestigious Daytona 500, which featured one of the Woods' most intelligent strategy calls.

The Wood brothers figured that if they made pit stops at slightly more than the typical forty laps—one hundred miles—they would end up, if calculations were correct, with one fewer pit stop than teams normally went. If Lund drafted near the front most of the race—which would allow him to stay in the running and conserve fuel—he could hold on and cross the start-finish line in front with just a few drops in the tank. A couple of big ifs, but it seemed a good plan at the time. Of course, Daytona is normally famous for throwing some unforeseen curves at even the most prepared teams.

"They had a caution flag at thirty-six laps, which is four laps shy of one hundred miles," says Leonard. "So the next time we go forty-two laps, and forty-two again, so we've made up our four laps, see, and [other teams] kept stopping at forty, so they're still four laps shy of one hundred miles. Well, it came down to the end, it's too late [for them] to make it up."

The Wood brothers further increased their chances of victory by doing something unheard of: They did not change the tires once the entire race. Lund would come in for fuel and minor adjustments at every stop and nothing else.

As the race progressed, the calculations seemed to be playing themselves out. "And we figured, well, we're the same as leading the race when we're back there in third place, just waiting for them to come down pit road. I mean, we knew and we didn't know, but if some unforeseen thing didn't happen, I mean, they were gonna have to pit; we were just waiting for them to pit, and here they came," he recalls with a hearty laugh.

Toward the end, with Lund in front and going wide open, Glen and Leonard kept their fingers crossed, lest mileage have the final word. In fact, it was close, as Lund's Wood Brothers' car did run out of gas—just after he'd crossed the finish line twenty-four seconds ahead of second-place finisher Fred Lorenzen. Lund's first-ever Grand National win had come in storybook fashion, courtesy of a textbook written by Glen and Leonard Wood. It was only the second superspeedway win the brothers had.

Because of their reputation, the Woods received a rare invitation two years later when car owner Colin Chapman asked if they'd be willing to handle the pit stops for driver Jim Clark at the Indianapolis 500.

They came to the Brickyard a couple of weeks early to study whatever adjustments might be necessary, which centered on Leonard's improving upon the new style of fuel pumps being used at that level of open-wheel racing. During the race, the brothers were able to cut the average pit stop time by two-thirds—or barely long enough to fuel up and do some tweaking when necessary. And like at Daytona, the brothers didn't change a single one of Clark's tires the entire race. The tires had treads on them, and according to Glen Wood, as the tread wore down, the car got faster.

Such haste in the pits allowed Clark enough time to race to victory lane. The fact that Glen and Leonard were able to come in and help make a victory materialize at Indianapolis, after doing the same at Daytona, is probably why you never hear the team referred to normally as simply the Wood Brothers. Much as Richard Petty will always remain The King, Glen and Leonard will forever be the Legendary Wood Brothers.

"You like a challenge, you know? Somebody saying you couldn't do something made you want to do something," says Leonard. "You gotta have that attitude that you want to be very competitive. You don't have that instinct, you might as well be in some factory. I mean, you just can't get along if you're not a real determined person."

The drivers who rode for the Woods always cite their honesty in business and innovation in the garage; in turn, the brothers lent confidence and great setups to the men who brought them NASCAR glory. There were few disagreements with drivers, but of them, one of Leonard's favorites involved trying to get Cale Yarborough, who drove for the team from 1966 to 1970, to conserve equipment by slowing down his legendary wide-open pace.

"I talked him into running slow one time, taking it easy," Leonard remembers. "He was running back in about third place, and somebody wrecked, and it threw something out [that] went up and cut his oil line off, put us out of the race; he says 'Never again!'"

Throughout the '60s and early '70s, the Woods' No. 21 car served as the office for some of stock's biggest names, but nobody traveled the road with them to greater success than David Pearson. With Pearson behind the wheel from 1972 to 1979, the Wood Brothers Racing Team came into their own. The perfect melding of driver and team produced 43 wins and 97 top-fives in 143 races, including 29 superspeedway victories.

"Now that was a driver that come along at the right time and the way we set cars up, it just fit his driving style," says Leonard Wood.

"It just worked perfect, I'm talking about from the first race on. Sat on pole, won the first race, and he was the easiest person to get around the race track I've ever worked with. Yeah—a great driver."

Of the wins they enjoyed together, none remains more memorable than Pearson's only Daytona 500 victory, in 1976, the race that forever exemplifies the stellar on-track rivalry between Pearson and Richard Petty.

The Woods had their car running well that day—better, in fact, than those of Cale Yarborough (who lasted a single lap), Buddy Baker, Bobby Allison, and Darrell Waltrip, who each dropped out of the race long before the end. That left Pearson and Petty to battle it out for the last quarter of the contest. Petty took the lead with twelve laps remaining, with Pearson hanging on his tail but getting no closer. The pair continued their circuits around the track with Petty's Dodge *seemingly* too formidable to pass.

"I remember [Pearson] calling in about two laps to go, and saying, 'I'm running wide open, it's all I can do,'" says Leonard Wood. "And he's the type of person that always told you he couldn't and could, so he was saying that's all he could do—well, how'd he pass him if that was all he could do?"

With half a lap remaining, Pearson gained the upper hand by pulling out of the draft and passing Petty. His determined rival charged back, and when Pearson ran up high on turn three, Petty darted back down.

That's when the descriptions begin to get murky. Did Petty get beneath Pearson and then get loose? Did Pearson tap Petty first? What's certain is that coming out of turn four, the cars, which had been running door-to-door, came together. Suddenly there was spinning and contact as both cars, now the worse for wear, made twisting beelines for the infield.

"The crowd roared real loud, and I knew something had happened," Leonard recalls of his attempts to see what happened from the pits. "And I'm waiting for something to come in sight and the first thing I saw was Richard's car coming down the track backwards. I didn't see David, and then I looked and he was down on the inside spinning around."

Pearson's composure was such that he never let go of the clutch. Petty's car lay seemingly dead in the infield, about one hundred feet from the checkered flag; Pearson, not much farther out, knocked his car into gear, and going about 20 mph, crossed the start-finish line in front, to the delight of the standing throng—and Pearson's race team, who'd earned their second and final Daytona 500 victory.

Unfortunately, three years after that triumph, the relationship between the Woods and Pearson began to sour. Pearson, who'd almost become like another member of the family, had begun talking about the possibility of retirement, and since he wouldn't confirm anything, Glen and Leonard grew frustrated.

Things finally came to a head eight races into the 1979 season, at the Rebel 500. During a late-race pit stop, Pearson had one thing in mind, which was to get back onto the track in front of leader Darrell Waltrip and return to the lead lap. In what has become a legendary instance of misunderstanding—especially strange given the clockwork fashion Pearson and the Woods worked in together— Pearson thought the team planned on changing two tires instead of the four Leonard and company had in mind. After the right-side tires were on, and the left-side lug nuts were loosened, Glen Wood's son, Eddie, working in the pits, yelled, "Whoa whoa!" to keep Pearson in check as Waltrip started to make his way out; the driver was convinced Eddie had said, "Go, go!" Go he did, although the journey was short-lived: By the time Pearson reached the end of pit road, he'd reached the end of the road, as the left-side wheels came right off the car. It might have seemed comical if Pearson and the Woods had been in better humor about their relationship. The incident became a final straw of sorts, and by the end of the week, David Pearson was out of the Wood Brothers' No. 21 Ford, which he had raced for the better part of a decade.

In time, all parties wished they could take the decision back; certainly, the way it was conducted didn't fit so classic a combination, especially given the unmatched success they'd all achieved together. It remains the brightest chapter in the career of the siblings, and of Pearson, who, with 105 total wins, stands second only to Richard Petty on the all-time list.

"I tell you, after that long you're bound to have a little disagreement, but man, I regretted all of that," Leonard Wood says now. "All of us have. He was one of the greatest drivers that's ever been. I think the world of him. We're the greatest of friends. I mean, he really pays us a lot of compliments. And I used to tell him how good he was, you know. I wouldn't do it if I didn't mean it. It came easy because it was the truth."

Eddie Wood was twenty-five years old when he tried to keep David Pearson in the pits that day at Darlington; by then, he'd already been working in the family business for eleven years, having started back when his main responsibility meant manning the broom handle in the shop. Eddie's brother Len also started when he was fourteen, in 1971, sweeping to earn $1-per-hour wages. You can't get much more humble than those beginnings, but they've led these second-generation brothers to NASCAR Winston Cup Series success, and an opportunity to build on a fruitful legacy. After years of learning the business—from spreadsheets to setups—alongside their father and uncle, they began to master some of the same behind-the-scenes fundamentals that made the Wood Brothers their name. Eddie and Len were integral parts of the team that helped such drivers as Buddy Baker and David Pearson attain their success, doing everything from carrying tires to changing gears. In 1979, their father gave them each five percent of the company; by 1985, it had risen to twenty-five percent, where it now remains. (Their sister Kim, who does the bookkeeping for the company, merited the other quarter, with Glen keeping the last.) By then, the brothers, as eventual inheritors of one of racing's good names, began preparing in earnest for the days when it would be up to them to keep that name competitive.

It seems now only fitting that the Wood team has, in recent years, fielded first-win rides for some of the brightest second- or third-generation names in NASCAR. It was with the Woods that Kyle Petty scored his first two victories, at Richmond in 1986 and at Charlotte in 1987. Behind the wheel for the Woods in 1991, Dale Jarrett scored his inaugural victory at Michigan. And beginning in 1999, with Len and Eddie firmly at the helm of the business, the younger Wood brothers had a respectable rookie-season run with fellow Virginian Elliot Sadler driving the famed No. 21 Ford.

Eddie and Len divide their power much as their dad and uncle did: Eddie takes care of business while Len stays mainly on top of the shop. And almost fifty years after grandfather Glen made his debut as a driver, Eddie's son, Jon Wood, began coursing his way through the Late Model Stock Division, gaining victories and consistency with seat time.

Glen and Leonard remain active in the business to a degree: Leonard still works every day in the shop on whatever is needed; Glen comes in almost every day as well, mainly to observe. Their triumphs may be past, but those days are still worth marking, and in 1999, the brothers and fellow owner Junie Donlavey were each given the Spirit of Ford Award, the automaker's highest racing honor. It was a fitting tribute to the Woods, recognizing not only their success and service, but the commitment the entire Wood family made to staying at the top of the sport.

"You gotta take it very serious," Leonard says. "It takes a lot of concentration and a lot of thinking. If you take your mind off of it, it's really hard to do it like it's gotta be done. And our families, my wife and Glen's wife both, stood behind us. I mean, they wanted us to win as much as we did ourselves. And if you don't have that behind you, you can forget it."

There's still plenty for the siblings to remember, housed now in a Wood Brothers Museum at their original shop in Stuart, Virginia. The museum may be a touchstone to a bygone era of racing, but first and foremost, it is a celebration of two brothers who, in a fifty-year partnership, kept their single-minded purpose intact, achieving great results through a simple formula. As Glen Wood puts it, "He would do what he did and I would do what I did, and we managed to keep all the wheels on it."

16
The France Family, Part Two

Lesa France Kennedy found herself with a dilemma. For years, fans had paid visits to the Daytona International Speedway, the most famous track in stock car racing and the two and a half mile-long bedrock of the France family-owned International Speedway Corporation (ISC). Although people admired the track, the experience of coming to the racing mecca left some people feeling short-changed.

"We had a little store there, and we had tours, but then [visitors would] say, 'What else is there to see?'" Kennedy remembers.

In the mid-1990s, she decided to give them more to see. She had first learned about the business of stock car racing from her grandmother, Anne B. France, while in high school, helping sell tickets at Daytona; after graduating from Duke University in 1983 with a bachelor's degree in economics and psychology, she joined the family business in earnest. Given her background, and the years she'd spent observing the great vision with which her father, NASCAR President Bill France Jr., and her grandfather, NASCAR founder William France, had made stock car racing into a bona fide American success story, an idea began to form. With NASCAR already growing into much more than an arena-driven sport, it stood to reason that a sports museum of some sort would encourage people to view the Daytona International Speedway as a year-round stopping ground.

"We thought, well, maybe we'll put a little theater in or maybe we'll do a couple of different things," she says of ISC's original take on the project. "But every time we knocked down a wall it wasn't big enough."

Once all the walls were knocked down, what emerged was Daytona USA, a 50,000 square-foot tribute to what has made Daytona, the town, and the track, memorable speed capitols. In Daytona USA, which opened its doors on July 4, 1996, the Pepsi Theatre screens a 70mm you-are-there movie about the Daytona 500, patrons race against top NASCAR talent in Sega Speedway games, visitors get to participate with crew members in a simulated pit stop, and that year's winning car from the 500 is proudly displayed on the premises, still wearing all the dirt and grit it did after its trip to victory lane. An equally impressive feature in the place is arguably the turnstiles, which spun for half a million visitors in the first year alone.

Kennedy had a great deal to do with the concept and development of the attraction, and she was there to accept when it went on to win the Themed Entertainment Association's Thea Award, its highest honor and one previously given to the likes of Disney and Universal Studios.

This, as much as anything, proves the "arrival" of NASCAR. In the better than fifty years since Kennedy's grandparents, William and Anne France, began NASCAR, it has gained tremendous popularity compared to what its drivers call the stick and ball sports. Given how often we now hear the description, NASCAR could probably slap a registration mark on the phrase "The Fastest Growing Sport in America."

If current president Bill France is the chief reason for these developments—and his first forays into television and sponsorship are the seeds of this growth—then his children, Lesa and Brian, haven't slowed down in terms of their own contributions. In a way, they represent halves of a productive whole, a familiar, familial pattern throughout the sport's history. NASCAR first made it on the map because William France's vision matched expertly with his wife Anne's business smarts. The company's influence and success increased exponentially because Bill France ran the show with a mix of his parents' best qualities, while his brother Jim, a solid, dependable businessman, helped keep the wheels turning at ISC.

Competition on the track will always be the major part of the sport's appeal, but to keep spreading the message of NASCAR, the heads of stock car racing's body will need the most creative plans possible. The next generation of France leaders seem well suited to the challenge.

Lesa France Kennedy was eleven when her grandfather, William France, turned the reins of NASCAR over to her father, Bill, in 1972. The transition hadn't happened overnight. There were the years of Bill's apprenticeship, where he learned every element of the business by doing, from helping to sell hot dogs to eventually helping sell sponsorship deals. By 1972, after six years of performing many of his executive duties, what he gained, really, was a new title.

"As I recall, my father had a lot of the responsibility already," Kennedy states. "I don't think it was overwhelming for him. The transition over time had been handled pretty well. I think that it's always difficult for someone in a control position, and especially a strong personality like my grandfather, to totally let go of anything. I think that's human nature. I wouldn't have seen it as anything but just normal growing."

After the president's title changed hands, the concept of normal growing for NASCAR expanded with the increased presence of television. After the first-ever, live flag-to-flag airing of the Daytona 500 in 1979, things changed forever, and Bill France had a triumph setting the tone for his tenure. A one-time driver like his father, France's no-nonsense approach to his tasks quickly earned him the respect of the circuit after he took over. It almost seems a matter of good timing that two of the sport's most popular names, Richard Petty and Bobby Allison, soon carved out a rough rivalry; by sitting the racers down, levying fines, and talking them out of their conflict, he instantly made his presence felt. In terms of the rules, he became, like his father, the sport's unmoveable force.

France's lead was made easier by the presence of his younger brother Jim, a main sounding board; after a business degree and a tour in Vietnam, Jim became an executive in NASCAR in 1970. The brothers' relationship—with a fifteen-year age difference between them—has been dominated by cooperation; as France children, they grew up with the goal-oriented sense of purpose their parents taught them by example.

"The challenges are probably the same challenges you face—whether you're working for your family or not—when you're a young person coming into a business full of a lot of ideas," Jim says. "You've got to go through the process of your career development up through the ranks, to where you get into a role where you actually are in the decision process. The way our company works is no different than any other company. You had to come through the process. It required developing the same patience and understandings of things I went through and Bill went through. Our business has never been a one-man show, even when they started, putting on an event; it requires a lot of people and a lot of skills, and Mom and Dad were able to organize those. But those people and skills were important to the growth of the thing and just because you're a family member, you didn't just automatically come in at some level . . . I think because of our training and rearing, [Bill and I] have pretty interchangeable views on things. It's made our working relationship extremely smooth."

William France began his motorsports career behind the wheel of a car, when he wasn't under the hood figuring out how to make the thing run better and faster. His sons, Bill and Jim, each more than dabbled in their own driving pursuits, and for the last several years, Jim, always prominent on the motorcycle racing scene, has been having a great deal of fun competing in Legends car races.

Regardless of how far Bill France's son Brian may travel in the business of NASCAR, he was never destined to begin his career the same way.

"I damn sure wasn't going to be a driver," he says with a laugh. "If you saw me parallel park, you'd realize that I made a good decision."

In fact, as a youth, there was a question of whether or not he'd even be involved in the sport.

"When I was a kid, I quite frankly thought this would not be an opportunity that would even be available to me," admits the senior vice president of NASCAR. "I didn't think it was any kind of big business. I just thought of it as events that blew into town and blew out of town. It wasn't until I was in my twenties, or late teens, that I thought about it as a place for me to make a contribution."

At that point, he traveled out to California to work in the company's offices there, specifically on the short-track business side, where he began to grasp some of the fundamentals and saw, as he puts it, "Some areas where I could make a little bit of a difference."

Unlike her brother, Kennedy has admitted to few thrills as big as when she donned a helmet and took a Pontiac to the asphalt of Daytona to go a few laps one day in the 1980s. But she inspired few thrills as great as the one her grandmother Anne felt when Kennedy returned from college in 1983, and instead of opting for grad school, decided to begin a career at International Speedway Corp. instead. The pair were, by all accounts, exceptionally close, and Kennedy credits both Anne and her grandfather with helping to shape her professional attitude.

"From Pop I learned not to accept 'no,'" she says of Big Bill France. "He just didn't accept 'No, it can't be done.' There always was some way. And from my grandmother, I would love to have the fiscal responsibility that she had—open-mindedness and fiscal responsibility."

Kennedy has demonstrated enough of the latter to be an integral element in the company's growth. She may spend most of her time working for ISC as its executive vice president, while Brian makes his strides for the NASCAR end of the business, but in the areas of marketing and development, the siblings have combined to bring about much greater levels of NASCAR racing awareness.

In addition to Daytona USA, in 1989 Kennedy established Americrown, Inc., an in-house marketing company, which specializes in providing food and souvenir services to the several ISC tracks, including superspeedways at Daytona, Darlington, California, Talladega, and Nazareth, Pennsylvania. Kennedy also has a huge involvement in track development for ISC; the company's current project, a 1.5-mile tri-oval Kansas Speedway, has a NASCAR Winston Cup Series date in 2001.

For his part, Brian France opened a NASCAR marketing office in New York several years ago to help the company keep up with the enormous marketing challenges of the business. By all indications, he has made a tremendous impact. In recent years, NASCAR Cafe restaurants have sprung up in Orlando, Myrtle Beach, and Nashville; NASCAR Thunder stores are selling licensed products throughout the country; and NASCAR SpeedParks are drawing families in with their go-kart tracks, arcades, and miniature golf courses. In 1999, Brian earned the "Statesman of the Year" award, a top marketing prize that's previously gone to the likes of U.S. Secretary of Commerce William Daley and J. W. Marriott Jr.

Though their spheres of influence are normally separate, the siblings understand well the pride and pressures associated with being third-generation successes in a family-run business.

"We have the same common goals in that we want the sport to grow, and we want both companies to grow," Kennedy says of the working relationship with her brother. "I can't really define it; we both have very strong views, and we're not shy about expressing them. I think people that have been around us for a while are very comfortable with that, but it's okay in that we know what our end goal is."

"If you look at most siblings—within a business, it's tough," admits Brian. "If you think about it, if you had a family member you worked with eight hours a day, it'd be a challenge for both, and it is a challenge. Now, we work it out because she's right; it is the end goal. I would be fooling if I said you do it without some ups and downs. But in the end, it works out good."

Better than anybody else, their father sees and accepts whatever competitive aspects make up Lesa and Brian's personalities, especially since their efforts are all directed toward that same goal: increasing the sport's popularity while still promoting the weekly race that brought the sport its original fan base.

"Both of them are kind of high-strung people in a sense," Bill France says. "I know they agree on an awful lot, but they'll also disagree from time to time. But very rarely do I get called in to break the tie."

Bill France remains at the hub of all decisions in NASCAR, despite the fact that he has transferred much of his day-to-day operational responsibilities. In February 1999 he announced the promotion of the highly regarded long-time NASCAR executive Mike Helton to the position of chief operating officer, with France himself remaining as chairman of the board and president. As a result, France now has more opportunity to concentrate on the sport's big-picture concerns, the issues that will continue to reflect stock car racing's evolution.

One of the biggest of these issues is track location. The landscape of NASCAR has changed dramatically since France took over in 1972. At that point, the vast majority of tracks fielding NASCAR Winston Cup Series events were in the South. In the 1990s, a number of new sites have shown up on the schedule, including Las Vegas, New Hampshire, and the venerable Brickyard of Indianapolis; the sport's additional forays into the Midwest include their track project in Kansas City, followed by another in Joliet, Illinois, thanks to a joint project between the ISC and the Indianapolis Motor Speedway Corporation. There is also discussion of development of a track in New York.

But whatever happens on the tracks, NASCAR racing will soon be presented in a different way on television, thanks to a $2.4 billion television contract signed in 1999 that takes effect for the 2001 season. In that deal, FOX and cable partner FX will broadcast races in the first half of the year, starting with the Daytona 500, and NBC and cable partner TBS will work the second half. Also in the works is the NASCAR Channel, a cable network offering features and race reruns.

The new deal was a departure for the sport. In the past, track owners were in charge of selling individual television rights to races, and six networks—CBS, ESPN, TNN, TBS, ABC, and NBC—each shared the wealth. "Our first five races were on four different networks at different times with no pre-game show and all different presentations," says Brian France. "When you turn on the NFL on Sunday at one o'clock, you know FOX, you know John Madden, you know some things. [We got] all those things and that's what we're excited about because that's going to help us build an audience at a much faster rate." The deal has the stamp of Bill France all over it.

"[My father] makes a helluva lot of decisions that are not necessarily good for him personally or financially, but that are good for the sport. He believes growing the sport ultimately will be good for everybody," adds Brian.

Perhaps Bill France's ultimate skill is in how well he works with people, both on his side of the table and across it. He can at times be warm and sentimental, or brilliantly shrewd and purposeful. There's not a driver on the circuit who doesn't respect his authority to level the playing field in terms of equipment to make competition spirited and safe. And R. J. Reynolds, sponsor of the NASCAR Winston Cup Series, is only the most prominent example of his success at keeping big business in the sport.

France's recent bout with cancer has certainly caused great concern among his family and colleagues. True to form, however, he is expected to make a full recovery.

In NASCAR and ISC, France oversees all, as his father once did. But for those working closest to him, he manages a balance between trust and great expectations. "He's very tough, not in an unfair way, just a very challenging guy who holds me to a high standard," says Brian France, summing up their working relationship. "We're different kinds of guys, but it works great. There's a lot of family businesses out there—some families look at it as, 'Hey, I don't want my son or daughter to work as hard as I had to do. That's why I did this, so they don't have to.' His view is the opposite of that: 'You have to do your part and then a little bit more if you're going to be in a family business.' That's how he operates."

Obviously, the formula has worked in Bill France's view. "From my standpoint, it's going pretty good," he states. "Brian's got pretty good latitude—in the financial, expenditure area, he's not second-guessed every time he turns around."

Adds Lesa Kennedy, "I think it's helped us out that we had different interests, but once again the common denominator is motor sports and I think Dad's given us all room to grow."

Arguably the biggest question Bill France will be dealing with in the future has everything to do with family: namely, who will run the businesses if he decides to retire. Knowing that France succeeded his father, many have come to assume that Brian France, as prominent as he is in NASCAR circles, will eventually take over as president and CEO. Others feel the appointment of Helton represented a vote of confidence. For Brian France, one indication of his deep admiration for his father lies in the fact that nothing is publicly certain on the topic.

"He just is real clear that we've got a big constituency now of teams and tracks and licensees and sponsors, television networks, everybody else who relies on our sport to be managed correctly," Brian says of his father. "He's not gonna just [turn the company over] because your last name is France. Some businesses work that way, you automatically get it. He's not gonna do that and I respect that.

"The question is, who's the best person to operate the business. Not necessarily who owns it, 'cause I don't think he's planning on giving his ownership to anybody other than his family—I mean, I hope he doesn't do that. But on the other hand, there are things you've got to do to operate it day in and day out. And depending on who has the best resume for that and who he feels is the best, I'm sure that's the decision he'll make."

All the decisions involved—including which person will eventually run the sport and whether or not the business will instead be run by a committee of leaders—will be made by Bill France with an eye toward future growth and respect for the sport's past. The one guarantee is that NASCAR will continue to be run by someone who dreams big and isn't easily satisfied. Says Jim France, "I go back to what my dad always said—things either get bigger or smaller, they don't usually stand still. [My parents] worked their whole life to try and make things bigger; I don't think they would put any boundaries on how big something would get. [My father] was a pretty good visionary, looking down the road or seeing around the next bend. If he was here today, he would be looking not where we are today, but where he thinks we might be at ten, fifteen years from now. It's kind of the way he was and I think he would be the same way today. He'd be thinking that this thing is still pretty small."

Acknowledgments

There are a lot of people who gave me the tools, the time, and the encouragement to write *NASCAR Generations*. They're deserving of my deep gratitude.

First, there's no way I could have done this book without the cooperation of the stock car drivers and NASCAR family members who not only gave me their time but also were willing to open up about the past.

Topping that list is the France family—Bill France, Jim France, Lesa France Kennedy, and Brian France—who supported this project from the start and shared many anecdotes about William and Anne France. In addition, the Allisons, Earnhardts, Jarretts, Pettys, Burtons, Elliotts, Wallaces, Waltrips, Bakers, Woods, Labontes, and Mark Martin and Frances Flock were kind enough to reminisce about wonderful, personal moments. I thank them sincerely, since it is the power of their tales that made me excited about the writing.

In addition, several publicists were relentless enough to find me the necessary time in their extremely busy drivers' schedules. A few who stand out include J. R. Rhodes, who represents Dale Earnhardt; Danielle Humphrey, who—until her move to the NASCAR public relations office—ran the schedule for the Jarrett family; and Dan Fromm, my main contact for all things Petty. And in the NASCAR marketing department, editorial director Jennifer White opened up some doors that would have remained closed without her aid. I am grateful for her wit and candor.

To begin my research, and to carry me through the writing by confirming facts and revealing interesting tidbits I explored in interviews, I went to some acknowledged NASCAR experts: the writers whose books came before this one. Those titles include Greg Fielden's richly detailed Forty Years of Stock Car Racing series, the indispensable *Stock Car Racing Encyclopedia* he co-edited with Peter Golenbock; Mr. Golenbock's incomparable books, *The Last Lap* and *American Zoom*; the enlightening and enjoyable books by Paul Hemphill (*Wheels*), Shaun Assael (*Wide Open: Days and Nights on the NASCAR Tour*), and Kim Chapin (*Fast as White Lightning*); a pair of insightful biographies by Larry Fielden (*Tim Flock: Race Driver*) and Bob Zeller (*Mark Martin: Driven to Race*); and Bill Fleischman and Al Pearce's fine reference, *Inside Sports' NASCAR Racing*. Any NASCAR fan would do well to seek them out. In addition, searching through the pages of magazines such as *NASCAR Winston Cup Scene* and *Stock Car Racing*, and excellent web sites such as nascar.com and thatsracing.com led to still more avenues worth exploring. I thank the editors of those sources. Specifically, I wish to mention Steve Waid at *NASCAR Winston Cup Scene* for securing some photos that appear here. Jim Fluharty at that magazine and Buzz McKim at the Daytona racing archives were especially helpful in providing images past and present.

A number of friends and colleagues kept this book on track. Russ Rieger did what only the greatest friends do: He worked in his spare time to make sure this book found a publisher. John Silbersack originally took it on at HarperCollins, and ever since he's been a good friend, an expert sounding board, and an indispensable guide in the book-writing business. Brian Silverman edited this manuscript without incident and kept me on the straight and narrow throughout. My lawyer, Franklin Douglas, did a terrific job of making the deal workable—and he did so with a sense of humor. And ultimately, it was the encouraging, accommodating Tom Dupree at HarperCollins who finally brought this book to its final destination.

Other people either made the writing possible or improved upon the product. John Bowers helped me craft the original proposal and has been a support for seventeen years. Bret Watson pored over the proposal and early chapters and, as he always does, improved on whatever I wrote. Jay Gissen, my longtime great friend, gave valuable suggestions. *TV Guide* editor-in-chief Steven Reddicliffe gave me his consent and encouragement. Jay Fader, my esteemed technical guru, advised me on all matters Macintosh. Laurie Kahn also read the proposal and early work with interest and her excellent, studied eye. Ray Wilson, always the first to read anything I write, provided his typically sound perspective. Tina Hwang and Gail North transcribed a number of interviews with skill. Thanks go also to Eric Feil, my longtime partner in editorial crime at *The Cable Guide* and *See*, whose exceptional efforts and typical good humor helped keep the ship righted and have always made the journey enjoyable. Our lieutenants, Jeff Iorio and Scott Barwick, also aided the cause. I thank Barry Krostich, best friend and accountant extraordinaire, for talking sense and keeping track of my papers. People like Ellen and Steve Yevak welcomed my family so that I could crawl away to write. And to my good friends and students at Literacy Partners, thanks for your continued inspiration.

Given that this is a book about family, I would be remiss if I didn't thank my own, which has always encouraged this effort. Judy and Mike, Ricky, Steven—thank you; I wish Sonny were here to see it. My wife's family has also done whatever they could to give me the time to write, and is a most welcoming cheering section; Ellen and Mike, Butch and Suzanne, Hy, Lee and Bill, thank you.

I must also thank my brother, a sibling who is not only not a rival, but is a great friend and voice of reason and counsel. So to Dave and to Deb, thank you. And for many years, my exceptionally supportive parents have wished—in thought and deed—for nothing more than my own fulfillment. Writing this particular book has only confirmed that having parents who believe and nurture you is your most important foundation.

Also, it deserves mentioning that there's no way I would have ever written this book had it not been for the candor and courage of Bobby Allison. Our 1994 conversation about his family was the seed of this project. Like many people, I continue to profit from his example.

Finally, there are the most important people in my life, who had to put up with my absence while I was busy looking into the lives of others. To Rachel, my sweet little Rainbow Warrior, and Nell, who was born a week before the writing began, I thank you for your love and patience.

And to Loren, whom I forced into single-motherhood for months; who meticulously transcribed almost the entire set of interviews and came up with ever more inventive ways to spell "Bowman-Gray Stadium," all while dealing with a newborn; who understood the concept of "investment time" and is the person who really made it possible for me to do this, I thank you and I love you.